T0165354

BAMBOUSHAY

Have a Good Time—Make Merry

DEBRA VALERIE GORMAN

Trafford rev. 05/07/2013

 www.trafford.com

North America & international
toll-free: 1 888 232 4444 (USA & Canada)
fax: 812 355 4082

CONTENTS

To my most patient family as I try to get
all our memoirs down on paper.

CHAPTER 1

I was born on December 17th during the Great Depression year of 1931.

Mom told me that when I was born I interrupted a Pinochle game, popped out, hit the footboard but never caused a disruption in the card game.

The Depression was a worldwide economic downturn in the decade preceding World War II. It started in the United States with the stock market crash of Black Tuesday, October 29, 1929, and quickly spread to almost every country around the world. Unemployment reached 25% in the U.S. and in some countries it was 33%. Construction halted entirely, farming plunged as prices dropped 60%. International trade fell to half or even less. Many businessmen jumped out of skyscrapers so they would not have to face the devastation of losing everything they possessed. The next summer a severe drought destroyed the heartland of the United States resulting in many families moving west to find any type of work. They were even willing to pick crops, anything that could provide food for the family. The Depression lasted until World War II when the country mobilized for war.

My father, John Paul Duss, was born in Lvov, Poland to a peasant mother and a postmaster father who would never degrade himself by eating with his children. Raising children was strictly the woman's work. My Dad, John, would never allow my only brother, Larry, to toil in the kitchen or perform any task that John considered to be a woman's work. Of course my Mother could walk behind a plow and perform other heavy duty work but that was different. It was allowed. Poland had been subdivided so many times by the surrounding countries that Lvov is now a city in western Ukraine, thus my last name is without a—ski ending.

My earliest recollection of our brick bungalow on Belmont Street in Hamtramck, Michigan was the proximity of the Catholic school, St. Ladislaus, which was just a couple of blocks from home. I was just a toddler of 3 or 4 years old when I started running away from home to go to school with the big kids. My Mother finally talked to the nuns and obtained their permission for me to attend classes. Despite the fact that all classes were in Polish, I couldn't wait to get to school in the mornings. I thrived in this stern school, completing three grades in one year.

"Your feet don't touch the floor" the nun said, as she placed a cigar box under my feet. It was so embarrassing.

Hamtramck, at that time, was a Polish town within the city limits of Detroit. It was first settled by German immigrants. The Poles arrived soon after the Dodge Brothers opened their manufacturing plant in the city in 1914. Hamtramck provided these reliable peasants with good sausage shops, bakeries, and restaurants that offered a menu they were accustomed to in their home country. Most of these Polish immigrants were hard working, happy people, capable of leaving their family and friends behind to seek a different life in the New World; a World that promised so much to the Old Country peasants. They ventured into the unknown, took that leap of faith across the ocean to a new beginning.

Pierogis were very popular with the Poles. These dumplings are similar to raviolis. The meatless variety was standard fare on Fridays when Catholics were not allowed to eat meat on that day in commemoration of Christ's death on the cross. The pierogis can be stuffed with sauerkraut, ground meat, fruit, or my favorite, potatoes and cottage cheese. The peasant meals other than Fridays included kielbasa, Kiszka,(blood sausage that usually included barley), Kapusta (sauerkraut soup), Gołąbki, (stuffed cabbage rolls) and Chruscikis—dainty wedding cakes, that were rolled thin, cut into long triangles, slit, one end pulled through the slit, and deep fried, then sprinkled with powdered sugar. These cookies were also known as Bowties, Angel Wings, or Wedding Bows, for they were always served at the marriage feast which could last for three days, or until all the food and drinks were gone.

The Depression was a bitter time for newly married couples. The banks closed their doors without warning. People could not get their own money out of the bank's coffers. Dad told me he didn't have the five cents to ride a streetcar downtown to find work so he walked across Detroit, a large city, spanning miles in width and length.

Because Poland had been divided so many times the villagers were obliged to become fluent in many languages, most were of the Slavic origin. Dad always told me he came to America alone but a later genealogy search showed that his Mother was also listed on the ship's manifest. He had no birth certificate or baptismal record from his church because a fire in the village destroyed all records during his youth. Records were not vital to farmers. He related horror stories of his father, a town dignitary, never condescending to eat with his children. The father would sit down to a steak dinner while the children ate gruel. His Dad, as well as my father, believed that raising the children and eating with them was strictly a woman's work. No wonder his mother sought a new life with her son in America. We were never told that she came with him. He never talked about where she settled down; whether it was with family or even what part of the country. We were always led to believe that she was still in Poland.

Dad was born in 1898 saying he was too young for the First World War and too old for the Second one. He would have gladly fought for his newly adopted country.

My mother, Monica Patrinella Witkowski, was the second daughter of a family of five girls, and one boy, the surviving children. No one knows how many died during those days of home births and midwives. Mom was born in Cleveland, Ohio on May 30, 1908. She was ten years younger than my Dad but that was a normal span of time between husband and wife in those days. Monica and her older sister, Sophia were both born in Cleveland, Ohio so I am not a 100% Polack, but almost. The children always understood enough Polish so the parents could not tell any secrets without them understanding.

The Witkowski family eventually migrated to the Detroit area. They settled in Wyandotte, Michigan where her Dad, the Grandpa I never knew, became a policeman on the city force. During this difficult period of the Depression Mom said she had to stand in line at the Mayor's office to get milk for her infant daughter.

My Godmother, Ciocia (Auntie in Polish, pronounced cho-cha) Dombrowski lived just a few doors away with her husband, Walter. She and her husband had no children, so I became their favorite toddler. I had four doting adults to spoil me. I recall having a serious crush on one of their nephews. Charles promised to wait for me to grow up so we could marry and live happily ever after. I remember kicking him in the shin on his wedding day because he didn't wait for me to grow up.

The Dombrowskis survived off of the dozens of pigeons they kept in the attic roost area over their garage. The roost had a small exit door so the pigeons were free to fly all day and return for the night. The cooing of the pigeons did not seem to bother the neighbors. Everyone was more tolerant in those challenging times. Each bungalow in Hamtramck had a detached garage behind the house and off the alley. The attics were used for storage or, as in my Godmother's case, subsistence food stores.

The two nephews refused to help my husband and I pay for the ambulance when Ciocia died yet they inherited her house as they were the only family left. They even took the quilt she made specifically for me. This was all the result of not having a will at the time of her death. She did not express her last wishes so they inherited all. There was never money left over for lawyers to make up a will.

Often a "sheeny man" would pass through the alleys selling fresh eggs, corn or tomatoes he had raised on his farm. Depending on how good his sales were, he sometimes bought old clothes, rags and even newspapers. He bought whatever one could find in a relatively bare house to sell for pennies. Each penny was treasured. Yet, I don't remember ever being hungry or lacking toys. During the Depression our toys were simple things like a jump rope, marbles, jacks, or a chalk to draw hopscotch squares on the sidewalks—we had nothing elaborate, expensive, and certainly not electronic. They were not invented at that time.

Dad finally got a job in the auto industry when Henry Ford offered five dollars a day for production line labor. The men were thrilled to earn five dollars for a day's labor. It was unheard of high wages. I don't know when Dad moved to General Motors where he worked his way up to become a model builder for the Cadillac car. Dad was a wood craftsman and in those days the steel was molded on wooden replicas of the finished automobile. The Cadillac he worked on was far too rich for his pocketbook so his favorite car was a Pontiac. One would not dream of owning a competitive company's automobile. And, of course, Mom could barely get Dad to do any woodworking around the house.

When Dad turned down a job with Walter Reuther, head of the United Auto Workers union, he drowned his regrets in a liquor bottle and progressed with his drinking until it finally killed him on Father's day, 1959. He died at the early age of sixty one. In the meantime, there was much sorrow and fighting in the family due to his drunkenness.

Walter Reuther was a major union leader who made the United Automobile Workers a key force in the auto industry. Reuther later became president of the CIO, the Congress of Industrial Organizations. Walter negotiated a merger with George Meany and the AFL, the American Federation of Labor. He also won major concessions and recognition for his unions with General Motors and Ford Motor. In 1933 he and his brothers, Victor and Roy, went to work for a couple of years in the Gorky auto plant in the Soviet Union but soon returned to America due to the lack of political freedom in Russia. Walter was a brilliant negotiator, most likely accomplishing too much power for the unions, so vital in the 1930s, but eventually leading to their downfall in later years.

"Hello, is this the police station?" asked a frightened child.

"Yes, it is." The officer replied

"Can you please hurry to our house, my Dad is about to hit my Mom and I don't know what to do.", cried the little girl.

"Help is on the way. Just try to stay calm", the officer said.

A nervous breakdown during my teenage years was another result of Dad's drinking. I always escaped the turmoil by simply fainting away. The family doctor advised that I should get away from my father for an entire summer. I was invited to spend the summer with Sophie, Mom's older sister, and her children at their cabin in Alpina, Michigan on Lake Superior. During my breakdown, I had also attempted to run away from home. I only reached a mile or so down the road. I would have gladly jumped off a bridge if I could only find one high enough to do some damage.

Mom's father, Ignace Witkowski, was a policeman on the Wyandotte city force. Mom told stories of how her Dad would warn all his bootlegging friends of a planned raid on the stills so his friends wouldn't get caught in the police web. The city of Wyandotte was riddled with underground tunnels during the Prohibition Era. Ignace was shot and killed by the Purple Gang of Detroit. His murderer was never caught.

The Purple Gang was originally known as the Sugar House Gang. The leader, Julius Horowitz, supplied sugar to the breweries. It was a gang of bootleggers and hijackers. The Purple Gang's talents also extended to the activities of extortion, jewelry theft, and gambling. Detroit was a major port for running alcoholic products during the Prohibition for it bordered Canada. The Detroit River, with a tunnel under it to facilitate the trafficking of liquor, was the only separation between Ontario and Detroit. Breweries in Canada, Mexico and the Caribbean flourished as the alcohol flowed into the United States. The smuggling of alcohol across the river was accomplished by ordinary people using many ingenious methods including rubber belts, false breasts, chest protectors, suitcases, even loaves of bread.

While I never was able to see any of the tunnels in Wyandotte because Grandpa was shot before my birth, my imagination ran rampant with visions of the entire city collapsing from the mesh that was dug beneath the streets. I could envision my teenage, "flapper-girl" mother rapping on a speakeasy door on one of her dates and telling the bouncer inside that "Joe sent me" in order to gain access to the dancing and drinking inside.

My Mom, told me she lost her hair three times due to Scarlet, Typhoid and Rheumatic fevers. Surprisingly it grew in differently each time. One of the fevers put her in the isolation hospital, Herman Kiefer, for months. Herman Kiefer Hospital was mainly for communicable diseases like tuberculosis, which was rampant in the late 19th and early 20th centuries. The hospital was also used for single, unwed mothers. They could be cared for at Kiefer when they were effectively "banned" from more respectable maternity hospitals. An orphanage was also on the premises where many Detroiters were taken from their unwed mothers and raised.

In the early twentieth century the girls were never taught about their bodies, hormone changes, sex, or menstrual periods. At least the Witkowski Mother (my Grandmother, Busha in Polish) never discussed the subjects with her girls. These matters were all taboo, never to be discussed by refined families and certainly not by a widowed Mother. When the oldest girl, Sophie, first saw the signs of her period she hid it from her Mom believing she had hurt herself in some way. The girls used rags to absorb the blood. They washed the rags and dried them in the warm attic off their bathroom.

After Grandpa, was killed, Busha was left with six young children to support. From her insurance proceeds, she bought a large home, one block from St. Stanislaus Elementary School. She added a neighborhood grocery store onto the front of the house. The store included various sundries, a few necessities like milk, bread, butter, and treats for children, such as candies and a soda fountain. She also, cleverly, made arrangements where she could watch the workers in the store, her own children, and even me years later, from a strategically placed rocking chair in her living room. She could see the reflections in the cooler doors. It was very difficult, if not impossible, to swipe a piece of candy or a bite of ice cream without her knowing it. We never could figure out how she caught us every time.

Mom, forever the Flapper Girl, never shy, was always full of daring. She got herself and her older sister, Sophie, in trouble at St. Stanislaus' school. The two girls were made to stand in front of their classmates and were ridiculed by the nun for rouging their knees. They were brought before the Principal, and scolded for attempting to entice the boys in the class. I am sure Mom was the instigator.

When Monica's older sister, Sophie, got married her picture was on the front page of the local paper. It seems her new husband, Andrew, had a previous marriage in Poland and the wife, or ex-wife, we believe, was contesting his new marriage. In the front page photographs the European woman appeared as the modern, flashy-looking, woman despite just arriving from the Old Country, while Sophie was the demure, maidenly looking wife in the picture. Large headlines blared over the picture "WHICH WIFE IS THE REAL ONE"? It was a major embarrassment for the Witkowski family.

My parents wedding, as most Polish weddings, lasted three days. Family and friends were required to stay until all the food and drink was consumed. Weddings were held at home or in the parish hall with everyone dancing polkas for hours. The accordion was the instrument of choice and produced a lot of music. I tried accordion lessons in later years until I started developing breasts—then it was too dangerous.

I was a typical looking Pole with brown eyes and mousy-colored brown hair. My Mom felt the same about her hair and used Henna dye to produce a reddish brown tint to her tresses. The hair style of the day was a plastered down finger wave, which worked well for her with the short hair of new growth that was coming in so many times. In my youth, however, she wound my longer hair around strips of rags each night to curl it. The rag was tied at the top of the curl and the whole process was easy to sleep on. This produced long tightly wrapped locks, which was my hairdo throughout elementary school.

Grandma had warned her entire brood that once they were married they were never to return home to settle their arguments. They were to work out their problems on their own. So when Mom and Dad had a serious fight one day, Mom called a moving company and removed every piece of furniture from their apartment. Imagine Dad's chagrin when he came home from work. She couldn't go home to Mother so she went to her sister's home until the argument was settled. Their arguments must have gotten worse for another time Mom said she tried to abort me by jumping out of their second story window—but it didn't work. I am still here to tell my story.

Belle Isle Park was one of our favorite family picnic outings. The admission was free and the park had acres of mowed lawn where Dad could teach me cartwheels and splits. These tricks became useful during high school years when I was quickly accepted into the cheerleading squad. Tap dancing was another activity that I enjoyed as a young child including an appearance at Radio City Music Hall in downtown Detroit. I felt like a miniature Rockette, although I was only three or four years old. I had a glittery, frilly, blue and gold costume with a pointed cap topped by a black pompom that matched my shiny, black patent-leather tap shoes. Fortunately, Mom and I had to travel downtown by streetcar. I was so proud of myself that I told all who would listen where we were going and who was performing that fantastic day. My idol at the time was the six year old movie star, Shirley Temple, who was also a tap-dancer. I could fantasize myself performing on the stage with her before a crowd of thousands. We executed a tapping duet.

Any news of that era was obtained by two methods: an ear pinned to the radio speaker or by news reels prior to feature films at the movie theater. It was 1934 and much was happening in the world. After a prolonged draught, along with misuse of the land, the Dust Bowl, or Dirty Thirties, laid waste to millions of acres of prairie land. Thousands of farmers were moving west looking for better land but finding conditions worse than they left. Many picked fruit in California for starvation wages.

World War I had ended in 1919 and the League of Nations was formed to prevent another such war, but didn't. After the First World War, the Treaty of Versailles' provision that Germany accepts full responsibility for the First World War and make reparation to certain countries caused the German hyperinflation of the 1920s.

Germans had to carry their money in suitcases to buy a loaf of bread. Wheelbarrows, as often depicted, were not the usual mode of transporting the cash. The Treaty was ignored by the early 1930s. It had not weakened Germany. In fact, Hitler was coming into power, flexing his muscles. He was appointed Chancellor in 1933 and quickly transformed the Weimar Republic into the Third Reich, a single party dictatorship. Within weeks Hitler would become the absolute dictator of Germany. There was so much to keep abreast of in the news in those days. My parents watched the news reels carefully and after the feature was over, I often fooled Dad, or so I thought, by feigning sleep so he would carry me home on his shoulders. Dads were so easy to fool at times, never Moms. We were heading for another World War that would affect all of our lives.

Grandma's second marriage produced a "change of life" baby, Andrea, an aunt a year older than me, who became as close as a sister. Andrea's father, Adam, had varicose veins in his legs that had not been treated so he developed gangrene in both legs. The process of removing black toes, then legs, a little at a time, was heart breaking to a teenage daughter that had to take care of half a man. All twenty five cousins were on their knees praying for his death for several days. When Adam was finally blessed with death it was on Halloween night with all his nieces and nephews called back from their trick or treating in the neighborhood. Adam must have thought he had already left the planet when he opened his eyes and saw the ghosts and ghouls kneeling around his bedside, praying that the Lord would finally take him.

$\mathscr{C}$HAPTER 2

Jay, Julius Leonard, was born on December 29, 1926 of two Lithuanian immigrants; both parents were thirty years old when their son was born following their daughter, Laura's, birth in 1918. A note found in his Dad's, Julius Joseph's hand described his childhood in a small Lithuanian village.

> I was born in Lithuania in 1896 (or thereabout). No records were kept at that time. I was brought up Catholic. Our home was a one room cottage. All cooking and sleeping was done here. We had clay floors and we slept on rye hay covered with a sheet. Chickens roamed freely in the room. I was a sickly child. When I was five or six, I was sent into the fields as a shepherd boy to watch the cattle. We had cows, pigs and sheep. I was frightened by lightning.
>
> I crossed myself after each bolt and prayed for an older brother to come and bring me home.
>
> My Mother had fourteen children, eight of whom lived. All immigrated to America except two, a brother and sister. Mother was an angel but Father was an alcoholic who never spoke or ate meals with

the children. He was mean and very demanding of Mother.

Jay's Dad was born with a leg that didn't develop properly. The circulation was so poor that they feared that he would lose the leg to gangrene. The child's Father could not concern himself with his son's birth defect. The oldest brother took Julius to Warsaw to see a doctor. This brother immigrated to America also but later returned to Lithuania for the custom was that the oldest son inherited the farm or whatever assets the family owned; the second son usually went into the priesthood and ascending the hierarchy, depending upon the wealth of his family. He lived comfortably on the tithing of his parishioners. The remaining children had to fend for themselves leading many to seek their fortune in the New World.

Most fell away from the Catholic Church in Lithuania because the Mother said she had been approached by a Catholic priest for sex. Their politics soon became communistic for they saw what Russia was doing for their country, although it was benefiting the USSR instead, but there was no convincing them. Life was so much better for the peasants when there was a rule to follow, plus some of the smarter relatives were being educated by the government.

Julius Joseph, Jay's Dad, left his Mother when he was only sixteen years old, never to see her again. Nor did he ever see the brother and sister that remained in Lithuania. With a few coins that Mother scraped together jingling in his pocket, and his name pinned to his jacket, he started on his three week journey across the Atlantic Ocean. The sea voyage included many bouts of seasickness for him and his fellow passengers in steerage. He, at last, passed the awe-inspiring Statue of Liberty and arrived at Ellis Island, where all immigrants had to land to enter the United States. To assure the government that he would not become a burden on the new country, Julius had been sponsored by his brother, Anthony, who had to promise to support and find work for him. Ellis Island was where the endless waiting began; waiting for inspections, waiting to be tested in math, waiting for results, waiting for family to arrive, praying that the doctors would not reject his shriveled leg.

When Anthony finally arrived, Julius was driven to another brother's home in the coal mining town of Wilkes-Barre, Pennsylvania. The year was 1914 and anthracite coal was king. Every immigrant could get a job in the coal mines. Julius had added a couple of years to his age so he could obtain work sooner than normally allowed. He descended into this terrifying black hole with his mining brother, Joe. Julius was so claustrophobic that he lasted only one day. This was not what he thought the New World was all about. A farm boy that had been a shepherd, accustomed to open fields and blue skies could never make his living in the dark bowels of the earth.

It was Henry Ford's offer to pay laborers on Ford's production lines, the unprecedented high wages of five dollars a day that took him to Detroit where he met Anna, a Lithuanian peasant girl who became his wife. They met at the Ida Chorus of the Lithuanian Club. A club they had sought, found, and joined immediately; a club where others spoke their native tongue.

Anna, the shy one, was so eager to marry that she gave Julius an ultimatum. Marry her or she will walk away. Fearing he would not find another pretty girl to pay attention to him he agreed to the marriage. His fear of not meeting another young woman was unwarranted for he was a gregarious person who loved to sing and to meet new people. Yet he was so self-conscious about his short stature and his leg that he could not overcome his bashfulness.

Anna spent the summers camping with her two children at Island Lake, about twenty miles west of Detroit, where her husband could join her on weekends. Island Lake was a small lake where Jay (or Junior, as he was known in those days although he wasn't technically a junior) could reach an unhabituated island by jumping up and down off the bottom. Why a young boy would want to reach the island was unknown but it was something to keep him occupied. The lake was surrounded by a state park that assured the safety of the mother and children sleeping in a tent.

The family was living in a modest two story home on Weatherby Street in central Detroit, where the Sherrill Elementary School was one block away, and the children could walk to school. Jay had his kindergarten and first grade at Sherrill. The Depression was in its throes. The five dollars a day wage did not support the family plus cover the interest-only payments on the house that the banks were demanding. The family had to leave their home and rent it out. They had to find a home they could afford. The only reasonably priced home they could find was on Trenton Street across from the municipal dump. Thus the low rent.

The public school Jay attended from this embarrassing location placed him into the third grade. He skipped second grade altogether. His new school was about a half mile from home and the youngster got lost on his first day walking home. School busses that transported children to school were not in existence at that time.

When home the dangerous city dump became the boy's playground. On one incident Jay and a couple of playmates were scrounging at the dump when one of the boys fell into a pit of trash filled with oil. The frightened boys ran to tell the victim's parents, who quickly rescued their son. That was the last time the boys were allowed to play at the dump. It was not a healthy playground for children.

The Greblicks found a family friend, John, who could co-rent the house with them because it had a large yard where John could raise his chickens and rabbits. There were few neighbors around to complain about the menagerie in the yard. Jay's Dad often went out with John to peddle the eggs, rabbits, and chickens.

After a few months in this depressing location the family moved to a more respectable single family home on Snowden Street. It was at this house that Jay remembers his first game of "Spin the Bottle" in the woods behind the house. When the bottle landed on him he was too bashful to kiss the girl. Had the boy inherited his Dad's bashfulness? He was a pudgy, hazel-eyed, blond boy with curly hair that was the envy of his Mother and sister. Lithuanians are more typically Slavic looking, of light colored eyes and fair skin, than the Poles who could be made up of many different tribes, including Germanic.

It was on Snowden that Jay almost lost a cousin. Jay and his cousins, Stanley and Leonard Bogus, loved to play in an abandoned warehouse building. Somehow Leonard, the oldest, scrambled up on the roof of the two story building and fell off. Fortunately, he fell into a swale of soft mud, not breaking any bones. That was again the last time the boys were allowed to play in that abandoned building.

Laura and Jay often speak about the good times they had at Joe Terza's farm. In the summertime the Ida Chorus spent many weekends there. Teenager, Laura, would not reveal the games played in the hayloft where the young people slept. The farm had an old quarry pit that Joe had cleaned out. He removed all the wire and debris from the water turning it into a popular revenue-producing swimming hole. The hole included a diving board and crystal clear water. Jay's summer job was to collect the twenty five cents per carload at the gate.

He was also to help around the farm. One of his chores was to walk the cows down the railroad tracks for a mile or so to graze on the tender grass along the track that got little attention from the railroad maintenance men. This journey was so engrained in the cows that they automatically turned toward home when they reached the end of the road. They knew they had to turn around at that point. It was amazing to a young boy; that animals could have such habit forming behavior instilled in their brains.

There was one other move after the Snowden house before the Greblicks could move back into their original home on Weatherby, the home that his Dad never lost to the bank. The interim move was into a smaller flat in a friend's home, the Daukus family, on Normandy Street. They were at Daukus' flat for just a few months when the Weatherby house became available once again. The renter's wife committed suicide by putting her head in the oven, and turning on the gas. Back then stoves did not have automatic pilot lights. Fortunately, there was no refrigerator motor that could cause a spark and explosion, just the typical wooden ice box. The wife basically died of suffocation.

The husband no longer wanted to live in the home that took his wife from him.

Attending the Sherrill School again Jay made a lifelong friend of one of his classmates, Steve Siskowski, with whom he would later run away from home as teenage adventurers to find the Lost Dutchman's Gold Mine in Arizona. Jay loved to read and learned of the mine in the endless library books he devoured. He coaxed Steve to leave with him on this grand adventure.

Laura, eight years Jay's senior, was already finished with high school and married by the time Jay graduated from Sherrill's eighth grade at thirteen years of age. He then got his first bicycle to travel the two miles to MacKenzie High School. The year was 1939 and there were still no school busses. Any child in the city living less than two miles from school was expected to bike or walk. While the first school bus was a horse-drawn carriage for a London Quaker school in 1827, it was not until after World War II that the public schools in North America were consolidated and busing for the rural areas began to flourish.

Throughout his early teens Jay was always the boy that traveled on his bike to visit his cousins a dozen miles away but never the reverse. The cousins were not lucky enough to own bicycles. Jay was quite mature for his age. His parents trusted him to travel alone for long distances. Or perhaps they did not worry enough about him or his whereabouts. This could very well have led to his adventure of running away from home with his buddy, Steve, three or four years later.

Laura and her new husband, Botvid, understandably better known as Buck, were living in one of the bedrooms at the Weatherby house. Buck was a chemical engineer and, noticing Jay's scholastic ability, talked the boy into taking the entrance exam for Cass Technical School where Buck had graduated. Cass was a three year technical school of such caliber that after graduation you could attend any college or university without taking an entrance exam. Jay started his sophomore year at Cass Tech but did not graduate for World War II interrupted most boys' education in the 1940s either by the draft or enlistment.

The attack on Pearl Harbor by the Japanese on December 7th, 1941 had every young man and boy eager to fight back. These two boys could barely wait until they were 17 when they could take up arms and defend their country.

CHAPTER 3

Leaving the familiarity of a small town and venturing into farming was quite a change for the Duss family, especially since their knowledge of farming was pretty much next to nothing. This would be on-the-job-training from day one. They found a large hip-roofed house on five acres of land with a two story barn, also with a hip roof, leaving a great space above the car on the second floor for curing hams or homemade sausages. The property had a large chicken coop, a corn crib, a brooder for raising baby chicks, a pig sty, and an outside hand pump to draw well water, a dog house and even an outhouse.

The farm was on Fifteen Mile Road, about a mile from Gratiot Avenue, where the public bus took us north to the closest town of Mt. Clemens. The town was known for its mineral baths that reeked of sulfur, or rotten eggs. People came from near and far to bathe in the hot sulfurous water to ease their arthritis. Often our well and house water had the same smell and taste. Our water discouraged families from staying too long on visits as it usually led to the "tourista" dance for the relatives, who were accustomed to the soft, city water of Wyandotte, Michigan. Our water also contained so much iron that an overnight drip would leave rust streaks to the drain.

This farmhouse had four bedrooms on the second floor and a small one on the main floor that Dad used so he could be closer to his booze in the refrigerator. There was only one bathroom, one black phone that was a party line where anyone on the line could listen in on your conversation. Party line users were polite and kept their conversations short in an attempt for some semblance of privacy. You had to ask the operator to dial the number for you. The numbers at that time were not all digits. They consisted of an area name and numbers.

One of the upper bedrooms was my Mom's. I never knew my parents to share a bedroom. Perhaps it was Dad's snoring, but more likely his drinking that kept them apart. Another upper bedroom was mine and the smallest one was my playroom that was reserved for future siblings. My bedroom faced the back yard where we allowed hunters to shoot pheasants in our recently harvested corn fields. I often heard bb shots hitting my windows when the hunters were stalking their prey.

Soon after we moved to the farm my parents decided to have a basement installed. This was no small feat in an existing two story house. The contractor had to carefully jack up the house on all sides with a dozen large jacks so as not to crack the walls. He and his crew then hand dug the dirt from the basement area. In their contract they also installed a concrete floor, a laundry tub and a sump pump because the water table was so high in that area. The front ten feet of the basement was walled with cement blocks in the middle. Half the space consisted of a coal bin on the driveway side of the house and a "fruit cellar" in the other half. The cool cellar stored all the jars of canned goods plus a couple of kegs of wine from our Concord grapes. Dad tried making wine from gooseberries and even dandelions, but the grapes always won the contest. The coal bin was loaded by chute from a truck in the driveway. We then could shovel the coal directly into the furnace from the coal bin. Our old wooden ice box also lived in the cool, dank space next to the laundry tubs with its own drain where the melting ice could trickle to the sewer and disappear. We ordered ice by the block, putting a sign in the front window with the 100, 50, 75 or 25 pound number at the top. The ice man knew how much ice was needed from what number was upright on the sign.

There was also a milk chute installed on the driveway side where the milkman delivered the milk in glass bottles with paper caps. If the temperature dropped too low the paper cap would rise a few inches above the bottle as the liquid froze. Mom often bought her butter from the milkman plus he had eggs for those not raising their own chickens. At times I walked to a neighbor's house, half mile away, where the bachelor farmer's Mother still used an old wooden churn to make her butter. I suspected she also had a loom hidden in the house where she could weave her own fabric.

While the basement was being installed, Mom and Dad planted dozens of fruit trees. At harvest time we had bushels of sour cherries, plums, peaches, and apples. We gave away as much as family and friends could pick. They canned and made jellies, as did Mom. There were also plenty of vegetables like potatoes, carrots, radishes, cucumbers, tomatoes and my favorite, sweet peas. The fruit cellar was always full of quarts of canned vegetables and handpicked mushrooms. We only picked those that were well known and edible. Whenever our stomachs grumbled we needed only to take a stroll in the garden or the orchard to satisfy our hunger.

In 1939 my brother, Larry, was born at home as most children were in the late 1930s. That was when doctors made house calls and siblings were sent to neighbors to play lest they see that the doctor's little black bag did not really contain the new baby. Of course, my belief at eight years of age was that the stork brought the babies but this puzzled me as I never saw any storks around the farm. I had, however, ordered a brother the last time we saw a stork at the zoo. I would stand at the stork's cage and shout that he should bring me a brother, to the amusement of other onlookers, so this event was no surprise to me. The stork was just following my orders.

Farm life provided so many memories, some pleasant, some not. The hens always pecked at your hands when you tried to harvest eggs from their nests. They sat on a glass egg to encourage the laying of another egg. We had to candle the eggs, that is, hold them over a light to make sure there were no blood clots starting the formation of a new chick. We learned that chickens need gravel to keep their gizzards clean, that the roosters are loud, the chickens pooped a lot, and shoveling out the straw and replacing with fresh was a never-ending task. The manure pile next to the chicken coop produced incredibly sweet strawberries. The berry seeds must have been in the straw we piled up outside the coop each day. I had no idea that chickens ate so many strawberries. The chickens could reach our grapes and raspberries from their fenced in area but there were no strawberry plants. Only those growing in the manure pile. Where could the chickens have gotten the strawberries?

Dad later built a cage to hold several rabbits. We kept them for food until we learned that rabbit food attracts rats so we quickly ate all the rabbits and gave up raising them. Our dozens of baby chicks were ordered from catalogs via the post office and arrived in large cardboard cartons with many circular holes cut out for air circulation. It was sad to see the weakest chicks crushed in the shipping process. I spent many hours playing with the chicks under their aluminum canopy that contained light bulbs to keep them warm.

The ducks were fun to watch waddling around the fenced-in yard but we shied away from the geese. The gander would not allow anyone near his harem. Dad advised that their wings are strong enough to break your leg as they hung on to your clothes with their beak and beat you with their wings until you left his females alone.

Along Fifteen Mile road there were a dozen large mulberry trees to climb and gorge on the ripe berries; the berries stained our clothes so Mom knew exactly where we were for the afternoon by the color of the stain. The stains were either mulberries or sweet cherries. Our property had two large sweet cherry trees. It was a challenge to climb the tree and pick the berries before the birds feasted on them. One year we attempted to cover both trees with cheesecloth. That was fun but futile for the robins always found a way to get under the cloth.

There was an immense black walnut tree on the rear portion of our five acres. The land was split by a county ditch that had a culvert allowing us to drive our tractor to the other half of the property where we planted field corn. We planted sweet corn close to the house but the corn never tasted as good as the field corn we swiped from the neighbor's farm. It was the sweetness of forbidden fruit as proven by Eve and enjoyed by the Duss children. Mom somehow knew that we had swiped the field corn when we asked her to cook it for us.

In our farming adventure we learned that black walnuts are not an easily accessible nut. You had to lay them on the concrete road and drive a heavy truck or tractor over them a few times before the green husk would split open and the small nut become available. No wonder they have such a strong flavor for it is so hard to get any meat out of this tiny shell.

When I started school at St. Louis Elementary, I had to walk a mile east on Fifteen Mile Road to catch the school bus traveling north on Harper Avenue for the five miles leading to the school. Dad was so proud to be in America that he wanted his children not to have a Polish accent. He hired a tutor for me since he thought I had an accent from my attendance at St. Stanislaus where all the classes were conducted in Polish. The parish priest was my tutor and I soon spoke proper American English enough for my Dad to stop the tutoring.

St. Louis Elementary was staffed by the Sisters of Charity, who tolerated no nonsense from the students. On the nice days I was allowed to ride my bike the five miles to school. Parents never had to worry about children riding bikes for any distance. The few cars on the road did not travel at speeds over 35 mph. There was never an incident of child molestation. I had heard of a neighbor committing incest with his daughter but I didn't know what that meant. But I did understand when another neighbor hung himself for reasons unknown. My classmates and I were frightened when one girl had serious epileptic seizures with the frothing and kicking. The classroom had to be evacuated every time it happened.

Opportunity arose to buy the adjoining five acres and Dad jumped at the chance. The fate of his family in Poland compelled him to own as much land as possible. The Russians evicted his family from land owned by his household for generations. Dad was now in America where the land could not be taken from him as it was in Poland. Dad enjoyed sitting at the kitchen window, admiring his ten acres. He was always dressed in his full length BVDs (a sleeveless, one piece, loose fitting underwear) and suspendered pants. BVDs stood for Bradley, Voorhees & Day, and the manufacturer of underwear for both men and women, starting in the nineteenth century with bustles for women. Dad wallowed in his ownership of land which no bureaucrat could confiscate. He had just a few years of formal schooling in the farm country of Europe but was an intelligent, well-read, and self-taught man. He had the Old-Country beliefs that the cooking, cleaning, washing and ironing were a woman's work. Men and boys had no business in the kitchen, even to help clean up.

Of course, it was all right for Mom to help with the outside work. She often walked behind the plow while Dad drove the tractor because Mom couldn't drive. She was well into her forties when she thought this was enough nonsense. After teaching herself to drive in the old Model T Ford coupe that we kept on the farm, she took the bus into town, and boldly walked into the police station to take her test. The sympathetic officer that gave her the road test said, after she failed the parallel parking portion, that she just needs to park further away and walk. He said his wife couldn't park either. Thus she became one of the millions of new drivers on the roads although it was much later in life than normal.

Henry Ford's Model T Ford was known as the Tin Lizzie or Flivver, the one that "put America on wheels". It was most likely the first automobile that my parents owned. It had a rumble seat that could only be used in fair weather for it was outside where the luggage trunk is today. You had to crank the Tin Lizzie to start the motor and be careful that the crank did not unwind and break your arm unexpectedly. I practiced in the Model T also and had my driver's license at fourteen years, when children that young were allowed to drive. I did run over a few of the fruit trees but they were young trees and easily recovered from the abuse.

Some of my traumatic memories are of puppies drowning in the outhouse cesspool when my toddler brother, Larry, threw them in to see if they could swim. Why he didn't chose the county ditch that always had water in it will never be known. He later accused me of pushing his buggy into that same ditch when I had to babysit him but thought I had better things to do. Or the time I scarred my nose when we were playing hockey in the frozen ditch. My skate caught my playmates skate and I met the jagged ice on the edge of the ditch with my nose. There was also the broken arm of my friend's brother, Fred, when he walked into my bat as we were playing softball. Nor can I forget and forgive the maidenly neighbor sisters that refused to let me bring my brother into their home. I could not tend to his serious wound when he jumped off their porch step and caught his back, just an inch from his spine, on the stubs sticking out from their steel post. It was the type of post that you hung barbed wire on for a pasture fence. What it was doing in their garden next to the steps we will never learn. He was bleeding profusely but I had to take him home on the carrier of my bike. The holier-than-thou ladies were afraid he might bleed on their carpet.

The most frightening memory is of the tornado that bowled down Fifteen Mile Road roaring like an approaching train. The four Dusses were on their knees in the kitchen praying as we watched the brooder coop spiraled fifty feet into the air then was gently placed back on the ground, yards away from its original site. The dog house also went spinning into the funnel with Prince, our Chow/German Shepherd dog gone, never to be seen again. The huge barn was moved a couple of feet off of its foundation but was able to be pushed back into place with heavy equipment. The house sustained no damage despite limbs and debris hitting the windows for the eternal length of the tornado, which must have lasted only a few minutes.

Another chilling memory is of the lightning bolt that passed through the house leaving a streak on the living room carpet for a few seconds, shooting out the front of the house, and then splitting the lone tree in the field across the road. Or the bolt that struck the widow neighbor's water bucket, with the bucket bursting into flames.

There was also the embarrassment of attending grade school in home-sewn dresses made out of chicken feed sacks, printed with flowered patterns for the poor people. Times had been tough on the farm for when your chickens, eggs, fruit, or vegetables are ready for market so is every other farmer's.

There were thrilling memories as well when Dad took us driving or I should say spinning on frozen Lake St. Clair after a rain that left the lake like a giant, perfectly groomed, skating rink; or the speed, heeling, and thrill of a ride on an ice boat. Larry to this day remembers his fright when Dad tossed him into deep water from the dock at a friends' summer cottage, figuring the child will either sink or swim. The boy was so traumatized that he would not take his shoes off at any beach for years afterward lest someone might throw him in the water again.

Mom's older sister, Sophie, took a dozen cousins every year for summer vacations to her cabin on Lake Superior. They were among our wealthier relatives. They had a large Packard car and owned a bar with their living quarters over the bar. She enlisted her kids and any cousins that happened to be available to help with the weekly fish fries held at the bar on Fridays. On one trip north I remember sitting on a watermelon for the all-day trek to Alpina. It was 250 miles, long before interstate highways or even paved roads. Sophie earned her angel's halo for having so many youngsters underfoot.

The cabin was only three rooms but we were pint-sized kids so it seemed immense to us. The boys slept in tents under the pine trees in the yard, the girls were in the cabin with Sophie. We picked huckleberries in the mornings and were rewarded with movies or burgers at the local diner in the afternoons. I remember crying when I returned home after a summer in Alpina and my baby brother did not remember who I was.

One fateful day I saved Sophie's oldest son, Eugene's life. Gene had contracted polio and while swimming out to the raft anchored in water over our heads he started to struggle. I swam out to him, had the good sense to take him underwater, stand on the bottom, turn him around and push him to the raft. I had to convince him to go back into the water, to try swimming again. I vowed after that incident that I would take life-saving lessons when I grew up. Despite this heroic deed I was never able to get my brother's shoes off of him whenever he was near water or on a beach. Dad's method was not the way to teach a child to swim.

CHAPTER 4

Jay and Steve were sixteen and seventeen, respectfully, when they left home for their western adventure. Jay had worked in an Awrey's Bakery taking bread from the hot ovens to save money for the trip. Steve also worked at the same bakery to earn the spending money he would need for this adventure. Both were in the Civil Air Patrol during their high school years and had uniforms similar to Army uniforms. Dressed in their uniforms the boys were able to hitchhike across the country. Rides were easy to catch, dressed in any uniform during this patriotic war. We had been attacked and the losses at Pearl Harbor justified the war. All drivers were willing to pick up military men going any direction in the country. The boys admitted they were in the Civil Air Patrol and not the military but the drivers accepted them—not knowing they were running away from home to search for gold in the Superstition Mountains around Phoenix.

When they reached Arizona they detoured to see the Grand Canyon. With the vigor of teenagers they decided to walk down the trail, but often slid straight down to avoid the long hairpin turns. They were heading to the Phantom Ranch at the bottom of the Canyon. They rented a room, had dinner and breakfast then headed back up the Canyon in the early morning. In their exuberance and ignorance they did not carry water with them. The trail in 1942 had no water so it wasn't until they reached snow near the rim that they could quench their thirst, with white snow only.

It was March when they left home. They had reached St. Louis before Jay called his Mother. She told the boy she knew he was not coming back after the weekend. The boys lied that they were going on CAP maneuvers so the packed duffle bags did not arouse suspicion, they thought. While out west the young men tried their hand at setting pins in a bowling alley and picking fruit in the groves. Steve advised Jay that he would soon be eighteen and rather than be drafted into the Army he was going to join the Navy. He joined as promised and left Jay on his own. The two were in Arizona for weeks but never did have the wherewithal, read money, to search for the Lost Dutchman's Gold Mine. Jay later got a better paying job as a welder, having had a class at Cass Tech. He was big for his age and passed as somewhat older than sixteen, Jobs were plentiful during the war with any type of skill that could be useful. He remembers one night spent in a flop house—where he paid only twenty five cents for a cot wet with urine. Home wasn't so bad after all, he figured, so he saved his money to return to the comfort of his parents.

At fourteen he tried to enlist in the Navy. Instead of ridicule, the wise doctors told him his eyes were not good enough for the service in order not to discourage the boy. They hoped he would return when he reached the proper age. Every boy shaves at an early age to encourage their beard to grow. The peach fuzz doesn't pay attention to the early shaving, however. Only time will make it change and then the boy-turned-man wonders why he ever wanted to start this lifelong shaving ordeal.

Jay realized that this was not the life for him. He wanted to finish his education. He packed his few belongings and started hitchhiking home. It was a weekend when he arrived home so he went directly to Terza's farm where he knew his parents would be. He told his parents he wanted to go back to school. They embraced their prodigal son and accepted him back into the fold.

Buck, Laura's husband, became Jay's mentor supplying him with chemicals and lab equipment either pilfered from his workplace or purchased from a chemical supply company in the city of Detroit. He was also responsible for leading the boy to a career in science.

CHAPTER 5

My high school years were filled with activities. My most exciting activity was cheer-leading. I was quickly accepted into the squadron because I could perform cartwheels and splits, taught by my Dad at Belle Isle Park. We traveled with the basketball and football teams resulting in my crush on the best football player. I had been wearing glasses since early school years when the nuns noticed that if I didn't sit in the front row I couldn't see the board. I truly believed the adage that "boys never make passes at girls that wear glasses". I resigned myself to the fact that I would certainly be an old maid, alone in my senior years. Despite my self-consciousness of wearing glasses, I won a popularity contest and became the Queen of Hearts for a homecoming dance. I was walking on clouds for the football player I had a crush on was my escort for the dance. What more can a teenage girl wish for than this dream date. I had a good mind and figure, with dynamite legs that helped in attracting male attention but I couldn't help worrying about my shortcomings.

Living on a small farm provided access to a neighbor's hay wagon pulled by a team of horses. My moonlit hayride parties were popular and well attended. The classmates always requested that my Mother and her two friends, Mrs. Koze and Mrs. Pickler act as chaperones because the three of them were so much fun. This speaks volumes about their personalities. I seemed to be developing into my Mother's personality; optimistic, fun loving, and daring with some wanderlust thrown into the mix.

The graduating class from St. Louis eight grade moved to St. Mary's High School in downtown Mt. Clemens. I was just twelve years old as a freshman and short so the nuns still insisted on a cigar box under my feet; it was embarrassing again to a girl that was younger than her classmates and wearing glasses to boot.

I had a great Chemistry teacher in high school, Sister Xaveria, who piqued my interest in Science. I had hopes of becoming a nurse after volunteering as a Candy Stripper at the hospital but this nun convinced me otherwise. Plus you had to be eighteen to enter nursing and I would only be sixteen when I finished high school. Sister Xaveria and my parents convinced me to go to college for the two years I had to wait. That was the demise of the nursing career.

High school classes included Latin, Physics, Chemistry, Home Economics, where I learned to cook and sew, plus whatever Liberal Arts courses were required for college entrance. To earn some spending money I had a job after school at a bakery in town, although the temptations were too great for a teenager. In later years of high school I was allowed to date and Mom would always be up and turning on the porch light the minute I arrived home. She, of course, had not slept until I reached the back yard.

From St. Mary's High School I proceeded to Marygrove College, a small Catholic girl's college on Six Mile Road in Detroit. The campus was about 30 miles from home so I had the privilege of living on campus in the dormitory, Madame Cadillac Hall. The experience of living away from home matures youngsters quickly without Mom and Dad to rein you in and advise you. My weekly allowance was two dollars but that was in the days when tuition was a fraction of present day's costs, including room and board.

I was the youngest in the freshman class until Teresita Perez arrived from Guam where she beat me by a month or so. Teresita said the Japanese bombed Guam on December 8, 1941, the day after Pearl Harbor. Her family escaped by hiding in the woods where they buried their family treasure hoping to recover it after the war. Most of the girls at Marygrove were there to earn their MRS degree that is to find a college man to marry. In the meantime the majority of the students majored in Education so they could have the summer off.

There were only three students interested in Chemistry. We took classes, did our homework, and crammed for exams together. Our professor, Dr. Brewer, marked on a class average. One period it was my turn to get the A, the next it was Carrie's and the third period was Jane's time to excel. There were only five students in our Calculus and Physics class, three in Organic Chemistry. Our dorm rooms were connected by a bathroom so there were four suitemates, unless assigned to a double room.

It was in our freshman year that my roommate, Wanda Keester, and I, learned to smoke. The school rules stated that if caught smoking on campus there was automatic and immediate expulsion. Wanda and I opened the window, sat on the ledge and smoked, daring to be caught. Our room that freshman year was next to the nun, Sister Ann, who was the live-in Mother Superior for the dormitory. We never got caught; fortunately, for I am sure my parents would have tarred and feathered me.

I was always amazed that my roommate, Wanda, grew up on a farm and had more brothers than sisters yet had never seen a naked boy in her lifetime. I wondered how her Mother hid the brothers when she changed their diapers. Because our campus had twenty acres or more of woods that surrounded the dormitory it attracted many peeping Toms. Ladders were often found propped against the dormitory walls or the nun's quarters. This girls' campus attracted the dregs of male society. One day Wanda and I were walking down Six Mile Road when a man approached us wearing a long overcoat. As he drew near he opened his coat and flashed us with a very erect penis. We reported the incident to the police and were asked to appear at the station to look at a rogue's gallery of sex offenders. Wanda was beside herself from the whole event. She had no interest in men after the police told us that they could not do anything until the man harmed us. Yet this same innocent girl was pregnant when she walked down her wedding aisle.

The dormitory was also a finishing school of sorts for we were taught to head the table at dinnertime serving the other seven girls correctly. Teas were often held on Sunday afternoon where we had to wear gloves, hats and high heels along with modest and proper dresses. Slacks were not allowed. If we were going on a date that required slacks, like horseback riding, we had to roll up the slacks to hide them under our overcoat. For every minute we were late coming back from a date for the ten o'clock curfew we were required to return from the next date fifteen minutes. On one occasion I had fifteen minutes total for the date, not even enough time for a coke at The Cup, a small shop across Six Mile Road, where everyone hung out.

An article in our college monthly newsletter stated:

> "In our opinion Dolly Duss has become entangled in an Ideal web of trouble. Saturday night Dolly had a date with a perfectly D-I-V-I-N-E man that she met at an "at-home" (dance). But come the dawn of Sunday morn and Dolly is off bowling from 12:00 to 3:00 with a new man. Promptly at 3:00 the gentleman deposits Dolly at the door of Madame Cadillac little realizing that within another suitor awaits to take Dolly of all places—bowling.
>
> We nominate Miss Delphine Duss as the "femme fatale" of the Freshman Class".

There were many dances held in the main ballroom with the men invited from the University of Detroit, a mile away, or Wayne State University further down the road. The heavy drapes in Madame Cadillac Hall must have hidden many a stolen kiss. The towering Sister Ann along with a few other nuns chaperoned the dances. No male ventured to place even one foot on the steps leading to the girls' rooms. We had lights out at ten o'clock and the only time I flunked a test was a history exam when I hid in the closet to study all night. I was too tired the next day to think straight or pass an exam requiring dates and events that had to be recalled.

I was thrilled when I met Rick, a West Point Cadet during my sophomore year's summer. Rick wrote me every day with interesting letters detailing his life at the Academy. I was thrilled when he invited me to the Army/Navy football game in New York City and a weekend dance at West Point. Most memorable was a stroll down Flirtation Walk, where only cadets and their girlfriends are allowed and a kiss under the Blarney Stone is to be expected. It was strange bidding the men farewell at their lights out time and the girls heading to the Thayer Hotel. There are memories of dances in the Main Hall and the boob imprint of many large buttons on the men's uniforms when the cadet got too amorous. Rick and I eventually became engaged. His parents even gave us a plot of land as a gift. Rick had hopes of becoming a minister and I could not visualize a minister with a Catholic wife or my being able to convert to his Lutheran religion. We had a tearful departure promising to meet in heaven one day. Subsequently I learned from an ex-teacher of Rick's that he was sent to Russia after graduation and was killed while on assignment.

I never forgot my near drowning when I saved my cousin, Gene's, life so I made sure I took lifesaving classes in College. We had to take the classes at another campus as there was no swimming pool at Marygrove. Every student was also required to be involved in social work of some sort and I chose the Big Sister program where we visited, mentored, and entertained a neglected child or orphan. On my two dollar a week allowance from my parents it took some ingenuity to provide this service to the child.

It was during these college years that my friends from high school and college were getting married. Despite all my worry about wearing glasses I had been blessed with six proposals of marriage and was a bridesmaid six times. I began to wonder if I would ever be planning my own wedding day.

I was the instigator of many tricks on the brides and grooms and expected a full payback on my day. In one wedding the bride and I were kidnapped by the bride's brothers and not returned until the reception was long over. It was not funny for the bride or groom. I wondered if another adage: "Always a bridesmaid, never a bride" would come true for me but I had not yet met the man that would be my soul mate for life.

CHAPTER 6

When Jay returned home from his adventure out West he re-entered Cass Tech for a semester and a half, then when he turned seventeen he joined the Navy in the spring of 1944. A train ride, compliments of the U.S. Navy, took him to Great Lakes Recruit Training Command, the largest military installation in Illinois and the largest training center in the Navy. Great Lakes RTC has been training students for eighty years, turning civilians into seamen and seamen into sailors.

After thirteen weeks of boot camp where the civilians were indoctrinated with naval history and etiquette, orientation, aptitude tests, hours of exercise to get into shape, rifle range practice, and more testing, the trainees were given two weeks leave to bid farewell to their families, many never to return home. Upon their return to Great Lakes, their assignments of either further training or active duty were posted on a large board for all to see. A man standing next to Jay, probably in his thirties and an enlistee in the Navy to avoid the Army draft, with a wife and two children, was assigned to a destroyer, the ships that surround convoys to intercept the German torpedoes aimed at more strategic targets. The man started to weep.

Because Jay had not finished high school he was not qualified to become a radio technician to repair radios. He was assigned as a radioman and would be at Great Lakes for twenty more weeks to become proficient in typing Morse code. After the further training he was sent to Curacao, Netherlands Antilles. During World War II Curacao and its neighboring island, Aruba, had large refineries that supplied most of the fuel for English, French, Canadian, and American planes. To the sailors stationed on the islands the area was known as Torpedo Junction. Many German U-Boats patrolled the region planning to torpedo the tankers. They did manage to sink thirty ships or more.

Curacao had a ten square mile tank farm that stored 18,000,000 barrels of crude and refined petroleum. The two islands, Curacao and Aruba, were only sixty miles from Venezuela with its newly discovered oil in Lake Maracaibo. The two islands provided secure harbors and were strategically located to protect the Panama Canal. The trip to Curacao was on a tanker out of New York harbor. For three days the tanker had to head back toward New York to avoid a storm at sea. Jay, standing on the fantail of the ship, could see water under the bow. It was a rough ride for a new sailor but he was blessed with never experiencing seasickness.

By the time Jay enlisted in the Navy in the spring of 1944 the war was winding down. He was still in Curacao when VE Day was celebrated by islanders with dancing in the Fort and the streets. The Germans signed the unconditional surrender documents on May 8, 1945, the day Europeans and Americans celebrated V-E Day, Victory in Europe. We dropped the first nuclear bomb on Hiroshima on August 6th and on Nagasaki on August 9th. Within six days of the bombings Japan announced their surrender to the Allies but didn't sign the Instrument of Surrender until September 2, 1945, when we celebrated V-J Day or Victory over Japan. It was not until 1951 that the Treaty of Peace was signed with Japan.

During 1945 the United Nations was formed to prevent another world conflict and to replace the League of Nations formed after World War I. It is questionable whether the United Nations is doing a better job than the League of Nations did to prevent conflict.

Returning home, after two years in the Navy, Cass Tech allowed Jay to take his GED exam, giving him the opportunity to enroll in college without completing normal high school classes or graduation. The school also allowed him to buy a class ring representing a graduation from their school.

Graduates of Cass Tech were not required to take entrance exams at any college because the school was so highly rated. He was accepted at Wayne University for the spring semester. In the meantime he met a Norwegian girlfriend of his cousin's future wife who lived in the Upper Peninsula of Michigan. He quickly switched to a school in Marquette, the Northern Michigan College of Education, to be near his girl.

Jay's Mother dreamed of her son becoming a dentist. Lacking plans for his future, he followed his Mother's dream and prepared for dental school. The new girlfriend then moved to Detroit for employment, so Jay, having no reason to stay in the Upper Peninsula soon followed south and enrolled at the University of Detroit, which had a dental school. The romance ended. Jay's parents, in the meantime, moved to Florida so he sought housing from the University.

The G.I. Bill of Rights provided the veterans with all their education expenses as well as home loans with no money down and low interest rates. The ninety dollars per month subsistence for food left the vets somewhat hungry at the end of the month, becoming quite tired of cheese and crackers. Jay then quit U of D as a full time student and sought work. He found a job at Ethyl Corporation in the laboratories on Eight Mile Road. Ethyl was the research laboratories for General Motors Corp. It was considered "country club" living but with a paycheck. Bagged lunches from home were consumed outside at picnic benches under immense shade trees on immaculately trimmed lawns. Ethyl wisely kept their chemists and scientists happy, well paid, and well trained.

CHAPTER 7

My graduation from Marygrove in 1955 made my parents proud beyond words. Many relatives tried to discourage my parents from spending the money on an education for a girl. Why does a girl need to go to college to take care of children and wash diapers? I was the first of twenty five cousins in the family to graduate from college. To major in Chemistry was unheard of in the 1950s. My Chemistry Professor, Dr. Brewer, met with my parents during the years at Marygrove and tried to convince them and me to proceed to a teaching position or into library science.

Dad always told me I could do anything I wanted to, so I intended to break new ground. There were few jobs for women in the laboratories but the war had just ended. I had no trouble finding employment at the Detroit Tank Arsenal. The Arsenal was the first manufacturing plant for the mass production of tanks in the United States. It was established in 1940 under Chrysler Corp. and the construction effort in 1941 was one of the fastest on record. The building was designed as a dual production facility to make armaments during the war and then to be turned into peaceful production at war's end.

The men in the laboratory were not happy with the hiring of the first female. They complained that there would be no more swearing in the lab and I would soon be hanging lace curtains on the windows. That never happened. In fact one huge black man told me stories of going to the West Indies and contracting with a woman to bear a son for him. I had just graduated from a strict girl's Catholic college. After sixteen years of education by priests and nuns I was stunned by the morals of one of these complainers. Another complainer had his come-uppance with a serious explosion in the lab while using potassium permanganate and sulfuric acid in his laboratory hood. This combination results in a very explosive mixture that shattered his hood and half the laboratory. Because the Tank Arsenal finally hired their first woman in the laboratory, I swore that I had no voodoo dolls on me nor did I put a hex on this man.

It was at the Tank Arsenal that I met Buck Schevo who became my mentor as well as Jay's counselor. He was also the husband of the woman, Laura, who would eventually become my sister-in-law. I soon left the Tank Arsenal for a better position and more pay at Ethyl Corporation. I was to work in the analytical laboratory, more to my liking than testing steel at the Tank Arsenal.

I too quickly learned that Ethyl was indeed "country club" living. The labs in the analytical building were designed for two chemists. A particular thorn in my side was the fact that I worked alongside a married man, doing the same work as he did, but got paid less money—because he had a family to support. This was typical for the mid 1950s. Women were just entering the work force, en masse. They didn't expect to get the same pay as the men and they begrudgingly accepted this fact.

Ethyl tested our gasoline products along with our competitor's. At that time we provided most of the tetraethyl lead additive for automobile fuels as an anti-knock agent. Our building had two engines that roared continuously in the rear room testing the gasoline. I learned that the TEL (tetraethyl lead) was so dangerous that if we spilled a drop of it we would have to strip completely, burn our clothes, and bury the ashes; the concrete floor would have to be replaced, and the lab completely tested before we could reenter. The danger, we were told, of TEL was discovered when two men cleaning out a storage tank went mad and then died. The heavy metal, lead, in the TEL causes insanity, and then death, not a comforting thought.

Every spring the various departments of women hosted a luncheon for all the other women of the company at a fancy hotel or restaurant. The hostesses were required to produce the entertainment in the form of skits or parodies about life and work at Ethyl. When it was the analytical labs turn to entertain I remember putting on a strip tease with long underwear, a skirt we made and mops on our heads for hair but Pat, (who worked in my lab with me) and I changed the dance routine but didn't advise the third girl on stage with us. The laughter was deafening and the kudos were many.

In the fall months the company held a dinner/dance at the Latin Quarter, which was the highlight of Detroit's social scene. Besides the elegance of the Latin Quarter itself, there were tuxedoed waiters, ice sculptors, mounds of shrimp, meat carving stations manned by chefs in their crisp aprons and toques, and an endless buffet table of desserts. There was always entertainment put on by either talented employees or hired professionals.

It was in this setting that I accepted an invitation to a Halloween party put on by Jay and his housemates. I had had a disagreement with my current boyfriend, Carl, who wanted me to convert to Lutheranism. I was serious enough about this man to take lessons in his church from his minister who tried to convince me that the earth was only 6000 years old. The minister was insisting on a literal translation of the Bible. I was trained as a scientist. After my astronomy classes in college I learned that the light we see today left the star thousands of light years ago. Every day fossils were being found that dated back millenniums. I knew that the minister's theory could not be true. I had previously dated a man that had studied to become a Catholic priest, then this Lutheran "mama's boy", a cadet that wanted to become a minister and even a good Pollack that would not cause any problem for my family. But Leonard was like a brother to me. He was the son of very good friends of my parents. Both parents dreamed of us being married. At this point I was looking for an interesting, exciting, and acceptable man. There must be someone around.

I knew of Jay before we dated for he had been seeing Pat, the woman who shared a laboratory with me. Pat had a young son from her divorced husband. She was five years older than Jay. She turned down his proposal advising him that he should look for someone younger. I was also aware that Jay had a reputation around Ethyl of being a flirt with all the women, which made him interesting.

I drove alone to the Halloween party and while dancing with Jay in the recreation room basement we were separated by his most recent girlfriend, Ellen. She was angry that he invited me and, displaying quite a temper, hauled off and slapped him loudly on the cheek. From that day on we were inseparable. We always dated at a quiet, discreet bar, Tassie's Tavern, on Harper Avenue, where we could talk for hours and get to know each other, or put some nickels in the juke box and dance the evening away. We never went to a movie where you sit in silence for hours. We played on the Twilight Golf League and the Bowling League together.

During one date, while attending a high school football game in Mt. Clemens, Jay proposed. I did not accept immediately for here was another non-Catholic. His proposal raised a rumpus with my beliefs. We had only been dating for three weeks. He knew he had found the right person but I wasn't sure. Why was I meeting all these men that would give me, my family, or my church trouble?

CHAPTER 8

My Dad had been working nights and never met Jay so when the man properly asked my parents for my hand in marriage Dad said:

"What did you say your name was?" We'll never forget that line.

We had decided that I would not need an engagement ring but my Mom was so disappointed that we made a concession. The first day I wore the ring into work my coworkers all said:

"You are not going to marry him, are you?"

It was a total shock to everyone for we had known each other only three weeks. I had not had any discussions with my coworkers regarding a possible engagement. They were all surprised, as well as us.

Over Christmas we planned a trip to Florida to meet my new in-laws. The trip was lengthy and arduous, long before any interstate highways. There were monotonous stretches through the mountains on narrow two lane roads. It took thirty hours of dangerous driving.

The Duss and Greblick families met and enjoyed each other's company until Dad, true to his drinking self, got smashed, as we feared, but expected. I often asked Mom why she stayed married to him and she replied that it was for the children. But one must remember that a woman of that day was not trained to be independent nor did she have a career that she could rely on to support herself and her children.

I had dreamed of being a June bride but fearing that my Dad would not be sober enough to walk me down the aisle, plus I was eager to leave their household. We moved the wedding date up to February 19th, 1955. I am sure my aunts and uncles thought I was pregnant thus requiring the earlier wedding date. I could see them counting the months on their fingers as I walked down to the altar of my church on my father's arm. Because Jay was not Catholic we had to be married at the side altar. The Catholic Church was not accommodating in the 1950s. When Jay proposed he said he would turn Catholic for me and I told him that I had enough to worry about with my own soul and didn't want the responsibility of his soul too. Dad did stay sober long enough to escort me to the altar. Jay's parents came by bus for the long trip to Michigan.

Despite having a "mixed" marriage we had two priests at our wedding: my pastor, Fr. Schram, who officiated at the ceremony and Fr. Shum, Jay's physical chemistry professor. Fr. Shum would read his Office quickly during class so he could go out in the evening for a few beers with his students.

It was close to Valentine's Day so my two bridesmaids wore bright red dresses. Jay's friend, Steve, his co-adventurer to the Lost Dutchman's Gold Mine, was his best man and my college age brother, Larry, was the other usher. Our reception was held at a country club in Utica near our town and church with a dinner for a hundred or so family members and friends. True to Polish tradition the ladies sang the beautiful Twelve Angels Waltz while the bride sat on the groom's lap. Along with the bouquet and garter throwing there was the incessant clicking on glasses to make the bride and groom kiss, a tradition enjoyed by most young couples who were starting their new life together.

The first year we were married we rented an apartment from the Boluses. The two story apartment building was on a busy street, Five Mile Road, with an empty lot next door so, with the landlord's permission, we sold Christmas trees during our first holiday together. We learned that all the trees are cut before the Thanksgiving holiday.

You were required to buy a rail carload of bundles, taking your chances on how many would be saleable. The proceeds from the tree sales bought our first washer, drier and refrigerator. Our possessions consisted of my old bedroom set, some egg crates for bookshelves, a console TV Jay rebuilt, a folding card table and three lawn chairs in the kitchen plus our pride and joy, a brand new refrigerator. When my mother came for her first visit we lined up the lawn chairs in a row to admire our new empty refrigerator. We were so proud of it, but when Mom left she slipped a twenty dollar bill into my palm so her daughter would not starve.

Jay was attending night school classes when I had a couple of disasters learning to bake. I had misread the cook book and instead of dividing my coffee cake dough into quarters, as the book suggested, I put the entire amount in the oven and watched in horror as the cake grew and grew and grew until it opened the oven door. Another time I used a tablespoon instead of a teaspoon of salt in my bread dough. My French bread could have substituted for baseball bats. I quickly disposed of the baseball bats, opened all the windows and had quite a time getting that wonderful smell of baking bread out of the apartment before he came home from school. With fans and the whispers of air that wafted through the windows of our second story apartment the air was back to normal before he arrived.

The next year we took advantage of the GI loan for Veterans and, with no money down and low interest mortgage of two or three percent, we moved into our first home. It was a three bedroom bungalow with only one bath, as most homes were in 1955, just off of Eight Mile Road, the last street in the Detroit city limits. Police were required to live in the city so we had several policemen on our street. The house had a large basement that we could finish off ourselves. A bathroom clothes chute deposited the dirty clothes next to the washer and drier in the basement, which was warmed by the furnace and incinerator.

I was earning only three thousand dollars a year as a college graduate with a degree in Chemistry and Jay, not having his degree as yet, earned even less. Yet on this meager salary we could save money, belonged to a golf club and even bought a riding mower. It took Jay nine years to complete his degree in night school. Our wedding postponed his graduation for a full year and his roaming sales job after graduation kept him out of classes for another year. Because Jay travelled all week we had a seven year honeymoon where he brought me a red rose every Friday. We delighted in the weekends together.

I remember my new mother-in-law telling me at my bridal shower that her son would definitely have children of his own. She was eager for grandchildren even though I advised her that one can never be sure. Sadly, I never was able to conceive and provide my loving husband with his own offspring. Not only did this break my heart but I felt I had let him down. I went through several years of tests and surgeries including a great deal of pain trying to get pregnant but was never blessed. Knowing how much I wanted children, Jay agreed to adopt a child. But we had a mixed religion marriage and no agency would consider putting a child, at that time, into a home where the couple did not go to the same church. So Jay proceeded to become a Catholic, this time for a reason that I accepted.

He became such good friends with the priest that was giving him lessons in the faith that the lessons were completed only because the priest was being transferred to another parish. They often watched football games together instead of studying. On one occasion they went rat hunting at the city dump. They wore miner's lights on their caps, dressed in their old dungarees and heavy jackets and set off on their rat hunt. They wore 22 caliber pistols in holsters on their hips almost hidden by their heavy overcoats. They were a frightful sight to behold. They left before dark. The daytime sun had warmed the soft mud of the unpaved road leading to the dump. During their "hunting and quick draw contests", the tires froze into the mud, the car became immovable. They walked to the nearest lighted home and asked to use the phone to call me for a ride home. Original cell phones were bulky, heavy, and not in common use in the 1950s so they had no means of communication with me. Can you imagine opening the door to two armed men telling a far-fetched story about hunting rats? The one man told the lady living alone that he was a priest at the local church as if that would allay her fears. The kind woman, with an unfrightened soul, let them enter and use her phone. This would never happen today.

Just before the priest was transferred we held Jay's baptism service at Our Lady of Sorrows Church. Jack Oldenkamp, who worked in the same building with Jay, was a proxy for my brother, Larry. Jay made an attempt to jump into Jack's arms insisting that Jack carry him down the aisle to the baptismal font. We laughed and then went home to celebrate his baptism with cocktails.

Our early married life was filled with parties, picnics, card games, visiting friends and families along with yearly trips to St. Petersburg to see the Greblicks. There were vacations to ski resorts via long train rides out west. We couldn't afford the sixty dollars for a bed so we sat in coach seats all night, played cards with Steve and Debbie Siskowski, and snacked on hard salami, that we kept cold in the coupling sections of the train. We enjoyed canoe trips to the Minnesota/Canada border—known as the Boundary Waters and Quetico Provincial Park in Canada. We first took a trip with a hired guide to teach us how to handle the wilderness. A few years later we returned with the Siskowskis when we knew what we were doing, or so we thought. A few years later we had to show Jim and Diane this special part of the world.

From the guide we learned about pitching your campsite on an isolated island because bears can swim. You have about a half hour after cooking bacon in the morning to move your camp to a different island. He taught us to fish for walleyes and have the fire ready for the fillets; that you can just toss your pancake mistakes into the fire. He showed us how to skin the bark off of a fallen log so that you have a smooth seat as a toilet; to bury your garbage so the animals wouldn't dig it up; and to carry out every can of mosquito spray you brought into the wilderness. No pressurized cans could be buried in this special backwoods; you had to find pump bottles. The mosquito spray was a necessity for at dusk, which in this northern region is often ten or eleven o'clock at night, you can hear the mosquitoes descending from the canopy to look for fresh blood. You hurry inside, close up your tent, and hope you don't find a spider in your sleeping bag. A few pine boughs under your bag can soften the ground and the pine smell improves the body odor.

Our cautious and hidden skinny dipping in the icy lake results in very short baths. You also learned that you do not touch the canvas tent anywhere while it's raining for you break the surface tension and the tent promptly leaks, usually right over your sleeping bag. Once you leave the outfitter's dock you never see an electric light again or hear an airplane, for the area is a no-fly zone. It was a true wilderness experience, quiet and serene, except for the slap of beaver tails on the water or the haunting cries of the loons.

French Voyageurs, who hunted and trapped beavers for their French and British companies, as well as native Indians, once walked these rocky trails portaging their birch bark canoes. Thankfully they left the trails unmarred for the generations to come. These jagged trails required high top shoes to keep from twisting ankles. Our men insisted that the aluminum canoes they carried were much heavier than birch bark. The lakes were so clean that we kept a tin cup tied to the canoe and drank cold water directly from the lake. The water was tea colored from all the vegetation but clean and drinkable. The water was so cold that we were required to wear small inflatable life preservers attached to our belts. They were designed not so much to save your life as to locate your body should your canoe tip over. The guide warned that the deep lakes were so cold that bodies sunk and never came to the surface. Canada did not want to clutter up their pristine lakes with a lot of bodies.

We also spent many weekends camping in our station wagon, while on fishing trips to lakes, ponds, and rivers. We planned skiing weekends with friends to relatives' hunting cabins up north. On one trip to John's uncle's cabin, we had the electric blanket controls switched and I sweated through the night while Jay froze. On the same trip Jay had to have a drink during the night and tried to use the hand pump in the kitchen to fill a glass. He was trying not to wake anyone with the noise of the pump handle so he slowly squeaked it until someone finally yelled out:

"Pump the damn thing."

We also rented a houseboat that could accommodate several couples and promptly went aground in shallow Lake St. Clair. We met our Ethyl co-workers once a month for parties at various homes. We started with a round of cards in order to have a couple of drinks before the serious partying started, usually with dancing and more drinking.

With Jay away all week, every week, I took up ceramics with a friend, Tag, and her Mother, Mary. We made so many gifts that people worried about what we had concocted next and wondered what they would do with our treasured gifts and who they could re-gift them to in the future.

*C*HAPTER 9

We were content in our GI house but we wanted to build our dream home so in the spring of our second year of marriage we found a lot in a newly developed subdivision in Farmington, a few miles northwest of our GI home. The developers bought an old apple orchard, where, in the springtime, we found morel mushrooms under the apple trees along with the white mushrooms you can buy in every supermarket. We were surprised and delighted to find wild asparagus also. Jay would never try any mushrooms until I had eaten them at least once but we both enjoyed the asparagus without trepidation. Our weekends were spent at the lot working on our new ranch home that backed up to thick woods where no other home could be built. The roads were unpaved and gravel. The subdivision had one deep well to supply all the homes with water, underground utilities, but we were required to install a septic tank and tile field.

We experimented with many new products in our home, like colored concrete blocks that were only two inches thick to resemble regular bricks but gave us an eight inch thick wall. The problem was going to be the inside wiring so we bought one inch thick Styrofoam planks that were one foot wide by ten feet long from Dow Chemical in Midland. A chemist at Dow happened to be Jay's customer for process control instrumentation, so he bought one inch thick slabs of Styrofoam from Dow. He had filled up our station wagon and had a four foot high pile on top of the car for the return trip to Detroit. The Styrofoam was cemented onto the inside brick walls but anyone working on the electrical could get a tingle occasionally if the plaster was damp under the Styrofoam. It was my job to do the wiring and get tingled. I never could wire the three way switches correctly so Jay had to redo all my efforts. I suggested that I handle the painting, and errands but some of this building business was out of my league.

We were thankful for friends and relatives that helped us build our dream home. One of Jay's cousin's, Mike Maksym, had a heating and air-conditioning business so his company installed our furnace in the crawl space. My brother, Larry, and Jack, who refused to carry Jay down the aisle to the baptismal font, helped us tremendously with the grunt work.

Besides the mandatory incinerator in the hot water closet we installed a barbeque at the other end of our large fireplace wall. There were four flues in the chimney; the furnace, fireplace, incinerator and barbeque. We picked a factory finished cork for our flooring that was guaranteed not to ever need polishing. It did not seem to suffer from our narrow spiked heels of that day's fashion. The cork was warm to the touch and dampened the sound.

With all the party loving friends we enjoyed we soon learned that this dream home did not have a party space so the very next year we added a 22 x 24 foot room on the back of the garage. The windows lighting the back of the garage were moved to the recreation room that had floor to ceiling windows on three walls to the north, west and east, a painter's ideal work area. An outdoor patio was also added at the same time with the living room windows now looking onto the patio instead of the pheasants that were constantly eating the corn we threw out for them. In our new rec room, against the garage wall, we had bookshelves built in along with a stereo system and storage benches below the bookshelves. The floor was tiled with white vinyl squares embedded with silver sparkles.

Many memorable parties were held in that room, including a New Year's party where everyone had to stay overnight due to a freezing rain. On the crowned gravel roads the cars would slide slowly into the ditch if the doors were slammed too hard. We often carried our metal cleat golf shoes in the trunk of the car so we could walk home, if necessary. On another occasion I had heard of a solution on the radio to have your friends arrive at a party on time by telling them the party starts at 8:06 or some other odd time, not just 8 or 9 o'clock. When we glanced out the window we saw all the cars lined up along the road. They were waiting in their cars for the exact time then all arrived at once to ring the doorbell. What were we to do now? We decided to have a drawing and the lucky person would win all the garbage from the party. When John neglected to take the garbage home with him we delivered it to his doorstep the same night.

Coming home from another party one night and after a few drinks, where we could no longer feel the cold air, we decided to make love in the car. We were on one of our dark, deserted streets just a couple of blocks from home. When the red lights flashed in the rear window, we hurriedly redressed before the policeman could reach the driver's window. He smirked when we told him we were just two blocks from home. Without writing us a ticket he told us to go home where we would be much more comfortable and warm.

Our small town of Farmington had the Great Lakes Winery on Grand River Avenue, the main road through town. To provide easy shipping, the railroad ran next to the winery. Before the laws preventing the disposal of waste matter from factories, the grape skins were dumped in a huge pile right along the main road. The skins, fermenting in the sun, drew great flocks of birds that enjoyed the strong juices and performed valiantly for the passing cars. They wobbled on the ground but funniest of all they had trouble sitting upright on the electric wires above. They were either hanging upside down or falling back into the lovely pile of grape skins when they could no longer cling to the wire. It's a wonder there were not more accidents along this stretch of the road because of the birds' performances.

My father's drinking habit caught up with him when he was only sixty one years old. We had tried medication that would make drinking distasteful but we were never sure he took the pills. Bottles of his Canadian Club whiskey were found stashed in various hiding places in the family home so we knew the end was inevitable. He had looked forward to retirement pledging to do various things that he always wanted to do but he never reached his Golden Years. He died on Father's Day in the Mt. Clemens hospital while I held his hand all afternoon.

His death certificate reads "hemorrhage of the esophagus" rather than cirrhosis of the liver, as expected with alcoholics. The doctor explained that the weakest part of the body will hemorrhage when the liver fails. His esophagus must have been raw from the drinking, the bromo-seltzer for headaches, the vomiting of the whiskey, and the immediate return to the refrigerator for another drink. I prayed for this man who could not find peace or happiness in his wasted lifetime. I recalled an incident where he was attempting to paint the windows sashes outside while drunk. He fell off the ladder landing on his hands, breaking both wrists. The chore of washing, shaving, and bathroom functions fell upon Mom, who had put up with this man for so many years.

With Mom now alone and my brother in college we needed some means of support for my Mother. Jay and I bought a Frozen Custard Stand in Utica, about ten miles northwest of Mt. Clemens. This new venture would teach us many novel skills. We learned that the difference between soft ice cream and custard is that there are eggs in custard as well as the sugar and cream; that chocolate covers up any other flavor including banana; that the machines had to be cleaned with Chlorox every night; that a popcorn machine produces about a 500 percent profit, but a hot dog machine is not so profitable. We learned to deal with running a business, health inspectors, and even the Detroit Mafia when they insisted that I use their laundry service. I was naïve and new at this game and defiantly turned them down. I read later that another business that refused their service was promptly burned down. We must have been too small of an operation for them to bother with us.

The Custard Stand which was to provide income for Mom and Larry but it turned out to be a second job for me. Jay was out of town most of the time. He was being trained by his new company, Fischer and Porter. I would drive to Utica after leaving the Ethyl laboratories; close the Stand at ten p.m., clean the machines, drive home near midnight, and then get up early for my day job. This adventure lasted for only a short period, as the routine was no longer fun, plus Mom followed Dad in death on August 2, 1960. She had just passed her fifty second birthday. We had found an apartment for her in Wyandotte near her family. She had rented out the farm house and while there checking on the property she said she felt dizzy, fell down and died. The cause of death was a cerebral hemorrhage. We had been married only five years and I had lost both of my parents. Unfortunately neither one of them saw a grandchild. I was still trying desperately to get pregnant, through numerous surgeries and painful tests. We even tried the gray market through an attorney and paid for the birth of an unwed mother's delivery. She then promptly changed her mind after seeing the baby.

At last, in Mid-August of 1961 we received a call from The Michigan Children's Aid Society. They had a baby boy for us. We were ecstatic. It was to be the youngest adoption in Michigan; he was just three weeks old. While he was waiting to come to his new home he was in a foster home where the Foster Mother did not recognize his crying problem as an indication of a hernia. We now were to pick up the baby at the Mt. Clemens Hospital after a hernia repair.

We named the baby after the middle names of both of the Grandfathers, James and Joseph. He became Jimmy Joe during his toddler years. We went through all the joys and sorrows of being parents. Running to the Pediatrician for every incident with the most serious being a scratch on the eyeball from the baby's own fingernail. Over the holidays we drove to Florida with friends, Mary and Gary Heffelfinger, to introduce the Greblicks to our new son. To prepare for this long road trip I bought my first disposable diapers. In Farmington we had employed a diaper service to assist a working mother. Cloth diapers were the parents' choice during the early 1960s plus disposables were too expensive for us. Later on, when the child doesn't need diapers any longer, we had a large supply of soft, well-used rags.

During the first seven years of our marriage Jay was always traveling, calling on customers in surrounding states. He was gone from Monday to Friday most weeks so every Friday he brought me a long stemmed red rose each week. Each weekend was a honeymoon. In those days when we were earning only $3000 per year, he had an expense account of $800 per month and was expected to spend it each month wooing his customers. He once took some special customers out to a fancy restaurant and nonchalantly ordered "steak tartare" as an appetizer. When the waiter brought the raw hamburger, he said: "You forgot to cook this!"

A few years after we were married Jay had his masculine "change of life" wherein a man, because he has not reached the point he thought he should be at, has a pseudo menopause. He was nervous and afraid of dying—to the point where we had to walk the roads, sometimes at midnight. This usually happens at about forty years of age but he was experiencing his early. He overcame this by learning self-hypnosis, but was so good at the craft that he was able to hypnotize others. Some, to the point where it worked so well that parents put their foot down with the children and sometimes the husbands too.

Because my parents both died young without accomplishing some of their dreams we began to talk about seeing more of this world we live in. We soon realized that the only way we could afford to do this is by sailboat. But we knew nothing about sailing. So we got every book out of the library that we could find on sailing, boat maintenance, and circumnavigating. We devoured them. Probably our most favorite authors were Captain Irving Johnson and his wife, Exy, who circumnavigated the world seven times in their schooner, Yankee. Each trip was with a new crew of young single adults that learned to handle a sailboat from truly experienced, world class, sailors. In none of the books we read could we learn just how much money a circumnavigation required. There was one mention only in an obscure book that stated—"you will need as much money as you are accustomed to for your regular life at home". But what did that tell us? We knew we had to be self-sufficient in numerous areas. With our skills and brains we thought we could do whatever was required—like mending sails, scrubbing barnacles off the hull, painting, sanding and varnishing. We were not too proud to work at anything along the way, if necessary, including digging ditches, but by God, we were going to go on this adventure.

Our education on sailing began in Michigan beginning with all the books we read, and faithfully watching the TV program "Adventures in Paradise", plus any National Geographic Society programs that might allude to life on the high seas. We at last revealed our dream to our close circle of friends and I am sure that some of them thought we were either joking or insane. One of the couples, John and Tag Hladchuk planned to go with us, along with their two young daughters. They insisted that any plans to be made included them. But when they saw we were serious about this adventure, they reneged. At our fiftieth wedding anniversary the remaining daughter said she was sorry they did not come with us as their life would have been so different and much better.

How would we break our ties to all these close and dear friends? Jay had been offered the opportunity to open an office in the Twin Cities for Fischer and Porter Co. so we took the transfer to break the ties. We would at last begin our lifelong dream.

CHAPTER 10

We left for the Twin Cities in 1962 shortly after Jimmy celebrated his first birthday in Michigan. Jay was taking a position with Fischer & Porter to open a new office in the Twin Cities. This provided the excuse to break the ties we had with our close friends in Detroit. Before we left the state of Michigan we bought a sailing canoe for our second trip to the Boundary Waters with Steve and Debbie Siskowskis. Jimmy was still in diapers when he was introduced to sailing in the canoe on the nearby quiet lakes of Michigan.

It was in Minnesota that Jimmy learned to ski. He rode up the T-bars between his Dad's legs. Young children seldom get hurt while skiing for they are never far from the ground plus they are so bundled up.

It was also in St. Paul where the boy had his introduction to water and swimming when we took him on our lunch hours to a gym that had a pool with a teacher for toddlers. He thoroughly enjoyed running to the opposite end of the pool from where I was in order to jump in and get his Mother to race across to save him. What fun he had taunting his Mom.

I soon found a job with 3M, the Minnesota Mining and Manufacturing Co. Minnesota Mining was as good a company as Ethyl Corp. regarding their treatment of employees. Each division at 3M had to be self-sufficient, in other words, make a profit. Each division was also expected to host parties for the employees in that section. I started work in the analytical laboratory in one of their older buildings that manufactured tape in downtown St. Paul. 3M was in the process of building their new research laboratories north of the city.

Many of 3M's processes are secret, such as the glass beads in reflective signs. Only two people knew the process. Because their profitable scotch tape was also a secret process, there was a great deal of corporate espionage occurring. The guards regaled us with stories of confiscated miniature cameras found in cuff links, tie pins, watches, even buttons. Because of all this espionage every employee had to wear a badge embedded with our picture even though the entry guards knew us well. Should we ever forget to wear the badge our immediate supervisor would have to meet us at the door and escort us to work. No one wanted that to happen more than once in a career.

Our first home in Minnesota was a rental in Fridley, high above the Mississippi River. There were wooden steps, about 100 of them, leading down to the river, where we kept our canoe lashed to a tree. The fast flowing river was about a mile wide in Fridley. There were islands in the middle of the river where we often picnicked with our toddler son. This great waterway begins its journey in the north at Lake Itasca, Minnesota. It travels through ten states and eleven people before it reaches the Gulf of Mexico.

We found the Twin Cities to be lovely towns full of friendly people but it was just too cold in the winter time for human beings. During this season we needed to keep a light bulb burning under the hood of the car in order to start it in the morning, despite being in a covered garage. You never grabbed anything metal without wearing gloves, even the door knob to enter the house. Scarves had to be worn over the face lest the cold air collapse a lung. During one of the Winter Carnival Parades, with the float attendees wearing only thick flesh-colored tights, our movie camera had to be warmed under a down-filled jacket or taken indoors in order to have the gears turn to produce films. We began to believe in the myth of Paul Bunyon and his giant blue ox, Babe. We were convinced that Paul Bunyon's words froze in a stream of icicles during the bitter winter cold, as in the myth. Minnesotans say the weather consist of eleven months of winter and one month of poor sleighing.

Occasionally in midsummer there were some nice days when we could take our canoe up the river to a sandy beach at one of the islands. In the springtime when all the tributaries add their snow-melt water to the Mississippi the flooding in the Twin Cities is awesome.

To fulfill our dream of sailing around the world we now needed to learn how to actually sail, and for that we needed a real sailboat. In Chicago we found a thirty foot Dutch Maid, hard-chine sloop, named "Truly Fair". We soon learned that a hard chine bottom (having no sleek hour glass keel) was not a racing boat. Before we bought "Truly Fair" in 1962 we became members of the Apostle Island Yacht Club. This Club consisted of a few serious sailors with racing boats, a large old fishing camp building with a pot belly stove, a protected marina for a dozen or so sail boats, and a second building housing toilets and storage areas. The Yacht Club was in Bayfield, Wisconsin, about 230 miles northeast of the Twin Cities. Every summer weekend we would leave St. Paul on Friday evening after work, drive four hours on narrow country roads, and arrive at the Clubhouse long after our bedtime. We stoked the pot belly stove with wood, hoping the coals would last until the sun came up, and then quickly crawled into our sleeping bags spread out on the wooden floor.

We soon fell fast asleep with toddler, Jimmy, in one of our sleeping bags. He was the mascot of the Yacht Club with young teenagers teaching him, at this young age of two, to become a true fisherman. The teens put a large fish caught by them on his hook, then prompted him to tell his parents that he caught the trophy fish. We believed him for a while. The toddler kept to that story, knowing full well that he did not catch the fish.

The boy started his fishing career early with just a piece of clothesline attached to a stick, while he was learning to cast. On shore he had to wear his bulky life jacket but when sailing he was tethered to the boat via a harness and line attached to a rope that ran the full length of the interior. He could go below on his own or join us in the cockpit. This allowed us to easily find the body should he fall overboard.

It was these same teenagers, Doc Pierpont's sons, who took us out on "Truly Fair" to teach us what all the ropes on a sailboat are called and their purpose. We learned that there are only two ropes on a sailboat—the one that is tied to the bucket that you dip overboard for water and the rope on the ship's bell. All the other lines have specific names like halyards, main sheet, jib sheet, anchor rode. etc; so that when the helmsman calls out "hoist the main halyard" the crew knew exactly what he meant and which line to grab. We thoroughly enjoyed the Yacht Club and the new friendships we were making. Some of these people even knew how to sail.

The Yacht Club abutted Halvor Reiten's boat yard that consisted of derelict boats and scrap metal of every shape imaginable. There were hulls of all vintages and in various stages of decay. Halvor could always find a piece of metal you might need. He would even mill the metal to your specifications. He was a salty, crusty gentleman, a senior citizen when we first met him. He constantly walked the few blocks from his home in town to the yard every day, and was always dressed in overalls and plaid shirts with a baseball cap hiding his grey hair. He thoroughly enjoyed the young people at the Club, especially a toddler exploring every nook and cranny of his dilapidated boatyard. His yard even had a large building where he could house Doc Pierpont's "Siskiwit" during the brutal winter months.

The Apostle Islands are a wilderness area of great beauty; Lake Superior is crystal clear with temperatures so frigid (between 32 and 55 degrees Fahrenheit) that we kept our beer bottles cold by hanging them overboard in a net bag. The crystalline water could not be enjoyed for swimming, unless there was an onshore breeze blowing the surface water toward shore. When the boats were launched in the springtime there were often icebergs still floating on the water. At times snow was falling when we put the sails away in the fall.

Our favorite island was Stockton Island that had a dock, of sorts; the wharf required the deftness of a ballet dancer to reach the shore prancing along on rusty I-beams, planks of rotting wood, or chunks of concrete, all askew. This so-called dock, as bad as it looked, was substantial enough to tie up to it for the night. On shore there was a dilapidated cabin that must have been occupied by the original Indians, who used this island for hunting and fishing.

Stockton is the largest of the Apostle Islands and the most varied. The Islands were shaped by the last Ice Age, 10,000 years ago, and the melt water of the glaciers formed the lake we call Superior, the largest of the Great Lakes. We were told by the local sailors that if we could learn to sail in the choppy waters of Lake Superior we could sail anywhere. It was August when Jay's parents, Floridians, joined us for a sail on our thirty foot yacht; snow flurries were falling when we were out on Lake Superior. This was August; snow should not be falling in the summer time. They were good sports and never mentioned the cold or how uncomfortable they were on our tiny sailboat.

Once ashore on Stockton we could walk about a half a mile to an eastern facing beach we called "the singing sands" shore, on the map this area is called Julian Bay. It was a brilliant white sand beach composed of silica grains that sang because of sheer stress. Many family members and friends joined us on this down-to-earth adventure. Some were seeing a true wilderness for the first time. They experienced beaches that squeaked when you walked on them. They had never spent a night on a gently rocking sailboat, or slept in a chilly, decrepit cabin. These same folks came from fancy homes with swimming pools and multi-car garages. Many were from warm climates; most were city slickers, used to all the conveniences of shopping malls and easily accessible supermarkets.

We stocked "Truly Fair" with healthy but fast preparing foods. She had a two burner alcohol stove that took some pre-planning to fix a meal of various ingredients. At times I would bring meals prepared at home. The stove once caught on fire while at the Yacht Club dock.

I quickly picked up the burning stove and tossed it overboard, then nursed my burned hands with the icy water of the lake.

We kept this Dutch Maid sailboat for two summers then decided that if we were to proceed with our dream we must move up to an ocean going sailboat of proper size for full time living aboard. We sold "Truly Fair" to a Minnesota couple, Leon and Barbara Lester, with teenage sons and daughters. It was September, 1964 when they drove to Bayfield for their sea trial. We were amidst the Apostle Islands on a sunny day with clear blue skies above, no ominous clouds in sight. A white squall was suddenly upon us. The winds were quickly up to 70 miles per hour, just below the 75 mph classification for hurricanes. White squalls seldom occur at sea but can happen on the Great Lakes of North America. The water started churning; the wave tops were shaved into spindrift. Jay sent the Lester family and Jimmy below decks, closed the cabin doors securely, and he and I sailed "Truly Fair" back to the marina.

To our surprise the Lesters bought the Dutch Maid and kept her for many years. They too enjoyed belonging to this rare yacht club composed of friendly, wholesome, sailors of all ages. They invited us back to sail with them on "Truly Fair", some years later.

Now we needed to find an ocean-worthy vessel, one large enough to live on for years, or however long a circumnavigation would take. We were determined to see more of this world we live in, especially after my parents both died young, never accomplishing their dreams. A male cousin of Jay's also passed away in his early thirties of cancer leaving two young children and a wife behind to raise them as best she could. We were determined to take our retirement while we were young and work until we die. That happens to be the stage we are in now.

I picked up a year old Sailing Magazine and called the owner. He was advertising a forty seven foot ketch. A ketch has two masts with the smaller mast behind the main mast and in front of the steering mechanism. The boat was located in Corpus Christi, Texas. Surprisingly it was still for sale, asking only $15,000. This was something we could afford from my parents' inheritance. The Duss farm sold for about $30,000 after probate. My brother and I split the proceeds. We now had enough to purchase a larger sailboat and continue with our plans.

The ketch was named "Sirius", the brightest star in the sky. We kept her name. She was built in Sweden as an ocean racing boat a dozen years before we took possession of her. She was an older wooden boat that we proceeded to pour our money into, as every boat owner does. She was our hole in the ocean that gobbled up money in big bites. She had tiller steering and a gasoline engine. We intended to change both of these items immediately. I couldn't handle the tiller and we certainly did not want to go to sea with a gasoline engine. We chose a ketch for it could be handled by fewer people. We also chose a single hulled sailboat with a heavy keel on the bottom because they can right themselves easily when completely knocked over. Catamarans or trimarans have a tendency to remain upside down boats. An upside down boat is really tough to sail, and not easy to live on.

Sirius had two berths in the foc'sle, an enclosed full length berth amidships opposite the elevated Throne, two upper berths in the main cabin and two benches that were supposed to be pull-out berths for ultra-slim crew; aft of the galley was a quarter-berth on either side of the companionway leading to the cockpit. These berths were not easy to access but were safe berths in rough seas. They were used mainly for storage. The mid ship stateroom was little Jimmy's own quarters. Sirius was built for a large racing crew but only slept two comfortably in the main upper berths.

The elevated Throne, or toilet, was a sight to behold and a task that became a challenge in high seas. One of the galley storage cupboards had a door that afforded some privacy from the cockpit view and a closet door in the foc'sle that provided visual privacy from any sailors in bed up forward. At least when one had problems with seasickness the afflicted person did not have to bend over quite so far since the Throne was half way up the port side. I envied the men who could use the fantail or a bucket on deck without fighting the pitching floor below; or the sharp crack of a wave hitting the side of the hull and tossing you off the seat. A regular automobile seat belt would have come in handy if we could only figure out how to attach it.

We concluded the purchase of Sirius and asked the Texas owner to deliver her to St. Petersburg, Florida. We returned to Minnesota to quit our jobs. We left Sirius at the city dock in downtown St. Petersburg where Jay's parent could keep an eye on her. We sold the house that we had bought in St. Paul. This was a three bedroom home we purchased when my analytical department moved to the new 3M Research facility. The home was strategically located on a curve in the road where the wind piled up snow drifts continuously in the driveway. No wonder the house was such a bargain when we found her. A St.Patrick's Day blizzard was the last snow we shoveled. Jay scooped our driveway out five times that day piling the snow way over our heads. We vowed that once we got the car out of the garage we were heading south, never to shovel snow again.

We quit our jobs in the fall of 1965. I stocked up at the 3M Company store with sandpaper, ribbons, and tape, enough to last for decades. We rented a U-Haul, added a hitch to our old Chrysler, crammed the trailer to its rooftop with possessions that we felt we needed aboard or could be used in Grandpa's apartment building. We drained our bank accounts of our entire ten year savings, and headed to Florida where we would be renting an apartment from Jay's parents. We marveled at how free we felt when we finally took that last leap of faith.

CHAPTER 11

Sirius had an ominous beginning on her new adventure. The Texas owner, foolishly trying to save money, did not fill up with adequate fuel. He was single-handing Sirius from Corpus Christi to St. Petersburg across the Gulf of Mexico. He radioed a Mayday to the Coast Guard in St. Petersburg that he was stranded in becalmed seas without fuel. We rushed to the Coast Guard Station to help load five gallon pails of diesel onto the helicopter so they could be dropped to the stranded sailor. We were relieved to finally see her silhouette coming over the horizon.

Jay found a commercial yard in Tampa, Marine Repair, that allowed him to work on the boat himself; yet they had extra hands to help when he needed it. Most of the other vessels in the shipyard were shrimpers that were alongside the docks or up on the ways. He arrived at the yard every morning at dawn and left when it got dark. This continued for four or five months as he changed the steering from rudder to wheel and the engine from gasoline to diesel.

The year was 1965 when we were preparing the sailboat for our long journey. The U.S-backed dictatorship of Batista in Cuba was overthrown by Fidel Castro. Castro was forming his communist government. One day Jay was approached at the yard by two dark haired, swarthy-looking men who asked if he might be interested in delivering a shipment of guns to Cuba. We had heard of ships getting too close to Cuba and the sailors arrested, at least the U.S. citizen was arrested but the Canadian was set free. We were adventurous but not that foolhardy.

In the meantime I was devouring every book from the library that I could find on food preparation for a sea voyage. I also used the food editors at the local newspaper, the St. Petersburg Times. Our story was so intriguing that it was on the front page of the Sunday Food Section. We were featured again when I agreed to be hauled up the main mast, sixty five feet above the water for painting. I didn't have the strength to haul Jay up the mast in the bosons' chair so the First Mate was elected for the job. Although I stipulated that the chore had to be done early so no one would see me, some jokester alerted the newspaper about this unusual situation. Photographers greeted us at the marina dock with cameras and plenty of film in tow. I suspect the call to the newspaper was from my sister-in-law, Laura.

I planned to have a year's supply of canned goods aboard; this amounted to roughly 800 pounds. Since the canned goods would be stowed in the bilges, which could have salt water seeping in, the paper labels had to be removed from all the cans, the contents labeled in indelible markers, and each can dipped in diluted varnish twice. This chore involved many hours of preparation. Our list included canned hams, lunch meats like Spam, canned pre-fried bacon, (we were introduced to this product on our camping trips up north), roast beef from Argentina with gravy, every type of vegetable and fruit available, plus an assortment of juices. One of the disasters was canned whole chickens in a juice-size can. The problem was that the chicken was squeezed until it fit into the can resulting in a million pieces of bone in the meat. A can of plain chicken meat was a much better deal. The V8 and tomato juice cans were the first to be used as the cans did not last long due to the acidic juices within them. Egg life can be prolonged by sealing the outside of the shells with lard but I chose to seal them on the inside by dipping in boiling water for a few seconds. Despite the saying that you will never eat a bad egg it was a good habit to break each egg into a cup before cooking it.

Some other tidbits I learned were: have a hand held opener without a magnet so it doesn't interfere with the ship's compass; that margarine will outlast butter; unsliced bread keeps longer than sliced; serve rough weather food in bowls and use spoons; small quantities of juice in tepid water makes it much more palatable; kerosene is a much cheaper fuel for a stove than alcohol; have the stove gimbaled (free swinging) for baking items; safety precautions are a "big" must; and a fire extinguisher in the galley is of utmost importance. The long hours of research for the trip have paid off tenfold but the proof will come when we are at sea.

We had several day sails in the Gulf of Mexico and Tampa Bay to reward the hard working crew members. The working crew consisted of Jay's sister, Laura; her daughter, Jerry; Grandpa, Grandpa's Russian brother-in-law, Max; and any other relatives that visited and worked on the Sirius. They all enjoyed sailing on her.

The porpoises in Tampa Bay performed on cue for us, frolicking in the bow waves of the boat. The popular TV program, "Flipper" was shown every week and little Jimmy with megaphone pressed against his lips would constantly call out:

"Here Flipper, here Flipper" expecting a porpoise to jump to his call as the trained ones did on the TV program.

The time for departure was approaching so we moved the boat to the Municipal Dock at the Pier in St. Petersburg. Only once did Jay's Mom come aboard, step on our newly sanded and re-caulked teak decks after many hours of painful work and, without ever going below, to see the spaciousness of the boat, with arms akimbo, said to the two of us.

"You're not putting a child down that black hole."

Those were our farewell sentiments from my mother-in-law. I really think they never thought we would actually go through with our plan. We would leave for a couple of weeks, meet some huge waves, come to our senses, and return home.

A short time before departure we saw a handsome, trim, muscular, young man walking down the dock. He stopped at our boat and announced that the dock master alerted him that we were preparing for a sea voyage. He asked if he could come along. Not knowing this young man we asked for references and in a few days we received a letter from the Dean of Cornell University, where Dave had been attending school. We learned that his parents had a cattle ranch in Texas, and that Dave needed some time off of school to find himself before he left for the military. We welcomed a strong young man aboard because Sirius was a large boat for a man, a woman, and a four-year-old boy to handle, plus we were total greenhorns.

Others wanted to join us for our trip from St. Petersburg to the Bahamas. Leon Lester, who bought "Truly Fair" from us in Bayfield, took vacation time to join us. Another sailor from our old yacht club, Doug Bosun and his wife, Betty, wanted to come along plus their friend from Minnesota, Jan Carson, was added to the roster. I didn't know what sailing experience Jan had but the First Mate decided she could use an extra cook in the galley, plus she played a mean guitar.

The fateful day finally arrived. Dave put up a smug sign on the bow reading "HAVE ROPE, NEED TOW". We at last pulled out of the slip at the city marina. As young and naïve as we were, we were ready to face any and all perils and pearls that King Neptune chose to toss at us.

CHAPTER 12

FIRST MATE'S DIARY

Thursday, March 3, 1966

After a week of rushing, working frantically, and running around we finally left the marina dock, headed to the Standard Station for fuel and realized that we didn't have a single chart that we needed. Jay dashed back in a borrowed car and got a chart from Perry and Ruby Stevens aboard the Estrellita, a motor sailor docked next to our slip. Not a good beginning. We reached the skyway bridge about 9:00 p.m. motoring. I served a cold supper and later we started sailing when we reached the end of the channel. The wind was on our nose so we ended up motor sailing.

The air below was stifling because of the new asbestos wrappings on the exhaust pipe. A jury-rigged air scoop was arranged on the forward hatch and the air freshened. I took no watches at the helm since we had Leon Lester, Doug Bosun and Dave Scott, the able bodied addition from Cornell, and Jay aboard.

Friday, March 4, 1966

We were able to sail all day under jenny and main sail. No seas. Beautiful day but Dave and Doug turned green even though the seas were calm. Leon was fine but Dave turned a darker green when he saw Leon chewing on a chicken drumstick. All men napped in the afternoon while I was at the helm. We were becalmed at 5 p.m. and started motoring. Dave was too sick to eat a delicious supper of hamburgers, mashed potatoes and mushroom gravy.

Leak in propeller shaft discovered at midnight so Jay slowed the speed down for water was coming in at a rate of one cup per minute. Jay not too sure of his navigating yet and was nervous. Doug, who was supposed to be the navigator, could not go below because of seasickness except to crawl into his sack so Jay was left with the responsibility. He was worried because we did not see any lights when expected before dawn.

Finally we got some radio fixes and were reasonably sure of our location. At 9:30 a.m. a heavy squall hit us from the northwest. We thought we would welcome the north winds since we were heading into southerly gusts so often but the north winds were 40 to 50 mph. The crew got the main sail down just in time. Seas got heavy and the bad weather stayed.

Started the engine to help us stay on course but it wouldn't start. Engine locked up because of salt water backing up into the exhaust when heeling to port. In horribly pitching seas, Jay managed to change the oil and get the salt water out of the engine. We were all ecstatic to hear the engine running. Thank goodness Jay doesn't get seasick.

Saturday, March 5, 1966

The only thing the navigator, Doug, could do was crawl into his sack. By this time the interior was soaked and a mess. The vents, windows and cabin leaked like a sieve. We asked the Coast Guard in Key West to stand by and headed there because of our trouble. They escorted us in. All collapsed in port after eating out at 11:00 p.m.

Sunday, March 6, 1966

All hands resting up, sightseeing, and waiting for wind to shift south again to make our trip to Miami easier. Baked yeast rolls for a very appreciative crew. We all tried Key Lime pie at several restaurants.

The men later went out for a drink. They were able to take showers at a men's locker club but I just had to sponge bathe on board with Jimmy.

Monday, March 7, 1966

We pulled out of Key West at 9:30 p.m. intending to follow a tug and barge through the Hawk's Channel. We were unable to keep up with the tug's motoring so we raised the sails at midnight. Vibration increasing in the shaft and Jay is worried.

Tuesday, March 8, 1966

At 3:00 a.m. Jay discovered that the engine vibration broke the aft port engine mount. We shut off the engine and sailed while Jay borrowed a screw from one of the other mounts for a temporary repair. Jay had to realign the engine and decided not to use it unless absolutely necessary. Unable to make headway, so dropped anchor at 6:00 a.m. so all hands could rest. It was a very uncomfortable anchorage. We decided to try sailing again at 8:30 a.m. Dave has been sick since leaving Key West. We decided to go into Marathon to make more complete repairs to the engine mounts. We bumped bottom entering the channel but not enough to stop us. Sirius' draft (distance to the bottom) was 7.5 feet but with the canned foods plus all the other supplies aboard we figured the draft was now 8.5 feet.

Wednesday, March 9, 1966

Leon decided to leave us for he had to be back to work on Thursday and couldn't be sure when we would reach Miami. We left Marathon at 9:00 a.m. and thought we would motor as much as possible in order to get to Miami for repairs. We could not sail because of continuous strong headwinds of 30 mph from the northeast now, just when we want it from the south.

Dirt in the fuel tanks stopped the engine again. By this time we were ready to shove this brand new engine overboard. Wind and seas picked up and we could not maintain four mph so we anchored just off the channel hoping that it would calm down at night but it didn't. All hands were so tired we slept through the night.

Thursday, March 12, 1966

We had only fifty miles to go to Miami so we struggled all day into high, rough seas. Jay navigated at night through touchy waters on approaching Miami. He is gaining more confidence in his piloting. I am glad Doug was not able to navigate for Jay was forced to do it and learn sooner. It was difficult to pick up the channel lights against the Miami skyline. It was late, 11:00 p.m., so we pulled into Mike Burke's dock (Windjammer Cruises) in the entrance of the Miami River.

Friday, March 11, 1966

We headed up the Miami River after arranging with Merrill-Stevens yard via radio to be hauled next Monday. Hate to waste all that time waiting but we have no choice. We headed up the river and enjoyed having the first bridge open up for us. You give three blasts on the horn and hope the bridge attendant isn't asleep at the switch and opens the bridge on time. We blasted for the second bridge to open for us and just as it began to open we went hard aground. Could not understand it for we were following the channel markers but learned later that they had drifted out of place. We swung Dave, the Cornell guy, out on the boom to heel Sirius over enough to float the boat again but it did not help. We were in front of the DuPont Plaza Hotel so we had quite a large audience. Fortunately, the tide was coming in.

After a while our tugboat captain from Key West came along but he was afraid to pull us off since the bottom was rocky and he didn't want the responsibility of damaging our vessel. He called the Coast Guard for us. They came to pull us off but insisted on using our rope, not theirs, so they too would not have the accountability of a damaged hull. They set us free, and then boarded us for an inspection and the signing of papers.

In Miami Dave left to visit an Aunt for the weekend. Doug rented a car, picked up Betty, his wife, and Jan Carson at the airport. They were supposed to pick us up for dinner but didn't show. They returned late at night. I figured Doug had had enough of Sirius's captain and first mate.

Saturday, March 12, 1966
Doug went off to the University of Miami with the women to see about entering the oceanography school. Jay and I worked around the boat. He got the exhaust ready to put in a flexible coupling which seemed to be the simplest answer, but costly. The yard quoted us a price that floored us considering we will have hauling expenses to check the bearings on the propeller shaft.

In the meantime we met an interesting sailor, Aat VandenBurg, from Holland on board a 100 foot sailboat, the Iduna. Aat is building his own forty eight foot steel ketch and will charter in the Caribbean eventually, as we plan to do once we get there.

Sunday, March 13, 1966
All hands returned to the boat for a delicious dinner of lasagna that Betty prepared. With three women aboard, we decided to rotate and have one woman cooking; one doing the dishes and the third would have a day off.

Dave decided to go on with us at least to Nassau before he had to report to the Army. It looks like all but Jan will leave us in Nassau. The Bosuns had to get back to work but Jan was a stay-at-home Mom. She was a pleasure to have aboard for she is always willing and ready to help and plays a great guitar.

Monday, March 14, 1966
The flexible coupling arrived and the yard told us they misquoted, the price would be much higher. Jay argued and got them to give it to us at their cost but it was still much more than they first quoted. At this point we had only $3000 left but at least we had a year's supply of food on board.

Early in the morning a shriveled old man in a bright yellow hardhat came to look at the boat and asked if we had sketches of the hull. Unfortunately, we did not have them with us so this threw the man all off. We were just hauled in Tampa and did not think we would need them but we see that a sketch should be aboard. I will ask Laura to send them to us ASAP. The afternoon came and nothing happened on the hauling. They just ignored our boat so after some screaming to the higher echelon, Mr. Hardhat finally took us over to the ways.

It was late in the day, but they started to haul us out. We got half way up, then Mr. Hardhat was unsure of himself so he paced, scratched his head, paced some more, until the quitting bell rang. They lowered us back into the water and went home. We were flabbergasted. Here is one of the biggest yards in Miami and they do not know how to haul a sailboat out of the water! We were fit to be tied and felt like going out to get drunk.

Tuesday, March 15, 1966

Mr. Hardhat and crew continued to haul out other boats and ignored us completely even though they promised the day before to come in at 7:00 a.m. and haul us early. They came in early all right but drank coffee until 8:00 a.m. at which time Hardhat told us he was not going to haul us, period. We insisted but he said it would be at our own risk. We could not believe it. We figure the price for hauling should take care of their responsibilities and insurance. The management called Marine Repair in Tampa for information. Their incompetence is unbelievable.

After lunch they tried again and finally got us up on the ways. Their methods of working are very primitive compared to Marine Repair in Tampa; at least Harold in Tampa knew his job. By nighttime we were so frustrated we went out for dinner and a movie.

Wednesday, March 16, 1966

The work on the boat went along slowly and after chewing our nails all day we did not finish on time to get off the ways before quitting time. Jay had the bottom repainted while it was up for there were some bare spots after only two and a half months in the water. If we don't get away from here soon we will both have a nervous breakdown and Jay will have an ulcer besides.

Thursday, March 17, 1966

Unbelievable, but we are finally off the ways and floating again. We filled up our tanks with water (all 100 gallons) and started away from the dock just before 6:00 p.m. Some men shouted from Merrill-Stevens that the bridge does not open until 6:00 p.m. We had to pull over and wait again. This was certainly an ominous beginning to a world trip. We finally found a gas station open after running up and down the river opening all the bridges.

Then it started raining so hard that the visibility was nil, so, again we pulled over and waited. At last we got back out on the river and once again tied up to the Burke's dock for the weather looked terrible to cross the Gulf Stream. There was a 30 to 35 mph northeast wind a-blowing. The Stream travels north so this wind would make the crossing very choppy. We stayed the night at the dock figuring if the seas are rough we better go in daylight and not fight the darkness.

Friday, March 18, 1966

The waves were already four feet or so when we left Government Cut. Jay and I vowed we would not be pushed by deadlines and here we were going when we shouldn't because everyone with us had to go back home and to work. I was surprised to see Jimmy seasick for the first time. Whenever we sailed previously the boat was anchored for the night. The seas were calm at anchor so there was time for the stomach to settle down. Dave, Doug and Betty were all tossing but Betty was far worse for she also had diarrhea. She looked like death warmed over. She lay on the cockpit seat clutching our all-purpose bucket as though it were her best friend. Doug finally tried to eat some Oreo cookies after a long quiet spell in his stomach but he was soon over the rail.

The Oreos promptly came back up. Jim asked what was wrong with Doug and Jan quickly responded

"That is what you call tossing your cookies."

CHAPTER 13

To our surprise even Jimmy got seasick on this passage. The seas, we estimated, were sixteen to eighteen feet and coming from all directions. Crossing the Gulf Stream took us several hours with the northeast wind producing choppy seas. The Gulf Stream, a deep Atlantic river running north is squeezed between the Florida peninsula and the shallow Bahamas Banks to the east. The Banks are only six fathoms deep. Leaving from Miami, as we did the Stream runs north at this location at about five or six knots.

We thought we had rough seas around the Keys but the Stream is by far, much more wicked. The waves came from all directions, and when you happen to be where two fifteen footers meet, it dumps a ton of water into the cockpit. You certainly learn to respect the fury of Mother Nature.

We anchored at Gun Cay when we reached the Bahamas and sailed on to Cat Cay the next morning to enter the Bahamas officially. We all welcomed a day of rest on solid ground after sailing across the Gulf Stream. Cat Cay is the official entry point for the Bahamas although everything looked closed except for Customs. It is a pretty place, privately owned with only gravel roads, English Colonial buildings, many coconut palms and beautiful sand beaches.

These islands were once the bastion of pirates like Henry Morgan and Blackbeard. As we strolled down the sandy roads we expected a pirate to jump out from behind a coconut palm tree. The swaying palm trees and tropical breezes awakened our vivid imaginations.

Betty picked up a starfish on one of the beaches. She quickly christened her, Stella, and insisted on taking Stella home on the plane to Minnesota. We could only hope that Stella wouldn't tear the bag and smell up all her clothes in the suitcase.

We started across the Bahamas Banks on Sunday morning. After sailing in deep Lake Superior, seeing the coral heads of the Banks unnerved the Captain and First Mate. You can see the entire bottom of the Banks. With our 8.5 foot draft we touched the sand a few times, even dug trenches through the powder. The water is so clear it is like sailing on a swimming pool. Even at thirty feet of depth you can see the intense colors of the coral.

After many days of hard seafaring in the Gulf of Mexico and across the Gulf Stream we had our first pleasant night of comfortably sailing with only the main sail and jenny. It was a perfect night; a soft breeze, the sky crowded with stars, the temperature mild, and an occasional flying fish danced above the water. We were in the Tongue of the Ocean, deep water again, heading to Nassau, New Providence Island, where we didn't have to worry about digging a trench in the sand.

We had taken that first step, left our homeland, arrived in our first foreign country, eager to taste the culture and cuisine of these once British Islands.

CHAPTER 14

In 1966 the Commonwealth of the Bahamas consisted of 700 islands and around 2500 smaller cays of low-lying islands, many were just rocks. Only about 30 islands were inhabited. The islands lie in the Atlantic Ocean and Caribbean Sea north of Cuba and Hispaniola. This is the island that is Dominican Republic on the east end and Haiti on the west. In the 7th century the Taino Indians (known as Lucayans and later called Arawaks) moved into the uninhabited southern Bahaman islands from Cuba and Hispaniola. When Christopher Columbus made his first landfall in 1492 on the island known today as San Salvador, it was the most eastern of the Bahamas. To populate the islands the Spaniards followed Columbus but they brought along with them the European disease of smallpox which decimated the Indian population. British colonizers then followed the Spaniards.

To establish organized government the Bahamas were made a crown colony of the British throne. Famous pirates controlled the island before British rule was established. Today the islands number over 300,000 inhabitants, probably a third of that number in early 1966 when we passed through the Bahamas.

The first political parties were formed in the 1950s. The British made the government internally self-governing in 1964. They appointed Roland Simonette of the United Bahamian Party as the first premier. In 1967 Lynden Pindling of the Progressive Liberal Party became the first black premier of the colony.

When we arrived in Nassau in March of 1966 we knew Pindling was soon to come into power along with the promised changes of his campaign. Beef, travelling just 50 miles from Miami was priced at almost $3.00 per pound. We knew that shipping was high-priced but it couldn't add that much to the cost of the product.

Fresh vegetables were scarce. Produce was non-existent. Green turtle steaks and conch were staple Bahamian food and reasonably priced, so we ate a great deal of these Bahamian staples. The Eleuthra island pineapples were sweet and dripping with juice. The pineapples were sold at the wharf by vendors with machetes that hacked away the tough outer skin and handed the fruit to the customer with the top used as a handle. This was a healthy and inexpensive fast food. Few people knew what a hamburger was in 1966; there were no McDonalds or Burger Kings. A stick of sugarcane substituted for a candy bar.

We found Nassau to be most interesting. The natives are exceptionally friendly and courteous; you never pass a local without saying "Good morning", or some other form of greeting. There are no taxes here, no income, sales, property, or business taxes. The government supports itself on duty taxes and a tax on rental properties. Tourists pay most of the revenues.

We wondered how the native supports himself, for we discovered that the cost of living is very high. Food, clothing and other necessities are costly, while the luxuries, like perfume, liquor, and cigarettes, are much less than in Florida. There are so many liquor stores on Bay Street alone that when you tire of walking around you can enter one of them, sit in comfortable chairs, and sample some of the open bottles displayed on the counters for their customers.

There was also the large, famous, Straw Market to explore. In order to get surreptitious pictures of the vendors I tried on the island print materials that can be worn many ways while Jay took telephotos from across the street.

One of the hotels had a huge Kapok tree on their lawn where you could climb stairs leading to an enormous platform nestled in the crook of the tree, sit at an ornate table and enjoy a cup of tea, with crumpets, of course. From this perch we watched a rugby game in the park below, while trying to figure out the rules of the game.

We marveled at the calm, uniformed policeman standing on a block of wood in the middle of a busy downtown intersection directing traffic. He was outfitted in a starched white jacket, white cap and gloves; looking so sharp in his dark trousers with the red stripe down the outer seams. He was the only traffic light in town. Life on these islands was so much slower and less hectic than bustling Miami, lying only 55 miles to the west.

The island closest to Nassau was known as Hog Island, later renamed Paradise Island, when a fancy resort was built on the property. The name Hog Island was certainly not conducive to tourism. Dave would often dinghy off to the sandy beaches on Hog Island to find any and all single girls.

One night Dave babysat Jimmy while the rest of us, Doug, Betty, Jan, Jay and I went to the Junkanoo Nightclub to see a floor show. We were quite a sight in the dinghy, all dressed up for the evening, carrying our dress shoes in our hands, along with flashlights and a bag of garbage to take to shore. The fee to overnight at the dock was five dollars a night. Much too expensive for our pocketbook, since Merrill-Stevens in Miami drained us of all our cash. So by choice we anchored out.

The first act at the Junkanoo was King Trevor, who danced on glass. He also limbo danced under a stick just eighteen inches off the floor holding Betty in his arms and a much thinner girl that was part of the act on his legs. Betty's face was ashen when she returned to her seat.

Doug and Betty, toting Stella the starfish, returned home to Minnesota during our time in Nassau. Then Dave went off to the military to fight in Vietnam. We could only hope to see this wonderful young man again someday.

Our three months in the Bahamas were idyllic. We worked on the boat for a few hours in the morning then played in the afternoon with our young son. We would beach comb for shells or etched glass, swim, snorkel, and explore the islands. When walking on the sharp coral rock that makes up the Bahamas, thick soled tennis shoes are a requirement. The coral reefs were exposed and became the Bahamas islands when the sea receded centuries ago after the last Ice Age.

Our favorite island was Highborne Cay in the Exumas.

Highborne along with Norman Cay were owned by Bill Smith from Pennsylvania, who had major holdings in Kewaunee Oil Co., which later became Kendall Oil Co. When we arrived the island was an Aloe Vera Plantation. Highborne's aloe was grown for burns, especially nuclear burns. Aloe is also added to many skin care products and cosmetics. The local natives use the gel directly from the plant as a daily nutrient, mostly to settle an upset stomach. Interestingly, the Highborne Plantation fields were divided into sections with two foot walls of field stones gathered in the process of clearing the land.

Not having to return to a job, Jan stayed a couple of weeks longer with us. We were to take Jan back to Nassau so she could catch a plane to Minnesota but a seaplane carrying four college age children of Mr. Smith's along with their friends landed at Highborne Cay so we were able to send Jan to Nassau on the seaplane. Nassau, as well as the Out Islands was jumping with college students on spring break.

The manager of Highborne's plantation was Dan Lawson, who was from northern Minnesota. His wife, Donna, and two young daughters lived in the main house on the plantation. Donna had a maid, Riata, which was a blessing for us for we could leave Jimmy to play with 4-year old Dawn's many toys. There were two other white men and a white woman secretary that worked for Mr. Smith plus forty natives along with their twenty children who received no formal education. The native parents wanted it that way for if the children were too well educated they might be inclined to leave the family circle.

There was a long concrete pier on the south end of the island that protected boats from all directions except the north. Once we maneuvered the tricky entrance channel from the west we tied to the pier. We were still planning on going on to the Virgin Islands but the longer we stayed the more rooted we became to the Exumas. Tied to the pier, it was common for us to sit on the sandy bottom at low tide. The crystal clear water often made the boat appear to be floating above the water like a kite in the sky.

Highborne Cay was a popular stopover for the charter boats because of the long dock and no fees. We were toying with the idea of going into the charter business here instead of the Virgin Islands. We enjoyed getting to know the captains on the other boats and having them accept us as competition. They were willing to help us get a work permit, which was not easy to obtain. The government did not look favorably on anyone taking a job away from a local person.

The water of the Bahamas is so crystal clear that the underwater visibility is often 200 feet or more. The water temperature, however, is affected by the Florida weather so while clear; it is often cold in the winter and early spring. We were enjoying the islands in the springtime of March, 1966. Our swimming adventures would last only a couple of hours in deep water. In the warmer, shallower waters we could pick up conch two at a time for they were so plentiful. The native boats would return to Nassau overburdened with conch. With some difficulty Jay learned the exact spot to break into the shell to release the firm hold the animal used to drag his heavy home around. We learned to enjoy this Bahamian delicacy. The best conch was eaten raw out of the shell using only the white meat dipped in cocktail sauce. Marinated herring is, after all, raw we told ourselves, whenever a guest was squeamish about trying the raw meat. Conch chowder, cracked conch, conch fritters are only a few of the recipes we tried on the Sirius. Turtle steaks were bought only at restaurants where the chefs knew how to handle the bloody meat of the turtle.

The only supplies we could purchase at Highborne was frozen meat and milk. We had to sail back to Yacht Haven in Nassau to purchase water or fuel. One evening we were grilling hot dogs and offered some to the group of local teenagers that worked on the plantation. We were chagrined when they grilled their T-bone steaks on the same grill that we cooked our hot dogs. Luckily, Highbourne Cay provided a grill on the dock for the charter boats. The grill was in front of Cheap Charlie's Oar House, Mr. Smith's storage locker on the dock.

These Halcyon Days were dotted with the exploration of nearby islands. Many of the islands in the Exumas are privately owned with shuttered homes that found no problem from prying native eyes or sticky fingers. The local fishermen attended to their work, never bothering the vacant homes or boats. You could leave your boat for hours unlocked, unattended, and return to find nothing amiss.

If the fishermen were collecting conch to sell in Nassau they would break a hole in the lip of the shell and tie five or six shells together with a coconut frond. They would keep them in the shallow waters until ready to fill the boat and return to the capital to sell their wares. They said one or two conch could walk away but having a group together, they could never agree to walk away in the same direction.

The older fisherman would often tell Jay that he must eat the translucent two inch visceral mass of the conch, in order to "put lead in his pencil". He never had the nerve to try it.

We periodically sailed the thirty three miles to Nassau to mail letters, pick up mail at Don's mailbox, or buy items we needed, like heavy duty fishing line to troll while sailing in hopes of catching our dinner; or a wooden "look box" to find the hiding places of the fish. This box was also handy for non-swimmers, sitting in the dinghy and peering overboard.

We witnessed a good sized tuna caught by another boat but a shark got to it before it was hauled in. The fisherman got only the head, the shark feasted on the rest of the tuna. We happened to be back in Nassau for Easter Sunday and after Mass found friends that had been transferred to the Bahamas. Otto, a minister, with his wife and two sons were to start a Lutheran Church in the islands. The minister was in the middle of his sermon when we found him holding his services in a closed theatre until he could locate a church site. Otto, in his white robes and statuesque posture, was a tall man. He certainly looked overbearing to a four year old boy. Jimmy tugged on my skirt and in a loud whisper, asked.

"Is that God, Mommy?"

Despite the five dollar cost Yacht Haven Marina was a favorite mooring for us when we needed water or fuel. The dock fees included the use of the hotel swimming pool. Jimmy swam every day that we were at the dock. I often checked his fingers and toes to see if they were sprouting webs. He was always required to wear his Styrofoam bubble on his back. Some parents objected to the bubble for the child had to have the ability to hold his/her head above water. I always remarked that at least we would be able to find the body.

When the boy wasn't swimming at the pool, preferably jumping into the deep end, he was in water around the boat that was at least eight feet deep, or the draft of the Sirius. Other captains suggested we write "The Deep Draft Guide to the Bahamas". We have gone so many places where common wisdom said we could not go. We went everywhere, but just stayed further away from shore. We saw many shallower draft boats aground. And there were times we dug trenches in the sand getting to an anchorage or close to a village.

While at the dock in the Bahamas, it took some getting used to a tide of one to three feet. One time the pier was above you, where you had to climb a ladder to get off the boat; then at low tide you descended the ladder or jumped to the boat deck. After no noticeable tide in the Great Lakes this was another item to master in these islands.

Without much arm twisting we agreed to head to Georgetown, Great Exuma for the Out Island Regatta. Over 100 yachts from all over the world attend the Regatta to watch this race. Over 250 native, decked-out, fishing boats vie for the prize money of $10,000.

When we were in Nassau over Easter we picked up another deck hand, Henry Smith, nicknamed Smitty, from New York, who wanted to sail with us to St. Thomas. We had to let Smitty go at Georgetown where he could catch a plane back to Nassau. He was fired due to his bossiness, always telling the Captain and First Mate that he was right, despite having no sailing experience. Besides we owned the Sirius, not him.

Staniel Cay, where we were waiting for clear weather to proceed to Georgetown, has a small settlement but boasts a Super Market, about twenty feet square. Fresh bread is baked to order by the ladies of the village and delivered to our boat at anchor by one of their husband's via dinghy. The bread is still hot from the oven and delicious. The ladies also take in the yacht's laundry with clothes returned brighter than the dingy Laundromats I had to use in Nassau. I suspect the local lady's laundry consists of three wash tubs and a scrub board under a shade tree in the yard with lot of elbow grease as the source of power.

Many of the Bahamas natives are descendants of slaves, or freed blacks, brought in by the Loyalists to work the unsuccessful cotton plantations on the islands. The cotton plantations failed due to poor soil, erosion and insect infestations. The Loyalists migrated to the Bahamas when the Civil War looked hopeless for the southern states.

Staniel is unique in that it has a yacht club operated by two former charter boat owners. The club's interior is decorated beachcomber style and is shaded by palm trees. It is a cool and pleasant place to socialize. The roof is thatch, as many building are on the Cay. We learned that you can put up a 5, 10, 20 or 30 year roof depending on the amount of thatch used. Surprisingly they are quite durable even in hurricanes.

Because there are so few people that visit the yacht club they don't attempt to keep a bartender. The honor system is used. You serve yourself, keeping track of your drinks, marking them on a pad on the bar. At Staniel we also swam into a cave filmed in the James Bond movie "Thunder Ball". It didn't take much to imagine Sean Connery stepping on the ledge above us or emerging from his mini-submarine rising from the bottom of the cave.

From Staniel we once again set out for Georgetown but strong southeast winds kept us and many other sailboats strung out along the Exumas not able to reach Georgetown, some sixty miles southeast. The waves beating into the Cut were fifteen feet or better, fetching straight from Africa, bringing with them quite a bit of weed from the Sargasso Sea, somewhat north of here.

Unfortunately, we missed the Regatta but it turned out there was poor attendance with many of the races called off because of the high winds. We reached Georgetown the end of April and anchored in a snug cove with Stocking Island providing a barrier isle about a mile from the main island of Great Exuma. Georgetown has a population of only 400 inhabitants but it has a post office, a commissioner, telecommunications, a few nice Inns, some food stores and an airport, making it an important city. The stores have no produce and the milk is the recombined milk that had been previously frozen. Bread is again baked to order and delivered to the yachts.

From the gleaning of books on sailing, I brought along Tide and Trend soap that is supposed to suds up in salt water but didn't. On advice from another First Mate I tried Joy dish detergent which thrives and lathers in salt water. I used it for all our salt water baths, laundry and shampoo. My dried out hair had taken on a sheen that I haven't seen since moving south from the cold north.

We rented Honda scooters one day and toured some fifty miles around the island stopping at every village for a cold beer or soda. On our way back we stopped at a farm and bought some fresh vegetables out of the garden and picked out a stalk of bananas. The stalk hung from the main boom and in a few days the green bananas started to ripen. Slowly at first, then later I was scrounging around for banana recipes. Jimmy enjoyed picking the bananas from the stalk. He also loved to collect coconuts. They are good snacks for him once he persuades his Dad into opening the stubborn coconut.

This four year old boy had achieved a great accomplishment in the past few weeks. He gave up his Styrofoam bubble on his back. His Dad had to be in the water for moral support or act as a buoy in emergencies; while his Mom was on the deck of the Sirius with a rope attached to the boy's waist so she could yank his drowning body off the bottom. Soon afterwards he gave up the rope and jumped into the water, without his Dad in the water. He leaped off the deck and even from the ratlines about eight feet above this level while his parents closed their eyes.

At Stocking Island we found a real treat, a source of fresh water showers. There was a beautifully landscaped home on a bluff that had never been completed. About eight years before our arrival a construction foreman committed suicide with a stick of dynamite. No native would work on the tabooed house ever after. It was a lovely house built into the side of the hill so that no room in it was square. The landscaping and roof were arranged to collect rain water into a huge cistern. The cistern had a hose sticking out of the overflow hole— no doubt from other sailors that had discovered this bonanza. You just needed to start the flow by sucking on the hose a little and voila, you had running sweet water. Most sweet water in the Exumas is rain water collected in this manner, except occupied homes have a pump to start the flow.

We attended church in Georgetown and noticed that the lady, Leslie Fick, walking down the hill with us had on boat shoes. We started talking and when she reached her yacht, Stardust, at the dock in Georgetown her husband, Harold, invited us aboard for his "Absinth Frappes". This couple was from New Orleans and retired from their scaffolding business. As we enjoyed the Frappes Harold made, we noticed a sailboat was careened on its side across the bay on the sandy beach. The owners were cleaning the bottom. We noticed a young boy playing alongside the yacht. Wendall and Laura Greg, along with their young son, Jeff, were from California. Harold soon invited the Greg family onto Stardust to join us for drinks. Wendell had sold his electrical engineering company to cruise the Bahamas for a few months.

We cruised with these two couples on the three boats for the next couple of weeks returning to Highborne to spearfish. Harold's boat had a cold plate and provided the ice for the three yachts; Wendell and Jay supplied the seafood dinners and Laura and Dolly cooked in Sirius' galley. The Gregs boat was the smallest, Stardust was the next in size, but we had the most room to seat six adults and two boys in the main cabin.

The best fishing seemed to be in the deep cuts between the cays where the tide rips through bringing a lot of food for the fish. Swimming in the tide rip is quite an experience for it is like riding down a slide. You must be extremely quick to dive when you spot a fish or you are far past it if you hesitate. I would run the dinghy down-current and give the men a ride back to the headwaters again for another try. The first night we had lobsters, or crawfishes, as they are called in the islands, no claws, just tail meat. The size of the tails amazed us. One tail would be more than enough food for two people.

On the second day of spearfishing Jay was paralyzed when he jumped overboard and saw a six foot shark. The shark remained on the bottom, minding his own business. It was probably a harmless nurse shark but it was unnerving to Jay, seeing his first shark while in the water. It was the barracudas that the men were unhappy to see and there was one practically every time they went fishing. They are curious fish, always hovering five feet from the men, following them, and watching every move. You are supposed to swim toward the barracudas to scare them away but they only move back after you ignore them. When you went back to fishing they were right there on your heels, watching. We are told there have been no recorded killings of men by barracudas, but if you have ever seen their teeth or vicious faces up close, or heard them gnashing their teeth, you wonder why you are not taking up a different easy sport like bungee jumping. When your entire body is in the water they are reluctant to attack for you are bigger than they are, but if just a limb is in the water they might attack for that smaller chunk of meat is not so menacing. They also like shiny objects so you never wear a watch while spearfishing.

We were rewarded for five days with tasty fish dinners for Wendell speared a thirty pound grouper. What a battle was fought by both man and fish. Wendell hit the giant fish and it took off for a hole in the coral at the bottom of the cut, about 25 feet deep. Wendell had to drop his spear gun and swim back to his boat to get his air tank to retrieve his gun and the fish. He was standing on the coral pulling with all his might. The spear bent in half before the fish's tail was finally showing out of the hole. I couldn't believe the size of that delicious monster.

We then spent a week at Highborne enjoying barbeques every night on the beach, including entertainment from the native boys with calypso songs and steel drums. We offered the natives some of our hot dogs and beans but they declined. They had steaks to feast on. Leslie would often take the two boys, Jimmy and Jeff, out in the Ficks sailing dinghy every day. We became lifelong friends with these two couples. Many joyful memories were shared with the two families.

After another enjoyable week at Highborne we headed back to Nassau to see a doctor about Jimmy's bloodshot eyes. He prescribed drops that seemed to clear up the redness. After Nassau we cruised with the Ficks and Gregs to Spanish Wells on the north end of Eluethra. We had to hire a pilot to lead us into the harbor. At this port we were told that with our draft we would not be able to get near the village. The pilot tried to keep his entrance route secret but we were sounding the depths from the dinghy. We would not have to pay another eight dollars to have him lead us out of Spanish Wells. We just dug a trench through the sandy bottom.

Spanish Wells is a neat, quaint town that looks like it was transplanted from a Scandinavian countryside. It fronts on a canal that carries more traffic than its one paved street. You can walk from one end of town to the other in less than an hour. After Spanish Wells we had to return to Nassau again to take Jimmy to a dentist. There were no doctors on any of the Out Islands. This trip was exciting for we saw two whales spouting water at least twenty feet high but were too slow finding the camera to get a picture.

It was suddenly June. We were back at Yacht Haven marina and figured we would have to return to Florida for the hurricane season. We also needed to earn some money since we depleted our coffers at the Merrill Stevens yard in Miami. Several boats arrived at Yacht Haven during this trip to Nassau. The captains convinced us to go on to the U.S. Virgin Islands to earn money, instead of heading back to

Florida. A skipper on board a boat arriving from Hong Kong via the Philippines, Indian Ocean, Africa, South America and the Caribbean spent time with Jay teaching him celestial navigation. They all convinced us we could and should make the trip now and that Sirius would do well in the charter business in the Virgin Islands.

We picked up a Jamaican native boy, Victor, who was 20 years old, 6'3", polite and hardworking, to help us sail the boat. This turned out to be a fiasco. The first three or four days he was so seasick he could barely hold his head up and after the seasickness waned he got his immense appetite back. He was so basically lazy that he could not concentrate on any one thing for more than a few minutes. Victor could not be trusted to stand his watch without falling asleep. He also truly believed that by placing a book under his pillow at night the knowledge in the book would infuse into his brain.

During this long voyage at sea I read Herman Wouk's book "Don't Stop the Carnival" and thought he was quite a comedian, revealing what life was like on a Caribbean island. Little did I know that he hadn't even begun to tell the story?

CHAPTER 15

The sun was shining and the sky was blue when we finally left the Bahamas on May 28th heading for St. Thomas, in the U.S. Virgin Islands, the next stop on our circumnavigation. St. Thomas was a U.S. Territory where we could find work more easily than in a foreign land. We were so naïve that we thought we could work anywhere we wanted to, not being too proud to do whatever was required, including digging ditches, if necessary.

We also knew that any boat that ventures onto the open seas must be equipped with electrical, plumbing and hardware items and that the owners must feel confident that they can handle any emergency. Having spent three months in the Bahamas, mostly in our beloved Exumas, we headed to the north part of Eleuthra where it would be easy to sail around the north end of the island and head for the open Atlantic.

The first two or three days were the toughest becoming accustomed to the constant motion. Even when the waves were calm there were huge swells. The motion of the swells made Jimmy's stomach and mine queasy but Jay never had a problem with seasickness. Victor was useless, never leaving his bunk in the foc'sle. On our first day of sailing on the open sea we watched a thunderhead cloud building up; it kept us enthralled until three water spouts dipped below the cloud only a couple of miles away. We doused sails in a hurry and motored out of their paths trying hard to swallow the lumps in our throats. Knowing we would encounter many more scary experiences we took on a "Que c'erat, c'erat" attitude. Anyone attempting such an adventure must have such an attitude to succeed. After the water spouts we were treated to three whales blowing water high into the air. This might be an interesting trip to the Caribbean, after all.

We were just two days at sea when the radio announced the formation of Hurricane Alma. Now we really had something to worry about. However, it was 1000 miles west of us so we felt no effect from this new threat. We intended to head east for 600 miles and then south but the sea current actually carried us quite a bit to the south-east of our intended track placing us about 100 miles west of St. Thomas when we finally did steer south. On the third day of sailing we hove-to, for the first time. The winds were forty to forty five miles per hour and we needed to rest. We tightened the mizzen boom and back sheeted the jib at the bow. The boat rode the waves much more comfortably when hove-to in this fashion. Not a drop of water came on the deck. We were like a cork bobbing on the water's surface. After we got our sea legs we always sailed in winds of this force with every wave sending spindrift back to the cockpit. Sailing over 1000 miles to windward with the easterly trade winds never dropping below thirty miles per hour is a wet trip.

During the day we would use the main, mizzen, two headsails or the large genoa sail, depending on the strength of the winds. At night we used only the mizzen and two headsails because only one person was on watch at a time. We could usually make the boat self-steering in this way.

We did not see much life in the open sea. There were a few flying fish; one even landed on deck almost leaping into my frying pan during breakfast. We did see many ships at night. One night we had to turn on the engine and motor out of the path of a freighter. There was no response to our horn blasts or lights shining onto their bridge. We concluded that the autopilot was turned on and no one was on the bridge. We tried several times to make radio contact with ships that were close to us but no one answered. It was like sailing in a fleet of ghost ships controlled by machines. It is no wonder there are collisions even on this huge expanse of water. No one looks outside. I have read so many books where the large ships give the small sailboats a positional fix so the little boat knows its position. We did not find this to be true. Perhaps it is different in the Pacific where two ships meeting on that larger ocean is truly a rare occasion.

Our sail from the Bahamas to the Virgin Islands took eleven days at sea without the sight of land. Jay and I knew that the earth was round and if we missed the islands we could sail on and hit the western coast of Africa. Victor was not convinced of this fact. We sometimes found an uneventful day where we could bathe by dipping a bucket of sea water while carefully holding on to the guy wires so we don't fall overboard. We would sit on the deck with feet propped against the rail and wash ourselves, even shampoo. Sirius carried only 100 gallons of fresh water. Whenever I cooked rice, pasta or potatoes I would use half fresh and half salt water. We used fresh water only for the final rinse when brushing our teeth.

After a calm day the next day invariably involved a couple of crises, like breaking the mizzen sheet, tearing the genny sail, or pulling up the genny track along with the toe rail cap. The most harrowing crisis was jamming the jib halyard in the block at the top of the main mast. The Sirius' mast was sixty five feet above the water. Someone would have to go up the mast and un-jam the halyard. Slender Victor was the first choice. When he was about half way up he promptly threw up on both of us below. When Victor was returned to the deck I would have gladly kicked him overboard if I didn't have to risk going to jail for making this worthless deckhand meet King Neptune. I didn't have the strength to winch Jay up the mast so the First Mate was chosen by the Captain to go up this swaying stick to untangle the line in the block. The last time I was hauled up this incredibly tall mast was to paint it. Sirius was sitting in a calm harbor at a dock. This ride was quite different. The seas were six to eight feet but the pendulum swing was much greater the higher you went. I really felt like I was reaching for the stars. I could almost grab the hand of God if only He would hold on to me so I wouldn't perish in the sea.

One day Jay announced, after eleven days of seeing only water on the horizon, that we should see land in the morning. The morning came and went, and the next morning came and went, but there was no land. He had made a mistake in his noontime sun sights and didn't want to admit it. We continued to head south. When we started to see flotsam in the water and land birds we knew we would spot Puerto Rico soon. We were tired and needed some rest from the tension of someone continuously moving the land farther away. We decided to pull into any port on the north coast of Puerto Rico and rest for a day before making the hundred mile trip east to St. Thomas.

We were near the 100 fathom line, a mile or so off shore, when we encountered two huge waves close together. We climbed up the first one but the second one broke over our bow. The force of tons of water washed me off my perch on top of the cockpit seat where I was taking compass bearings and threw me against Jay at the helm. The powerful wave washed all loose things off the deck. We almost lost Victor off the stern, but he managed to hang on, too bad. We were still ankle deep in sea water when we pulled up to the city dock in Arecibo, Puerto Rico.

Arecibo is not a port of entry for Puerto Rico so yachts seldom call here. We became the town event for the day. People were coming out, sitting on the dock and watching us. Most could not speak English so we felt like museum pieces. Victor jumped ashore and kissed the ground making our audience laugh. Juan, a prominent businessman, helped catch our lines and when we asked for cold beers he said he had already sent for a six-pack. This Good Samaritan took us up town in his car for shopping and then to his home for warm showers. The next day Juan ran many errands for us and made things much easier with Customs officials. Juan earned his halo that day and we will never forget his welcome.

We left Arecibo at night when the winds are calmer for it is a dead beat to windward along the north Puerto Rican coast. We pulled into San Juan harbor the next morning to wait again for the calmer night winds. The Customs men did not bother to board us for they were too busy. San Juan was hosting the Inter-American-Caribbean Olympic Games and there was much demonstrating that day over the Cuban athletes not being allowed ashore. Castro had sent the athletes in a Cuban ship, which was not allowed in the harbor. As we sailed past Castro's ship we prayed that the demonstrators would not get violent before we left port.

It took another twenty six hours to sail the last one hundred miles to St. Thomas. Again it seemed that the Virgin Islands were being pulled eastward by King Neptune and his mermaids.

The Charlotte Amalie harbor is on the south side of the island. The red range lights on the hillside were difficult to spot with the town lights glaring in our eyes after sailing all night on the dark ocean. We followed the channel markers into the main harbor, dropped anchor, and collapsed into our bunks for a well-deserved night of sleep. In the morning light we saw the hill towering over the harbor. We gulped when saw the Prince Rupert Rocks in the harbor entrance. We passed the rocks so glibly last night.

Charlotte Amalie is the capital of the Virgin Islands. The U.S. Virgins consist of St. John, St. Croix and St. Thomas, plus another hundred cays and rocks. The Virgins are much more picturesque than the low-lying Bahamas Islands with their crystalline waters. The sailing in these islands are in deep water without the fear of hitting coral reefs. St. Thomas is only 3 miles wide by 13 miles long with steep hills and sharp hairpin turns. To add to the excitement the driving is on the left side of the road, as in England.

In 1966 the West Indian Docks to the southeast still had a coal loading apparatus that filled the cargo ships heading to the United States through this port. To the west was Water Island, containing a rail to haul larger ships, a submarine base and a commercial port. To our east was the Yacht Haven Marina and Hotel and to the north was the town of Charlotte Amalie with houses climbing the hills only a couple hundred feet, or easy walking distance from the town center. A dock ran the entire length of the town where the pirates once offloaded their brigantines directly into their warehouses. This large protected harbor was once a volcano. During World War II a net was stretched across the entrance to trap German submarines. At this time down island cargo ships used the city dock to load items going to other Caribbean islands, including automobiles, generators, machinery, canned goods, produce and items from the United States.

CHAPTER 16

The islands of St. John and St. Thomas were offered for sale by Denmark to the United States in the 19th century for five million dollars. The Danes later bought St. Croix from France. That sale to the United States was never consummated. After World War I the U.S. was afraid that Germany would acquire the islands for a submarine base. For that reason and to protect the Panama Canal the U.S. bought the islands from Denmark in 1917, but the price was now twenty five million dollars. Here was another example of strategic planning by the politicians in Washington. In 1966 the population of the three islands was about 100,000 legal residents and about 10,000 illegals. The ratio was about 85% black, 15% white.

When we arrived in June of 1966 the homes only climbed the hill behind town about half way up the mountain. At the very crest was the Louisenhoj Castle. In its early days the Castle was a former plantation great house, belonging to the Magen's family. In later years Arthur S. Fairchild restored the Castle to its majestic beauty. Louisenhoj, with three foot thick walls, was built out of local stones with only the gatehouse visible from the road. To the south this property has a view of the Charlotte Amalie harbor and St. Croix in the distance, to the north a view of exquisite Magen's Bay, Hans Lollick Island and the British Virgin Islands in the eastern distance. Upon our arrival Louisenhoj was owned by the DuPont family, who established their ostracized gay relative in this isolated spot. He became the "queen" of the gays on the island.

It is often easier for a woman to get a job in a new location. I saw an ad in the local paper requiring a seamstress at one of the local shops that offered to sew a quick simple dress for the tourist while she shops. I had done some sewing at home, interviewed for the job, and was hired immediately. I had six local seamstresses working for me. The local ladies were all good seamstresses for the stores in town were priced for the tourist; there were no department stores with reasonable prices for the natives. The women sewed out of necessity plus they were accustomed to designing their elaborate costumes for the Carnival Parade each year. St. Thomas' Parade was second only to Rios' Mardi gras parade.

The end of July was Jimmy's fifth birthday and after pricing a nine inch cake for $5 and a half sheet cake at $10, at the downtown bakery, I decided to bake two cakes for his party myself. Jimmy had so many friends on the docks that at the boy's request I baked a white and a chocolate cake. I have never had luck with cakes even on a gimbaled stove in a harbor that rocked from the waves of passing boats.

The white cake was in round pans and would be the one we decorated. The chocolate one was in an oblong pan. I figured icing would cover up the flaw of a droopy center. The layers of the round white cake were so uneven that they would slide off one another when I tried to ice them. After a couple of slides one of the layers broke in half. I was heartbroken. I salvaged what I could and put the round cake in a Tupperware container. I decided to decorate the chocolate one and serve that one first, then resort to my white one, if necessary. When I glanced away, Jim and his good friend, Maria, were turning the Tupperware over to see what the bottom looked like. There goes the white cake. Then an hour before the party I was calming my nerves in the cockpit when I heard a crash down below. Jim had been spinning the pan on the table; it spun off the table, and landed on the floor, upside down. I was close to tears. A Knight in Shining Armor came to my rescue. Jay calmly walked the two blocks to Pueblo's, our local supermarket, and bought a delicious 8" decorated cake for $3.60. I guess I should have tried the local market rather than the bakery downtown. But then we wouldn't have had such an exciting party, or story to tell.

After two weeks of working downtown I had my paycheck in hand attempting to cash it at the Marina office. They sent me to the bookkeeping office for approval and when I walked into that office I was immediately asked if I wanted a job. I said sure, figuring how much easier it would be to work on the property, and not fight the traffic downtown or finding a parking place. I could be taught to keep books, to learn this trade that is the lifeblood of these islands.

The new job involved many facets. Besides the accounting office, there was front desk exposure, management chores, handling the maid service, and even some switchboard work with a rat's nest of cables that plugged into the various rooms. The operator could eavesdrop just like on the party lines of years gone by. In the meantime Jay found work with Island Yachts performing maintenance work on the boats. This worked out well for he could keep an eye on Jimmy playing on the docks while I worked in the accounting office.

Jay's schedule was loose so he also seized the opportunity of day chartering. He could take six people for a day of sailing and swimming at twenty five dollars each. Six is the maximum number of guests allowed by the Coast Guard on private yachts unless the Captain has a license to take more than six. We were living on Sirius so I would walk the two blocks to Pueblo's to shop for him after work, then made sandwiches the evening before the charter. Jim and I would join him on the weekends. We usually took the guests to Christmas Cove at a small island, on the east end of St. Thomas.

In August, 1966, we were stocked up on Wednesday evening for a six person charter on Thursday that Jay and Jimmy were taking out on Sirius. However, Hurricane Faith was approaching the islands. It was not a nice welcome to the islands; the storm was just two months after we arrived in the Virgin Islands. The St. Thomas harbor is not considered a hurricane harbor so all yachts must head west to the island of Culebra or east to St. John. All boats are required to leave the docks at the marina lest they pull down the structures. On the east end of St. John is a harbor configured with five fingers and a shallower thumb. The thumb is the preferred spot for the water drops off rapidly near shore.

We left early on Thursday morning so we could acquire the prime location in Hurricane Hole. There were already several swifter yachts or ones that left earlier than we did in the thumb. We had three anchors in the water and five lines to shore tied to the mangrove trees. A captain's meeting was required to untangle this spider's web before we could return to St. Thomas.

On the Sunday following our return to St. Thomas we finally had our first day charter of just two local people. The man was a Professor from Michigan State University taking a year's sabbatical to perform Welfare work here on St. Thomas. During his Dartmouth University days he was a classmate of Dr. Seuss, author of the children's books that we read over and over to Jimmy who giggled loudly at the witticisms of Dr. Seuss.

I had made inquiries of adoptions on the island and might have given up too soon figuring there were not many white children available. With the local natives there are very few adoptions for there is always room for a child in some relative's home. This Professor, it turns out is the man we would see at the local office regarding adoptions. He makes arrangements in the States for white children. In the meantime I had written to the Catholic Charities in St. Petersburg where we had applied before we left that area. They too are looking into us bringing a child to the islands. We wanted a daughter to round out our family but were not sure they would place a baby on a boat. We had gone through such a thorough investigation in Michigan for Jim.

Harvey Aluminum on St. Croix had interviewed Jay and was interested in him for the job of assistant plant superintendent. We were not sure we wanted to move to St. Croix but we were grateful that technical people were not easy to come by in these islands. St. Croix is a larger and flatter island that includes a golf course known as

Fountain Valley built by Laurence Rockefeller for his resort. The island is twice the size of St. Thomas so more plantations were located on St. Croix, the largest of the U.S. Virgins. Laurence Rockefeller also owned two thirds of St. John, the smallest of the three major islands and it took him over twenty years to donate the land to the National Park and obtain his tax credits for the donation.

The Virgins are an unincorporated territory of the United States with citizenship granted to the residents but they were not allowed to vote for the President. They had a non-voting representative in Congress with his vote counting only on unimportant matters.

Taxes are paid into the Virgin Islands Bureau of Internal Revenue, using the same 1040 forms as the Federal Government but the revenue does not go to Washington to be co-mingled with the Federal funds. The postal rates are the same as the States as well as the library and school systems. In 1966 the Governor was appointed by the President of the United States. Because Joe Kennedy made part of his fortune from the rum distilled at the Paiewonsky family's distillery on St. Thomas, John Kennedy, then President, appointed Isidor Paiewonsky as our governor. In later years we elected our own Governor, but Uncle Sam no longer matched dollar for dollar with what the local Internal Revenue office collected.

During our first Christmas on St. Thomas Jimmy insisted that his Dad build a chimney for Santa to arrive. We assured him that Santa would slide down our mast instead of using a chimney. It was during this first year on the island that Jay worked for V.I. Communications, a privately owned public utility supplying radio communications to the various islands. This company was also the marine operator for the Virgin Islands. Jay soon became the radio and electronics repair expert on the island. It seems you can wear many different hats on a small island, as long as you can read and understand what your customers cannot.

The climate is always perfect. 80 degrees during the day and the 70s at night. The islands are only 500 miles north of the equator so the days and evenings are about equal in length. The sun is penetrating because the air is so clean, but in the shade the constant trade winds are cooling. A light sweater is needed only when going to the mountaintop at night or an air conditioned restaurants or theaters. Our thinned blood thinks it is cold at 68 degrees.

We only saw Sahara Desert dust in the summertime when the trade winds blow the dust across the Atlantic. Surprisingly, there are no mosquitoes or even flies. Most of the restaurants are outdoors on patios or yards and food can be left out without bother from pests. The government sprays for mosquitoes regularly. That is when you want your home located on the upper side of the road. Homes seldom have windows, only screens and shutters to hold out the rain. Drinking water is collected on the roof and stored in cisterns, usually built under the home. By law a home must build ten gallons of water storage capacity for every square foot of roof area for a single family, fifteen gallons for two families. The cisterns are usually located under the living room area as no cistern can have a bathroom or waste drains above it in case of leaks.

A local doctor once told me that the children mature faster in this climate of full sunshine and are usually two years ahead of their contemporaries in the States. The girls mature earlier and start their families at 14 or 15 years of age. They leave the children with the grandmothers who are only thirty or thirty five years old, who by this time may be living with the father of one of their children. The young lady goes out to work and supports her children until she gets pregnant again.

The islands are a matriarchal society. The women can have inside, outside or yard children. The inside children are the result of a real marriage, the outside children are from a father outside the marriage and the yard children are the ones where the father is unknown. The men may or may not acknowledge their children but usually do not support them. Their goal is to impregnate a St. Thomian woman for the child has automatic U.S. citizenship. Eventually that child might support an elderly father.

During our second year I continued to work for Yacht Haven Hotel and Marina while Jay found a technical job at the V.I. Water and Power Authority. He became their chemist and results engineer. Besides providing the erratic electricity for the island, about 1.5 million gallons of water are desalinated from sea water. The demand for water and power was growing so fast that water still had to be barged in from Puerto Rico. Each island, however, has to produce its own electricity. There is no easy connection to a grid system like in the States. A new Israeli water distillation plant to increase the water output to 3.5 million gallons per day was being installed at the Power Plant. As in any new installation there were bugs in the system that had to be found and ironed out.

The evil-spirited Jumbies were causing the problems and spooking the natives; they didn't want to work in this scary place. Paul Carlson, the superintendent, finally hung a bag of acorns, which the natives had never seen, from the ceiling. He told the curious men that the acorns were food for the Leprechauns, the good spirits that would take care of the Jumbies. And it worked; there were no more problems after that.

There were only five white men working at WAPA and as they left or retired the policy of the government was to replace them with locals. We wondered how much longer the power would stay on when that day came.

Living on a boat at Yacht Haven made transportation easy for Jay. He went to work via dinghy and the outages did not interrupt our meal or reading for we worked off of battery power and used a kerosene stove for cooking. The hotel had its own generator, as most did for they could not rely on WAPA.

Working in the hotel business in the Caribbean can be enlightening and frightening. In the islands incidents are tolerated that would never be acceptable in the States. For instance after guests complained about their lousy chicken dinner the manager refunded the chicken portion but the guests had to pay for their salad.

My boss, John, the comptroller, and another employee went to lunch at noon. An hour after they ordered the waiter told them there was no more crabmeat for their order. Nor was there any shrimp. They ordered chicken salad and got tuna.

Or the time the manager, Ted, was kicked out of their room by his girlfriend, Ann, after a fight. Ted could not go back to his boat for he was housing the entertainers on his craft. He glibly went to the front desk each night, took keys for an empty room and slept in it until the fight was over. This made the arriving guests and the housekeepers angry. The guests checking into the room complained to the front desk, which reflected back on the maids.

Another time the cook entered the accounting office to report that the manager, Ted, skipped out and Ted's girlfriend, Ann, said she would be running the restaurant. The cook wanted to know who the heck the boss is now.

When Ann started dating a stateside boyfriend Ted ran around on his scooter looking for her. He ran off the road at 80 mph and a cabbie brought him back unconscious. This happens when you are one of the minority in a community that is 85% black and are easily recognized.

The icing on the cake of humorous stories at Yacht Haven was when the owner, Mr. Poe, shot air pistols at the native kids to keep them off the beach. Poe was arrested, put in jail, and we had to visit him weekly to get the payroll checks signed. Our management was not really retarded because they didn't have the sense to be retarded. They signed leases with new tenants even when the previous tenant still had time left on their lease.

We could hardly contain ourselves while watching the local firemen attempting to put out a fire across the street from the hotel accounting office. The high powered hose had gotten away from the firemen and they were all trying to catch the wayward snake instead of turning off the water.

Living on an island as small as St. Thomas, allows you to retrieve a stolen vehicle easily. Kathy's jeep was stolen during the heavy drinking of Carnival by six Puerto Ricans. She sat on the waterfront and watched for it to go by. And there it was coming from town. The car had to stop for traffic; Kathy ran and caught up with the jeep. The six thieves scattered in different directions and she got her vehicle back.

Another time my coworker, Dick, had his scooter stolen at Trader Dan's bar. Dick notified the police then decided he'd get drunk. He kept his eye on the road while drinking and, lo and behold, there goes the scooter. Dick runs out on the road, jumps into a native's car and tells him to follow the scooter. Dick got his scooter back and then gave the thief a ride back to town to the Carnival Village so the partying could continue.

One of the most popular bands, Milo and the Kings, played nightly at Yacht Haven during the final week of Carnival. The dancing started at 11:00 p.m. and ended at 5 a.m. We could only attend every other night but the music throbbed throughout the marina every night. It was our first exposure to Carnival on St. Thomas and we fell in love with the marching song of that year, "Fire, Fire in De Wire, Papa". This was a relatively calm Carnival with only four cars stolen, two shootings, and a couple of fist fights. In later years we would join a troupe and dance down Main Street until our feet were blistered.

Some famous yachts grace our harbor these days. The Double Eagle, better known as the Kiwi on the TV series "The Wackiest Ship in the Army", arrived from California and will remain to charter until the owner decides to take her to the Mediterranean. The Tiki, from "Adventures in Paradise", the program we watched faithfully and used as a model for our adventure, is being outfitted in San Juan for charter this season and should be in St. Thomas in a month or so. There was also a huge windjammer ship, the Mystic Whaler, which we often called the Septic Baler. It usually operated out of Mystic, Connecticut but she decided to try the warmer climates for the winter. This region of St. Thomas was fast becoming the world's most popular chartering area. The weather is dependable; there are good winds for sailing plus many islands to explore within a short distance.

Our biggest problem on a small tropical island is supply. The simple items that you take for granted in the States, where you can just run down to the hardware or department stores, have to be ordered from the States. Despite how urgently you might need the item it can take a while to reach the island. Or your order might sit at the airport for a week before they actually call you to tell you the part you ordered by air freight for speedy delivery is finally on the island. You can't just hop in the car and tootle on down to the mall.

To refill our coffers quickly we decided to let the Sirius go out on bareboat charter, without a captain and cook. Our sailing friends warned us against letting our home, a boat of this size, go out without a captain but we wanted the extra money. Two years later we would learn that the friends were right, we would rue the day of that decision. In preparation for letting Sirius go out on charter we repainted the entire boat, put up new rigging, and redecorated the interior.

Jay had to work one Sunday so I was handling the winch to lower the hired native boy who was painting the main mast with white enamel. Suddenly it was raining white paint on my head. My first concern was to get the enamel off the teak decks. We did such a good job that Jay didn't notice what had happened, only that I had premature white hair. I was advised by dockside quarterbacks that I needed to use Crisco to get the paint out of my hair, and then lots of shampoo to eliminate the Crisco. The marina showers on the dock provided the warm water. I used an abundance of elbow grease that day, plus I had thought again about throwing another black boy off the ship, hoping he couldn't swim.

At last I heard from the St. Petersburg adoption agency. They had a baby girl available for us. She was dark haired, dark eyed, but had an enormous red blotch on one half of her face. We happened to have a neurologist on the island at this time so I took the letter and picture to him for advice. He said the birthmark could indicate brain damage at birth. I wrote the most difficult letter of my life turning down this baby. We would have to wait for another girl and delay our planned trip even longer.

I then consulted a local attorney and explained our desire for a daughter. Most of the pregnant stateside women hid in the islands during their pregnancy but returned to Miami for the birth of their child, where the medical facilities are not so primitive. The mother's concerns are warranted when they see chickens and goats wandering in the yards of the hospitals or public health clinics.

We knew we had to have a home on land to appease the social workers. Jay was offered a building site above the power plant where the rent was free and the water would be pumped to our home from the plant below. The water was hot right out of the de-salinization plant so showers had to be taken at night and the drinking water cooled before it could be used. We hired a wonderful young girl from St. Kitts, Ingrid Grand, as our live-in maid. She would be living with us so we needed a bedroom for her, one for the children and another for us. We ordered a three bedroom, two bath trailer, twelve feet wide by sixty feet long, from a company in the States and were immediately offered the dealership. We became dealers mainly to obtain a discounted price. We never sold another trailer.

When we went to the bank for a loan we had to have good friends, Don and Ida Walterson, vouch and co-sign for us because we were new to the island and the bank feared that we could "take this trailer off the island and disappear with it." Little did the bank know what a chore that would be—even placing the unit on a steep hill two hundred feet above the water was a distressing experience.

One day I had a call from the local Social Welfare Dept. asking me if I had heard from the adoption agency in St. Petersburg. I told the lady that I was still waiting for a child. She said that there was a woman that stayed on St. Croix to have her baby. A miracle had happened, here where the population is 85% black, there was a white baby for us. She was a blue-eyed blond baby of Irish, English and Scottish descent and they would like to place her with us, if possible. A nurse would be bringing her to St. Thomas on Antilles Airboats, the inter-island seaplane. I could see the baby on Friday morning and there would be no fees connected with the adoption except for the attorney's fee to draw up the papers. Because this mother named the father we would need a paternity release from the father. If he doesn't acknowledge the child the courts can declare abandonment on his part.

In all it took four months before all the paperwork and documents were finalized and our new daughter could come home with us.

Growing up on the docks at Yacht Haven turned Jimmy into an avid fisherman. All the children that lived on boats, and there were many, learned to fish with bread balls, catch a small fish on the bread and then cut him up as bait for larger fish.

I remember finding two girls peering into a box gawking at the little boy sitting in the box explaining to his Mother that it was very hot so he had to take his clothes off. I am sure he was showing off the parts of his anatomy that differed from the girls.

The three of us had discussions on names and we settled on Diane Denise. Jim had already been telling his classmates at the Catholic School he was attending that he had a sister, Diane, for quite some time, I learned. The baby became known as Dee-Dee during her toddler years and only those that knew her back then are allowed to call her that today. She was so fair skinned that we had to be careful of the sun. Her hair was so blond and silky that women and children would come up to her in the supermarket just to stroke her blond hair and to feel straight hair, so unlike their own. Often I was chastised by the local ladies because I didn't have enough clothes on the baby in the cool supermarket or a hat on her hair to "keep the night dew" off of her.

Now that we were blessed with a daughter we would have to postpone our plans of a circumnavigation once more at least until Diane is a little older and can appreciate seeing new people and worlds, and for her Mom's sake, out of diapers.

CHAPTER 17

Setting up a sixty foot trailer on a lot that has a twenty degree slope was an unforgettable experience. There was the leveling of the site, drilling of holes in the large boulders so that a sturdy rope can be attached to giant size augers cemented in the rock. The ropes can then be thrown over the single wide trailer to keep it from rolling down the hill into the water in high winds. There were walking paths to be laid to the back door for carrying groceries, and on the water side a large slab poured to have a sitting/picnicking area at the front door. Two hundred feet or more of piping had to be brought up the hill for our water supply from the power plant below.

All homes on the island are oriented so that the view is at the front of the house with the main entrance at the back of the house. If we were building a regular, stick-built home we would also have to build a cistern to store the rain water collected on the roof. The cistern is tucked into the hillside, usually under the living area so that no waste water drainage can leak into the cistern. The overflow pipes are screened to keep thirsty rodents away from the water. Island law states that ten gallons of storage capacity is required for a single family home and fifteen gallons for a two family residence for every square foot of roof area. Most homes are two families; an apartment is rented out to help defray costs.

We sailed on Sirius every weekend that we could. We went on Mandoo one weekend and found my watch exactly where I had left it four weeks earlier when Jay and I hauled the dinghy onto the beach to scrub the bottom. The watch was hanging on a tree limb exactly where I had left it after a hurricane with strong winds came near the islands.

One Sunday we had several nuns, the Sisters of Charity, who were teaching at the Catholic School where Jimmy was a student. This was just when the Church was becoming more lenient with the nun's dress. They could dress as they wished, not needing their long white habits; they could also revert back to their family given names, and show their hair. We took them to an island few boats sail to so they would be comfortable swimming. So that Jay wouldn't feel outnumbered we asked another family to come along. I was surprised to see them change into bright colored bathing suits and only a sun bonnet for some, the others wore no head covering. We had our misgiving before we went out but we can truthfully say that was one of the most enjoyable days we have had with guests aboard the Sirius. The Sisters brought lunch, at their insistence, which was quite a feast.

We came home that weekend with seven lobsters and two large groupers. The lobsters in the Caribbean are not like the Maine lobster, there are no claws, just tail meat and are called crayfish locally. When we were living on the boat at the Yacht Haven dock the men could get dinner every time they dove on Prince Rupert Rocks at the harbor entrance.

Other boats arrived at the island in the same dire straits as our finances. When we sailed into the harbor we had thirty dollars in cash and one credit card. We did have a year's supply of canned goods aboard. Whenever we had a dock picnic one would bring the can of beans, another, the rolls, someone else the hot dogs and condiments, or the desert. A lad from a large ship, the Taormina, which was built in a Navy hobby shop, begged for an egg one morning when he smelled them frying in my galley. He hadn't had an egg for weeks, he said.

I had cut up all the voracious credit cards when we left the States but we did have the American Express card to buy Victor a one-way ticket back to Jamaica at the Immigration Department's insistence. We were not sorry to see him off at the airport that day.

It was normal for young boys to climb trees and Jim was no exception. He had a tree house in the huge mango tree in the back yard when we lived at Mandoo Manor. When I called him for dinner one night he reached for the rope he used for quick descents, missed, and landed on his wrist twenty feet below. The compound fracture required surgery the next day. He was constantly climbing the mast on the Sirius. During another speedy descent, he burned his hand severely on the rope. But I had read that Mothers should not tell their children to avoid doing something dangerous lest they get hurt. I could only close my eyes, pray, and let them proceed.

We had an interesting experience another weekend. Our friends Don and Ida, owners of the Mandoo, a sixty foot charter yacht, were taking a year off of chartering and were running a resort on Mosquito Island, one of the British Islands. They also owned the Mandoo Manor. The Manor is a home they bought for Ida's parents to live in to take care of their daughter, Mary, while she attended Antilles School. The Manor was located above the school so Mary could walk the two blocks to the facilities. The parents were to take care of Mary ashore while Don and Ida chartered the Mandoo. The parents both died before they had a chance to move to St. Thomas.

We were visiting with Don, Ida, and Bert at the resort one weekend and were about to leave the dock to hunt for lobsters when the phone rang. The manager of a bareboat charter brokerage was calling looking for Bert Kildare, owner of Mosquito Island. Bert and his wife, Monica, had bought the island in 1963 with an inheritance she had received. Bert had come ashore on this uninhabited island with laborers and machetes to clear the land. Within five years they built a resort that could sleep twenty and a restaurant that seats one hundred yachtsmen and their guests. Many charter boats stopped there for dinner.

This was quite a feat when an island is as remote as this one. You have to generate your own power and rely on rain for the water supply. Bert's first love is diving on old wrecks. He knew of hundreds of shipwrecks on the Anegada Reef. This reef is so treacherous because it extends for five miles from the island of Anegada, a low island like the Bahamas. You are on the reef before you can see the land of Anegada, the easternmost island of the British Virgins. The reef has been the graveyard of an uncounted numbers of ships dating back to the Spanish galleons loaded with gold. Someday Bert hopes to find a ship laden with these treasures. Bert is so familiar with the reefs in this area that he was named Receiver of Wrecks for the Queen of England. He has also rescued dozens of boats from the reefs surrounding his Mosquito Island. He even labeled them the $25, $50, $200 and $250 reefs, depending on his services. The man only needed a patch over one eye to label him a true pirate.

Two doctors and their wives chartered a thirty foot Chris Craft Capri sailboat and missed the channel through the reef. They were approaching the island from the west in a setting sun with not much visibility in the water and hit one of the reefs. They were on a lee shore with the waves carrying them further and further aground. Coming from the States the men assumed they would have the protection of the Coast Guard within a few minutes. Not so in the islands. You can only have trouble between the hours of 8:00 a.m. and 8:00 p.m., in calm weather, and not too far from St. Thomas in order for the Coast Guard to help. After much distress, the doctors finally roused the Coast Guard on the radio and were told that considering where they were, in the British Virgin Islands, they needed to get in touch with Bert Kildare. When they told the Coast Guard that they had someone injured, (a wife had mangled her hand in the ropes on a winch), that they were hard aground, the dinghy motor would not start, and they didn't know how they would reach the shore, the Coast Guard told them to paddle!

The Guardsman finally condescended to call the manager of the couple's bareboat operation and that is how Bert was alerted. When we arrived on the scene a sixty foot power boat was attempting the rescue but after bending several cleats on both boats he gave up. Jay swam a tow rope to the grounded boat which was now in knee deep water. Bert waited for a large wave and surfed them off at just the right moment. It was an incredible achievement.

I had thoroughly enjoyed getting back to gardening at our trailer lot, even though our soil was dry and rocky. However, in the tropics it is so rewarding. Everything grows at amazing speed. I started planting in June and six months later had good sized bananas, coconut palms, sea grapes, papayas, and grapefruit trees. Jimmy and I also planted a vegetable garden. We started the seeds in cut off milk cartons; they sprouted in four or five days and within two weeks the plants were large enough to set out in the prepared plot. We grew tomatoes, cucumbers, Chinese cabbage, beets, green peppers, carrots, pumpkins, melons and squash plants. We could only imagine what the plants would do in dark, rich soil. When you wanted flowers you took a cutting from a bush, soaked it in water for a week until it starts to root, then planted it in the ground; presto, in a few weeks you have a flowering bush. Among the flowers that graced this property were many varieties of hibiscus, oleander, moss rose, canna lilies, periwinkles, zinnias, candle tree, Pride of Barbados and bougainvillea.

The walkway is lined with miniature wild orchids that I picked off the rocks on the water's edge at the foot of our hill.

We had trouble growing sweet corn. Hungry worms were eating the seeds. An old native farmer told me the reason we had trouble is that we didn't plant them during the full moon. We tried again at full moon and the seeds sprouted in four days.

We added a pet to our family, a brilliant green baby iguana, whom Jimmy named Sam Green. Jay caught him on a bush at the Yacht Haven Hotel where I worked. The day Sam was caught, he struggled when Jimmy was holding him and his tail broke off. The tail grew back in a few months but iguanas are very slow growing, we learned. Sam must have just been hatched when we brought him home, for he was only about six inches long in the body plus a six inch tail. Sam is a land iguana like the ones in the Galapagos Islands that grow to about four feet in length in the body. They are supposedly good pets. Sam is quite tame and loves to be petted. He will sit on your shoulder and sleep for as long as you let him. He loves to be held under a slow running faucet for a shower. We force fed him honey from a toothpick. Iguanas are herbivorous. Their diet is primarily hibiscus flowers, although they love pineapple and maraschino cherries. I was waiting for the day when Sam was full grown and greeted strangers at the door.

We lost Sam one day when he crawled onto the flowered drapes. We searched and searched for him to no avail. He was loose in the house. Jay had pulled an all-nighter when there was trouble at the power plant. He was sleeping during the day when he felt something on his cheek. He brushed Sam off his cheek and on to the pillow next to him. They were both surprised by the encounter.

Unfortunately, we have often seen native children killing iguanas. They seem to be afraid of them, adults as well. We left Sam with a neighbor's maid when we went sailing one weekend and she either killed him or set him free outside.

Island living has its frustrations and the most classic example recently was that after months of trying to get a phone at the trailer I finally had one installed on September 18th. It was not connected until December 4th but in November I received a bill for local service. I wanted to keep the bill and frame it but Vitelco, the Virgin Islands Telephone Company, insisted I mail it back to them for correction. My thought was they didn't want any blackmail evidence around. In another incident we recently had direct dialing installed at Vitelco. A St. Thomas man tried a couple of times to dial a friend in New York. He kept reaching a wrong number so he asked an operator to assist. When the operator asked the woman they reached where she was, she said Greenland. The operator then asked the woman to call the New Yorkers number and have him call his friend in St. Thomas. Within ten minutes the man in New York called the island and his first comment was:

"Joe, where the hell are you?"

This incident reminded me of the owner of the Beauty Shop at Yacht Haven who complained to management that he had to pay for local phone calls made by customers from his Shop but then learned that the swimming pool lights, that burned all night, were on his meter.

After persevering for eleven months I had finally gotten a government job with the Department of Health. I was now the island Parasitologist. It was a completely new field for me but they are in such desperate need of qualified help in any technical field that they decided to hire me and send me to the States for training, which never happened. At least this job is in the science field and has the advantage of civil service work, which in the Virgins means four weeks of vacation the first year, three weeks sick leave and twenty six paid holidays. The sick leave is used every year lest it be lost. You call the boss and tell him you are going to be sick next Wednesday then take the day off.

The holdup was that the job required a Master's Degree, which I do not have. The powers-to-be had to waive this requirement before they could hire me. The work is going to be quite a challenge, and I expect to meet a great deal of controversy. I have learned that there are absolutely no controls here of health certificates for food handlers and untold numbers of people are working without certificates. I will have to register all the food handlers, test them for communicable diseases (and many have them), stop them from working if they need medical care; then make sure they come in for regular checkups. We will first have to fight for stronger legislation to back up the Health Department then get the cooperation of the police to enforce the law. It seems like I might need a bodyguard for this job. This will involve thousands of people on all three U.S. Virgin Islands. We must also get the cooperation of the other Caribbean islands for it is from these various islands that the diseases are brought into our area. Down-island aliens make up the greatest percentage of the workers in the food industry.

My office at Public Health had a view out the window of the balcony at the mental ward of the old hospital, where chickens and geese had free reign of the grounds. I was constantly distracted by the women who would raise their skirts at the men trying to seduce them. It was a tough place to concentrate.

The St. Thomian calls anyone not born in the islands "continentals", regardless of color or race. Europeans are also continentals, but down-islanders are aliens. A black prominent local doctor's wife, who was born stateside, told me she experienced as much prejudice as I might feel. Her husband was trained in the States as a heart surgeon but could not practice his specialty as he had no trained doctors or nurses to perform the surgeries with him. The government had helped him with his education in return for a promise to come back to the islands and practice family medicine for five years. Dr. Harth was our family doctor and an exceptionally good one.

The Caribbean Islands are a true melting pot. You can have the governor and your maid at the same party. Dress is always casual so there is no distinction between rich and poor by dress code. This was the atmosphere we were searching for, where all are as equal as possible. This would be a good place to raise the children.

CHAPTER 18

Over Easter break in 1969 we took a vacation trip south to visit Ethyl friends, John and Susan McDonald, now living in Valencia, Venezuela, about 100 miles from Caracas. This oil rich country had four-lane super highways travelling thousands of feet up the mountains that easily rival any in the United States. It was a far cry from the donkey-size roads in St. Thomas where the roads are mostly unpaved or non-existent climbing the hills we call mountains. Our roads are so bad that there is only one speed—slow. Tires wear out in 8000 miles and brakes in the about the same mileage. Our potholes are serious problems for all automobiles. We have few casualties from collisions. In fact, there were none in the year 1969. Any fatalities are usually from cars leaving the road and tumbling down the steep hills. We were surprised to find that South America is closer to the Virgin Islands than Miami to the north.

Susan brought her seven year old daughter, Kelly, to the airport to greet us. Kelly would keep Jimmy company. We rode the Teleferico cable car to the Humbolt Hotel for dinner. The Humbolt, overlooking Caracas, is located at an elevation of 3000 feet on the mountaintop. It is usually nestled in the clouds. Humidity is such a problem in the hotel that there were fireplaces in every room. The hotel is only accessible by the Teleferico. The ride up was spectacular, watching the sunset, then the sparkle of lights from the city so far below. Once inside the smell of wood burning brought back memories of ski lodges up north.

John McDonald had taken a job in a manufacturing plant as their chemical engineer. The family resided in a lovely home of monstrous size, with two maids and a gardener for the same price that I paid Ingred, $150/month. Each maid had her own bedroom and bath from the four bedrooms, three baths for the McDonalds. The gardener lived off property and came daily. When we couldn't communicate with the Spanish speaking maids we would hunt up a McDonald child. Even the three year old could do a good job for us.

Valencia does not enjoy the trade winds that we have in the Virgins. The stores all close from noon to three o'clock so everyone can go home for a siesta. Valencia has a population of 400,000 or more with probably 50,000 cars and only two red lights, in insignificant spots. What a free for all on the roads! The mountains are barren for they are burned periodically to get rid of the snakes.

In the U.S. Virgins the mongoose was imported from Madagascar or most likely Africa with the slaves, to take care of the snakes. Now we are overrun with mongooses. They look like a rat except they have a longer tail and a slenderer pointed face. They are very shy and flee from people.

When we think of South America we think of gold jewelry so Susan took us to a reputable jeweler. We went berserk in the store with our Christmas shopping. This was when the States was still on the gold standard. Gold was $35 an ounce. The jewelry piece is placed on a scale and you pay by the weight of the gold. The artist's work is ignored. For me, Jay bought a Cacique coin of 22 carat gold that I had set in a gold holder. The Cacique is a Venezuelan coin commemorating the Indian Chiefs. Pure gold is 24 carat but too soft to use as jewelry. Most jewelry is 18 carat gold.

We missed our tossed salads. Lettuce, like in Mexico, is unsafe to eat in Venezuela, while fresh fruit is practically given away. I found the cost of food at half the price of St. Thomas. Four people can have dinner in one of their many good restaurants including a drink and tip for just over $20. We enjoyed a good Chinese meal again after many years of abstinence. How strange to speak Spanish to a Chinese waiter.

We wanted to see some of the rugged interior country and to photograph piranhas or caribes, as they are called in Venezuela. John McDonald borrowed a neighbor's fishing gear and, not being a fisherman, did not know that he needed a license to fish. We tucked Jimmy and one of the McDonald boys into the car and John drove us about one hundred miles into the llanos, or plains. Along the way we saw beautiful multi-colored wild parrots and searched in vain for the Venezuelan national flower, the orchid.

We planned to go to a river at a remote village and catch piranhas with hot dogs. We were within a mile of our destination when the National Guard stopped us. These are the "untouchables" that are paid so highly and honored so much that you cannot bribe them. The young men had casually draped machine guns over their shoulders—too nonchalantly for our comfort—stopped us on the road. They checked our papers and then saw the fishing rods in the car. They fined John for not having a fishing permit and confiscated the equipment that John borrowed from his neighbor. They told John he would have to appear in court on Monday in the village to recover his equipment. We were sure they would steal half of the equipment, but didn't. They reluctantly allowed us to fish for the piranhas across the river from the police station where they could keep an eye on us. They couldn't believe that anyone in his right mind wanted to photograph this vicious fish.

John pleaded with them to not make him return on Easter Monday because he had to work that day. Every time he nervously moved out of the line of fire the gun would follow him. In the village the homes were mud adobes. The poverty was overwhelming. The children had such pot bellies that all I could think of, now that I was a Parasitologist, was all the parasites they must be harboring in those extended bellies.

Surprisingly, there were many villagers swimming in the river where we caught the piranhas. The locals insisted that the brightly colored fish with vicious teeth would not bother you as long as you are not bleeding, or if there are only a few piranhas around. A school of them, however, will clean the flesh off your bones in seconds. Be sure not to scratch yourself on the rocks.

It was Good Friday so Susan and I took the boys to say a prayer in the village church, while John continued his pleading with the police to ease up on his penalty. The church was empty, dusty, and looked unused but the prayers worked. We got all our tackle back without a fine.

Another highlight of our trip to Venezuela was a visit to the Nelson Rockefeller ranch. The McDonalds knew the manager of the ranch so we were treated to a very relaxing Easter Sunday afternoon. Nelson Rockefeller visited this ranch, Monte Sacro, only once a year for a couple of weeks.

The ranch is an 11,000 acre spread. It consists of a rich valley surrounded by mountains topped with clouds. The ranch house is simply decorated; the furnishings are rugged and masculine, as any millionaire would decorate it. After Nelson bought the ranch he brought in professional cowboys from Texas and rounded up the cattle on the property, which had not been rounded up for five years. The cattle were enough to pay for the ranch! The old adage that states "It takes money to make money" is so true. Monte Sacro also makes money raising oranges, bananas, potatoes and coffee. Rockefeller can also be given credit for improving the quality of chickens in Venezuela. He brought in the United States know-how of raising chickens on a large scale then sold the business to a Venezuelan after it was prospering.

This country is so oil rich that there are no sales or real estate taxes, only a ten percent income tax. Gasoline was fifteen cents a gallon in 1969. You do not need a prescription for drugs. Thievery was the big problem because of the Robin Hood theory: "it is alright to take from the rich for the poor or for my family". Children are never harmed and seldom the adults but you will be robbed blind if you are not careful. House doors are kept double locked with padlocks all day. High walls surround the outdoor play areas with shards of glass imbedded in the top of the wall. Of course the thieves need only to throw a thick blanket on the glass for protection as they break in.

We returned to St. Thomas sneaking in the gold coins we purchased in Venezuela then learned that we could bring them in to the States as collectors of coins.

We had been warned by our sailor friends that we should not allow our boat, Sirius, to go out on bareboat charter. We were enjoying the extra income and thought we were so careful in the screening of our charterers. The charterers included the America's Cup racer, and Charles Owens of Owens Yachts in Jacksonville, FL. We figured they must be careful sailors.

On Friday, February 28, 1969, Sirius, our forty seven foot sailboat, was shipwrecked. The charterers made a bad judgment and anchored the Sirius in a poor place outside of the Christiansted harbor in St. Croix. We should not have allowed the Sirius to visit St. Croix. This harbor is tricky and it's a poor anchorage inside the harbour but this particular captain was outside the harbor and completely exposed to the open sea. It was calm in the afternoon when he anchored but, unforewarned, a seventy mile per hour wind came up that nightalong with a six inch rain. The wind was from the northwest placing him on a lee shore. He dragged three anchors and ended up on the beach. It was soft sand so there wasn't much damage to the hull except for a twist put in her from lying on her side. The panicky crew stepped ashore and fled to a hotel. The winds did not subside for two days before she could be hauled off the beach. In the meantime we hired guards and asked the police for protection. But we were thirty five miles away and didn't feel secure, despite these efforts.

Jay called the Hess Oil Co. on St. Croix which owned a tug boat that could pull her off the beach. The Sirius was insured for $30,000 dollars. The maximum allowed under salvage laws is one third of the insured amount. That information was leaked to the tug boat captain somehow. His charge for the hauling was exactly $10,000. The hauling off the beach only took 35 minutes. During the days that she laid on her side the waves had washed the sand away from her hull so she stood up easily when the tug began to pull on the hawser that was wrapped around her life lines without regard to the damage that would be done to the pulpits or stanchions.

Sirius lost her rudder, dinghy, and motor, and was in dry dock in St. Croix for six weeks. The major damage took place inside the cabin. The marine plywood dried out so her wood began to warp and delaminate. It would be two more weeks in dry dock, or the end of May, before she slid back into the water. She did not develop any leaks so we knew she had a sound hull giving us more confidence in her for our ocean passages. We still had dreams of making our trip around the world but one tragedy after another kept us anchored to our tiny island.

During the summer of 1969 the young man, Dave, who sailed with us to the Bahamas, visited us for six weeks. He was returning from his tour of duty in Vietnam where he had been a demolition expert. Out of his troop of 24 men he was the only one that returned home. He needed a change of scenery.

When Dave arrived we were renting a three bedroom home, Mandoo Manor, from our friends, Don and Ida Walterson. We had Maria, their daughter, living with us while they went out on charter. Maria and Diane shared a bedroom. Doug bunked in Jimmy's room or on the Sirius which was back at the dock at Yacht Haven Marina.

Maria, nine years old, and Jim, eight, had the rough life of travelling every weekend to visit the Waltersons who were running the resort on Mosquito Island. They would leave school on Friday afternoon, hop on a seaplane to Virgin Gorda Sound, take a taxi over the mountain on Virgin Gorda to the north side of the island, then be picked up by small boat from Mosquito Island. They would play from morning to night with sea turtles, or their pet, Geep, which was a cross between a goat and a sheep, thus the name. On Monday morning the trip would be reversed so they could arrive at school on time. It was truly a rough life for these youngsters.

The islands were a great place to raise a family. The children were always playing outside; there was no television, or at least none in the daytime. One evening, I remember so well, we were in the middle of a good movie and the owner of the only TV station announced that he was tired and wanted to go to bed. He would show the rest of the movie to us the next night and proceeded to close down his station.

Power outages were another element that had to be tolerated in life on a small island. You could never be sure the power would stay on when cooking a meal for invited guests, or while in the shower shampooing your hair, so candles were always handy. You also learned to substitute items in recipes. You might need cottage cheese for a fancy recipe but none was available on the island, you learned the art of substitution. There was always plenty of booze, however. A coke would have to be spread between three of four drinks because it was much more expensive than the liquor. We could buy a case of good rum for eight dollars a case or a demijohn of wine, about four gallons, for five dollars in St. Bart's, a French island.

Another riveting experience is seeing your first large shark charging for the fish you just speared. Jay and I had gotten away for the weekend on the Sirius and were enjoying our favorite sport, spear fishing, in our favorite bay, Rose Bay, on the north side of Norman Island. Each charter captain had their own name for this special bay, depending on their experiences there. This un-inhabited island had a cluster of cows that came to the beach at dusk and actually drank the sea water. We had named the bay Rose Bay after the blush wine we drank on another weekend. We were feeling no pain, and had never put on a stitch of clothing for the entire weekend. Jay was reluctant to go into the water because of the barracudas attaching small dangling things.

Leaving those pleasant memories behind and getting back to the shark, I was a few strokes ahead of Jay on the way back to the dinghy to get our supper into a safe haven. I glanced back to see where Jay was, and saw a six foot shark racing toward the bleeding fish Jay was trailing on the spear. Not knowing whether it was possible to scream while holding a snorkel in your mouth, I screamed anyway.

"Oh My God!", I screamed.

The scream was so loud that the shark made a ninety degree turn and went off into the deep water. Jay was oblivious to the whole affair thinking I was screaming at the large barracudas hanging around. We went back to the Sirius and calmed our nerves with very big rum drinks, and quietly watched the sun set in exotic colors across the water. After this incident we learned to hold the bleeding fish up on the spear and out of the water. Now we could worry about the blood running down our arm. Can a shark jump out of water?

We both changed jobs the summer of 1969. I, at last, found a job in the actual field of Chemistry. The W.G. Andrew Corp., a pollution control company, opened a wet chemical lab recently and needed a chemist. They ordered the equipment and it sat for months with no one qualified to run the lab. I learned of the job from Jay's new boss, Ed Tower, whom I had for worked, only part time, until they hired Jay.

Mr. Andrew was a plumber in the States and, with a wooden box on the back of his pickup truck and a heavy duty pump, began emptying septic tanks on the island. He ended up with a large, fancy, newly-erected building on a hilltop in the submarine base, a number of employees, and a booming business in an area where no one wanted to work at "honey dipping". His work was very lucrative.

I began the process of reviewing all the Chemistry I thought I had forgotten. I enjoyed the job thoroughly, especially travelling to surrounding islands. I had set up a prototype sewage treatment plant in the laboratory and tested various cleaning products provided to the maids at the hotels to learn the reaction the products had on their sewage treatment plant.

"How can you stand this job with your analytical nose?" Jay asked.

"If a plant is working properly it should have an earthy smell", I replied.

In this manner, Jay was introduced to the field of wastewater treatment, which became a large part of the business he would initiate in a couple of years, Water Management, Inc. Jay had taken a job with the college of the Virgin Islands at the Caribbean Research Institute as an administration officer for the five boats the college owned plus the campsite at Lameshur Bay on St. John. Lameshur was the site of Tektite I, an underwater capsule for studies of coral reefs and saturation diving lasting anywhere from twenty to sixty days. He had been preparing for Tektite II. The aquanauts were returning for more studies. But Jay had reached his "level of incompetence". He was not an organizer and did not enjoy this new job. The logistics of handling five boats and supplies for the habitat and campsite overwhelmed him. He resigned from this interesting but overwhelming job, not knowing what he would try next.

In the meantime, I had tripped over a curb in the dimly-lit parking lot of the marina one night and crushed three disks in my lower spine. The pain worsened until I could no longer function so I headed back to Detroit to the Henry Ford Hospital, where Dr. Brush, a good friend of Laura's fiancé, Don, was Chief of Surgery. We felt he would have my best interest at heart. After days of tests the problem was determined. I would need a spinal fusion. The orthopedic doctors wanted to put be in a body cast for six months. I said no, I live in the tropics and could not tolerate a body cast, please operate and correct the problem.

My hospital room overlooked the entrance to the Emergency Room where the police were bringing in shooting victims almost daily. The black nurses tending me in the hospital said,

"Do you feel safe living in the Islands?" I responded with,

"Do you feel safe living in Detroit?"

Little did I know how serious a spinal fusion in 1970 can be? A bone was taken from the pelvic girdle and used to fuse the vertebrae together. The pelvic area, which is very vascular, gave me more pain than the fusion. I was not allowed to move out of bed until I was fitted with a metal brace three days after surgery. The brace did not allow me to bend over at the waist. I was to wear the brace for six months, night and day, taking it off only to shower.

We had given up bareboat chartering Sirius after Lloyds of London, our insurer, insisted on a hired captain. House rentals on shore were expensive when the boat was not earning her keep so we moved back on Sirius in May. I called my employer, the Andrew Corp. when I felt strong enough to return to work and they told me they would not need my services any longer. Because of current financial difficulties they hired someone for half the salary, with only two years of college and no experience.

It did my heart good when she was fired and the Andrew Laboratories biggest customer, David Baxter, manager of two Laurence Rockefeller's resorts, Caneel Bay on St. John and Little Dix Bay on Virgin Gorda, British Virgin Islands, came down to the docks looking for me and asking advise from us about the test results he was getting from the new technician. Within a week, we were invited to Little Dix Bay. We spent four days at Little Dix being wined and dined, given a car and the hotel at our disposal. We had two rooms, one to reside in and one to set up laboratory equipment purchased by Little Dix. They didn't trust the results from the Andrew technician.

Because Rockefeller had deep pockets the manager was worried about a tourist blaming the hotel for any slight problem. We were asked to come once a month, unannounced, to test the water and kitchen facilities for cleanliness. On one occasion the chef was adding more alcohol to the flambé dish on the buffet. The flames shot across the room and caught the closest lady's hair on fire. These were the days of bouffant hairdos and much hairspray. Flambés were never served on the buffets again.

Everyone was leery about me handling the companionway in a brace so when the owner of Shibui, Mark Rand, happened to walk by our boat. We were at the end of the dock and one doesn't just walk by our boat. He asked our family to live on the Shibui property while he closed the hotel during the summertime for repairs and conversion to condominiums. We accepted his offer without hesitation. I had worked for the Rands previously but this time I would be the manager of the hotel, with free living accommodations. The free living quarters, even without utilities included, would ease our lean pocketbooks significantly. Extra benefits included a fifty percent discount on airfares to Puerto Rico and complimentary rooms while on that island.

*I*nspired by a visit to Japan, Shibui is a hotel of a couple dozen Japanese cottages on a hilltop overlooking the busy harbor. Some units had massive boulders left on the hill; the cottage was built around the boulder. Each cottage had a kitchen, bedroom, living room, sunken shower/bathtub, sliding shoji screens as exterior walls, and balconies with spectacular views of the harbor, airport, and submarine base. When the water was low we would have the maids remove the stoppers for the bathtubs.

While the hotel was closed for the six weeks of renovation, the children had the use of the pool, a golf cart, and a five acre property to explore. There were many trees to climb and lots of fruit to pick—mangos, limes, papayas, soursop, sugar apple, and genips. The gardeners were kept on the payroll to maintain the hotel's beautiful grounds so abundant with flowers and fruit trees. The teahouse, where breakfast and lunch was served to the guests, also had a the same view as the cottages. The teahouse was located on a knoll next to the office. Because of its unusual beauty, Shibui was on the regular island tour of the cabs taking the myriads of tourists to Mountain Top, where the banana daiquiris were world famous. The daiquiris were served on a large balcony with a view of the British Virgin Islands to the east and to the north Magen's Bay, with its mile long sandy beach. Beyond Magen's lay the un-inhabitated Hans Lollick Island. Magen's beach has been voted one of the ten most beautiful beaches in the world by National Geographic Magazine.

Shibui is so popular with the guests that many return year after year. For the holidays, nameplates are mounted on their favorite cottage. The guests are always welcomed with kimonos, straw slippers, fresh flowers, and a bottle of rum or champagne. The Rands owned four hotels on St. Thomas with the new linens starting at Shibui and working their way down to the lower priced hotels as they became worn.

The cottages used bright red towels and the maids hesitated to wave them outside lest they attract the bull Mr. Pedersen kept on his property up the road from the hotel. Every weekend Mr. Pedersen, a wizened and elderly native, rode his donkey down to town for his weekly shopping trip. The donkey had a wooden box on each hip to hold the purchases and seemed to make the eight hundred foot climb without much effort.

When the hotel reopened in November I began working full time. We moved into the two bedroom manager's cottage providing much more room. This cottage, however, is at the lowest area of the property and far removed from the office containing the safe. When thieves took the safe out of the office we were relocated to a two story cottage directly across the driveway from the office where I could keep a closer watch on activities. Jimmy reveled in his job of driving the golf cart around to all the cottages to turn on the lanterns that lit the stairways and then reverse the procedure in the morning before heading off to school. His sister, Diane, also enjoyed the chore and often rode with him in the cart.

Interviewing the gardeners for W2 forms was another lesson in island mentality.

"Reginald, how many children do you have?"

"Mam, I have five by one woman and five by another woman", he replied.

"Are they living on U.S. soil?" I asked.

"No, Mam, dey is back on my island of Montserrat. But I sends dem as much money as I can, whenever I can."

"So you know you can't take them as deductions from your taxes here on St. Thomas?"

"Yes, Mam, I knows dat. But dey can live much better at home wid da little money I can send dem, den dey can here."

St. Thomas was known as the New York City of the Caribbean, where ambitious islanders could migrate north. They made enough money to support the families they left behind. The service people on St. Thomas consisted of a mixture of natives from each and every island in the Caribbean.

One fateful morning after Shibui opened for the season I saw a jeep full of young adults steal my son's bicycle. I hopped in my car and chased them down the hill toward town, honking my horn and driving like a mad woman. When we reached the main four-lane highway I tried to cut the jeep off a couple of times by veering around in front of them to cut them off. They just backed up and went around me. They turned sharply left into an area of town I felt I should not approach. The passengers hopped out of the open jeep and scattered in different directions. I decided to go to the police and report the incident. The driver was the son of a prominent contractor and when the desk sergeant learned who had rented the jeep he asked me,

"Do you know what you are doing pressing charges against this young man?" I replied defiantly,

"Yes, sir. I do. Please proceed with the charges."

We had a private hearing for this young man in the judge's chambers and the judge said,

"Young man, do you realize the chance these people are giving you? They are not pressing charges and insist that you go back to the College of the Virgin Islands."

To his credit the father called later and thanked us for giving his son another chance. The young man gave up the crowd he was hanging around with and was attending school again.

CHAPTER 19

After our invitation to the Rock resorts at Virgin Gorda, we realized that with our chemical background there was a niche to fill on these islands. I had tried filling the need for a Parasitologist on the island but to no avail. Jay had tried running a department for the college but learned he was not an administrator. So now we were presented with a chance to use our college training and at the same time fill a need on the island. We started our own company, Water Management, Inc., where Jay would use his sales background and represent various companies in the Water and Wastewater treatment arena. In the meantime I could run the analytical tests in a laboratory.

We quickly learned the ins and outs of running a business. Jay read every book he could get his hands on regarding water and wastewater treatment. After my short experience in the Andrew laboratory with wastewater I learned what cleaning products could harm the plants. Jay persuaded the hotels to turn over the running of their plants to our man, Leo. They gladly and quickly decided that it was easier to hire an outside firm than try to get their maintenance men to handle the sewage plant. We found that no one in the government knew how to run their plants, nor wanted to. They wouldn't even change a chlorine cylinder, a simple chore that even I can manage.

With the help of a hired bookkeeper, I learned to keep our books. I also learned to handle audits with the Internal Revenue Service. St. Thomas uses the same tax forms as the States but all revenues stayed in the local coffers rather than be lost in that Black Hole in Washington, D.C. also known as the General Fund. An audit with our local IRS office could be called for any number of reasons. One time I had to prove that my children were my children, and living on U.S. soil. Many down-islanders were claiming dependents living on other islands. This was not allowed by the IRS. At other times audits were called merely to produce receipts. I learned to keep every receipt pertaining to our business. The Internal Revenue auditor admitted that the IRS knew that businesses kept two sets of books, one for the tax man and a real one they could use to prove the business was making money. The last auditor I had told me,

"If I get your return to audit next year, I will quit."

We had only been married sixteen years when we had a tragic loss by a thief. How can anyone describe the loss of all your possessions? The years of dreaming of an unforgettable adventure, the planning, reading every book in the library on circumnavigations, the cramming of all our "stuff" into our ketch, and then the call early in the morning from our sales assistant, Bill, who lived above Shibui. Bill could also see the harbor from his home and the bay where we kept Sirius on an anchor in front of the Island Beachcomber Hotel, the lower priced beach hotel that the Rands owned. The day was July 8, 1971.

"Dolly, didn't you have Sirius anchored on a mooring at Lindbergh Bay in front of the Beachcomber?" Bill asked. He was a Seventh Day Adventist so I knew he hadn't been drinking.

"Yes", why?" I asked hesitantly.

"It's not there!"

My heart jumped into my throat. *This cannot be happening, I thought.* Jay was on the local ferry boat headed to Tortola, the capital of the British Virgin Islands. *She must have broken lose from her mooring. She must be on a beach somewhere. But the weather is calm.* Thoughts bombarded my brain. I ran up to the Teahouse where I could see the

Beachcomber. I spotted a sailboat heading west toward Puerto Rico. With the help of the FAA tower and an Antilles Air Boat pilot, who flew his seaplane low over the boat, we learned it was not the ketch, Sirius. When Jay got back to St. Thomas he hired two airplanes to search for the boat. Someone reported that a sailboat left Lindbergh Bay late at night and was heading east toward the British Virgins. *Perhaps a bunch of hippies took it for a joy ride, I thought.* An hour later another Antilles pilot called me and said he thought he spotted a sailboat on a reef off the east coast of Puerto Rico. The boat was on a cay near the El Conquistador Hotel in Fajardo. It was the Sirius! He also said he spotted a group of men on a neighboring cay. *The culprits! I thought.* But I was wrong—they were the vultures. Because the Sirius was hard up on a reef the pirates felt they had rights to anything that wasn't fastened down and even what was fastened.

I was frantic. I was incessantly on our phone pleading with the Coast Guard helicopter to head immediately to our emergency. Instead they went to a plane crash reported to be near St. Croix, but it was a false alarm. By the time the FBI, the only cooperative federal agency, moved in there was no one near the site of our crash. As soon as Jay returned to St. Thomas he hired two airplanes to search all the coves in the British and U.S. Virgin Islands. Both planes headed east; if they had only headed west they might have found the Sirius before the pirates got to her. It was so frustrating prodding everyone to move quickly. Jay spent two hours on the phone trying to have someone in authority stop the stripping of the boat. But none of the police boats in Puerto Rico were working.

By the time Jay was able to reach our yacht the next day the engine had been unbolted and taken; the sails were cut off the mast and the boom; everything that wasn't fastened down was stripped from our boat. The boat that was our home for so many years of adventures. Our hearts were crushed. Jay was able to rescue the binnacle, compass, and ship's bell just as it was being removed. By the time the Coast Guard cutter arrived that same day we knew she was too far gone to pull her off the reef. This spot would be her grave. And we would have to watch her break apart every time we flew over her to Puerto Rico or the States. For weeks I could not bring myself to write about the tragedy or even look at Lindbergh Bay or the empty mooring at the Beachcomber without a tear forming. The bay became a tombstone marking the end of a very happy and important chapter in our lives that took many years of work along with dreams.

It was about ten days later when the FBI captured the thief. Simeon turned out to be a seventeen year old Dominican. He was on St. Thomas illegally. He figured he could enter Puerto Rico much easier on a private yacht, abandon her in the harbor, then move on to the United States without a problem. No passports are required for Puerto Ricans travelling to the States.

The thief was still in jail at the end of 1971. Juvenile court wanted to release him because of his age but the FBI insisted on prosecuting. He didn't have a pot of his own so we could not recover anything from him. We could only see justice done by incarcerating him. The FBI jokingly said we could keep him as a slave but I am afraid that Jay or I might strangle him—then we would end up cooling our tempers in a cell for life.

We had no insurance on the Sirius at this time due to my high expenses with the spinal fusion in 1970 so we had to tug up on our boot straps and start all over again. And start all over again, we did. We were so busy with our new business, Water Management. Jay had left the college in 1970. I was earning money as the manager of Shibui. Our living expenses were covered by the Rands. At long last Jay was able to try his wings in his own business. We became manufacturer's representatives for water and wastewater equipment, pumps, chlorine, sewage plants, and anything to do with pollution control such as sewage treatment, chlorination, desalination, ultraviolet disinfection, and even solid waste disposal with compactors.

The compactors looked like they would be our bread and butter. Puerto Rico had just outlawed all incineration, like New York City. The smog from the incinerators burned your eyes when you visited the island, which depended on tourism. New construction was required to use compactors. But to run a company in Puerto Rico you must have a Puerto Rican partner, which Jay found easily. The one he found, however, was quite naïve. Carlos thought when we received a large new check book for the business that there was plenty of money in the account because of the size of the checkbook. Jay was kept busy in Puerto Rico with his new company, Refuse Compactor Systems, Inc. They were getting large orders from construction companies building high-rise apartments. I was able to run Shibui plus start our business because in November the hotel was not busy yet. I kept the books and did the secretarial work for Water Management in my spare time. We had a microbiologist, Bill, the man who alerted me that the Sirius was stolen. Bill was handling the monthly maintenance contracts from the various St. Thomas hotels, some lab work, and working on sales commissions for any new business.

During this stressful period our nursemaid, Ingrid, added some levity to our lives. A couple of years ago Ingrid went out with someone other than her boyfriend, Ramon, because Ramon wouldn't get rid of the pregnant girlfriend living with him. Ingrid told Ramon and us that she drank poison. She ended up in the local hospital getting her stomach pumped. She told us, but never Ramon, that it was wine and not poison. Shortly afterward they became engaged and she moved in with Ramon.

He told her he would not marry her unless she could get pregnant by him. They had trouble getting pregnant, even going to specialists in Puerto Rico, but Ramon had to be the problem for Ingrid had two children previously—one when she was only fourteen and the other soon afterwards. It makes one wonder whether the pregnant girl living with him before Ingrid moved in was really pregnant by Ramon or just getting support from him for someone else's child. A year later Ingrid was finally pregnant but there were still no wedding bells. The months passed, she grew bigger, and still no bells. A baby girl arrived in September. She now had to actually have the baby not just get pregnant. On November 13, 1971 we finally witnessed the tying of the knot in our Catholic Cathedral. The bride wore a white satin and lace dress with train and veil, white flowers, bridesmaids, groomsmen, the works. I wondered if the new baby would come to church. Jay was the official photographer and the bride insisted on some pictures holding the baby. We cornered the bride at the reception and asked if we could now tell Ramon about the wine incident? She said NO emphatically. To top it all off the guy she went out with that started the wine incident was at the reception and he and Ramon are good friends but Ramon doesn't know he is the one she went out with. Is the new baby really Ramon's baby?

The island philosophy is quite different from what we were brought up with in the States. Island society is very matriarchal, with the girls having their children at a very early age. The grandmother then takes care of the children while the young girl is employed and sends money home to support her mother and children. The men are macho only when they get the girl pregnant. They may or may not acknowledge their paternity. They often brag about how many women they have impregnated. They may or may not support their children. This often leaves the children alone where the mother and daughter both have to work to make ends meet. The children left alone get into trouble, especially when they reach their teenage years.

In the 1970s I had no fear living as part of the minority. The island was predominantly black yet I could attend the theater at night or PTA meetings at the Catholic school downtown without fear. You did not have to lock your car or home. The hotel on St. John, Caneel Bay, did not have keys for their rooms. It wasn't until the drugs started passing through the islands as a transshipping point that everything changed.

CHAPTER 20

I left the Rands when they became too demanding. I started working for David Jones Real Estate in town. With the setbacks of 1971, the stealing of our yacht, "Sirius", and the loss of everything we owned, we had to do a lot of the work ourselves to build a home on shore where thieves could not steal it.

We rented a house in Hull Bay that belonged to David Jones, who wanted to occupy his own home by November 1st. We had a very restrictive time constraint to build our first home on the island. We started construction in August, so to build a home in four months on a small island is a magical feat up there with miracles. The local lumber yard might be out of 2x4s one day or a shipment arrives on island with a couple of your windows missing. To save money we did our own electrical work and Jay is still sorry that he had me do some of the wiring for him. Evidently he didn't learn how I can foul up the three way switches from the first house we built in Farmington, Michigan. He was much happier when I handled the painting.

After six years on the island, life was no easier for the full-time resident. Our dairy cattle have no grazing fields so all grain has to be imported. We always told tourists that those were paper cutouts of cows that we see on the hills.

We can buy German or Danish butter at half the price of Florida but Borden's Dairy found the island's milk so lacking that they started recombining powdered milk. The local milk has so little butter fat that Danish butter had to be added to the dairy milk. To this day son Jim will not drink milk because of the powdered milk taste he had as a youngster.

We have no sales tax, no state tax, and low real estate taxes because a few local families own most of the vacant land. What compensates for the complaints is the near perfect climate, blue skies, crystal clear water, and the birds waking you up in the morning.

Building a home on a small island in a short period of time was truly frustrating. To save money, after the loss of Sirius, we agreed with our St. John builder to bring the materials to the site. This agreement ended up to be quite a nightmare. There were only two lumber yards on the island and whenever a shipment arrived the lumber was gone the first day that it arrived. One day both yards might be out of 2x4s or they might not have the length you need. You often had to buy a longer piece and waste two feet, perhaps. Or the island might be completely out of cement or glass. Jay even made a trip to Miami to order the lumber but by the time the shipping costs are added plus the time to clear the shipments through Customs, it wasn't worth the extra toll on our sanity.

The year was 1972. Our friends from the Bahamas, Harold and Leslie Fick, became our financial guardian angels. They loaned us the money to buy a lot on St. Thomas to build a home, where a thief could not steal it, and the children would have a more normal life ashore. We chose a lot in Wintberg with a view of Magen's Bay and the Atlantic to the north. In front of the home there was a flat area where we could eventually mount a basketball hoop on a power pole. The children could ride their bicycles to neighbor's homes to play where there were many children in the neighborhood. The school bus picked up our two children right in front of the home.

We chose a house being built in Puerto Rico in a factory. It was designed to be a modular home and placed on the site by a crane. With our steep land, of about a 20 degree slope, using a crane would have been expensive and nerve wracking so we bought the plans and found a builder on St. John to construct the main building. We would take care of the finishing touches.

There was a living/dining room/kitchen module and two modules consisting of two bedrooms and a bath in each. The master bedroom had its own bath with a walk-in closet, next in line was the children's area separated by a bath. Jim was thrilled with a loft above his closet and the fourth bedroom's closet. He climbed a straight ladder to reach the loft, where Mom and Dad did not climb. He loved this hideaway, away from his parents. The fourth bedroom was used as our office which was near the entrance gate. The living and bedroom modules were separated by a redwood deck, twelve feet wide and sixty feet long. The ends of the kitchen and living rooms had an outdoor area of twelve by twelve feet where we dined outdoors using a pass-through window from the kitchen or enjoyed the sunsets in the evening at the living room sitting area. The deck was so long that Heidi, our Doberman, and Penny, our Poodle, got plenty of exercise just running on the sixty foot deck. They often chased the Thrushy birds that insisted on making a nest in the rafters. I swept up twigs every morning during their nesting season but they fetched more twigs and rebuilt it every day.

We enjoyed many guests during the years we lived in the house we named Treetops. We hung a sign on a roadside tree and we sometimes had visitors knocking on the gate asking if we were a restaurant. There actually were some houses that had a night view of the harbor with all its lights that were used as restaurants. We had this home built entirely of redwood thinking we would have no termite problems but we soon learned that redwood rots so it is not the solution for a tropical climate.

There is no grass or the need of a mower on a hillside. We kept the site as natural as possible with stone walkways and stairs. The pathways throughout the garden were lined with small stones. The lot had huge boulders which we planned to spotlight. It was so easy to start plants for landscaping, even trees, by taking cuttings, rooting them in water for a couple of weeks then sticking them in the ground. You have your own plants in no time with very little expense, especially when friends give you cutting or you relieve the roadways of excess plants.

The open deck lent itself to many party settings. We hosted a Hawaiian luau insisting on islandy costumes. We found when people are in costume the ice is broken much quicker and more fun is had by every attendee. One of the guests, after too many rum drinks, forgot to turn right to ascend the stairs to the road and walked straight off the landing. He fell a couple of feet into the garden, brushed himself off and insisted that someone snuck this ninety degree turn in since he arrived. He swore he didn't have enough drinks to cause this mishap, but we all knew better. We also hosted a sit-down, catered, dinner for government officials who didn't bother to RSVP or show up on time, ever. In fact, being late is so fashionable on the island that any time for appointments and parties is known as St. Thomas time.

The most interesting party at Treetops was a Roman Orgy that was fun to plan and a huge success. We insisted on costumes. They could be as simple as wrapping a sheet around you to make an easy senatorial toga. I had gone to the library to look up menus and decorations from Roman times (this was before computers and the Internet). Jay built two large columns for me as our entrance pillars to the Roman feast. I lined the columns with marble contact paper. They looked quite authentic. I bought two damaged ten foot doors at the lumber yard for a couple dollars each. I propped the doors up on cement blocks, surrounded the twenty foot table with cushions. We all sat on the floor as long as possible. One couple that owned a fruit stand volunteered to bring a case of grapes for my Roman feast. He and his wife wrapped themselves in their pink bed sheets to attend the party. On the way they had car trouble and as Mick was bending over to look at the engine with just his pink behind turned to the road along came his native employees. After their smirks abated they fixed the car. The grapes finally arrived for the Roman Orgy.

There were gladiators with their concubines, puffed up Senators, chariot drivers, even their valets. Jay was Julius Caesar and I was his queen, both dressed in shimmering white satin and royal purple trimmed with gold braid.

Another party was the talk of the island but was held at a villa that lent itself more to a Speakeasy party. The parties I threw were such fun with the planning and execution that a group of ladies wanted to co-host with me. At this particular party everything cost a nickel at the buffet. We provided the liquor, guests were to bring their own set ups. They drank their drinks in plastic tea cups in case the police raided the party. The guests had to check their guns at the door. They either obliged or were frisked. In large refrigerator cardboard boxes we had risqué peep-shows of old silent movies that also cost a nickel. The costumes were all 1920s and all cooperated.

During the planning stage we tried to have the police raid the event but we couldn't get them to cooperate, probably because they were not invited. We even tried off-duty cops and private security companies. Anyone in a uniform would do, but we had no success. Instead, two weeks after the party all guests were sent a summons to court to report to a judge and explain why they were drinking during the prohibition era.

Guns had to be checked at the door and hung on pegs so they could be easily identified and returned to the owners. Costumes that I can remember readily the owner of a refined real estate company in a smoking jacket and tuxedo trousers. There was also a newspaper boy with knickers, tam hat and a newspaper bag slung over his plaid shoulder announcing to all that would listen the latest news of the depression, like who was jumping out of the high rise buildings next. The smoking jacket man was accompanied by a woman in a sleek, red silk, tight dress.

The invitations went out as follows:

ANNOUNCING

the opening of the new

HARMONY VILLA SPEAK-EASY

at the

Milner Residence

Prohibition Party   Talk of the 20's

October 30, 1976   8:37 p.m. sharp!

Re-live those fun-filled days. Rub elbows with Al Capone, Baby
Face Nelson, Legs Diamond, Bugsy Moran. Meet the Flapper of
the Year. Note: guns must be checked at the door.

BATHTUB GIN - ENTERTAINMENT - DANCING

"White Lightning" and "Rot Gut" provided. Bring your own "set-ups"
and your favorite flapper or beau. Prizes for the best '20's
costumes. Door prize and more! Bring nickels (no wooden ones) for
surprises and pay-offs.

SAFE. No cops or reformers allowed, but take precautions not to
be followed - double up on transportation if possible and keep a
low profile!!

Must present following password to be admitted..."23 Skidoo".....

R.S.V.P.   4-6841   Sponsored by the Opponents to the WCTU
           4-3460   (Women's Caribbean Teatotalers Union)
           4-3420

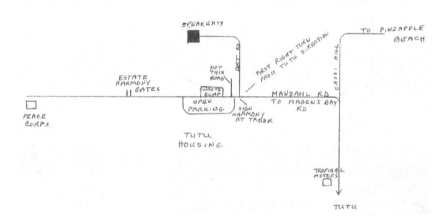

The year was 1972 and the locals continue to teach stateside
continentals their ongoing folk lore. One day, while waiting to admit
Diane to the hospital for her tonsillectomy, a young native mother
carrying an eight week old baby was also waiting in the admissions
office. I was reading our local newspaper when she approached and

asked for a small piece of the paper. I thought she wanted to read and handed her half of the newspaper but she said no just a small piece. She just tore off a small corner of the page. She wet it on her tongue and stuck it on the baby's forehead. I asked if the baby had a cut but she said no the baby had hiccups. The paper would stop the hiccups. I smiled and thought it was a joke but, by Jove, the hiccups stopped at once.

While working at Public Health I heard many tales that the mothers found to work well for their children. If a baby fusses at bedtime you must pick some branches from a soursop tree, hang them over the crib, or at least plant a soursop tree outside the bedroom window. The leaves do indeed contain a barbiturate as later research has proven. There are shrubs that can de-worm a child, or even cause an abortion, depending on how long you boil the leaves for tea. I no longer questioned the wisdom of the old women.

$\mathcal{C}$HAPTER 21

During the summer of 1973 we returned to the Canoe Country with the children. Because we had small children, the outfitter suggested that we lash two canoes together to form a stable catamaran. We used thin birch trees for the lashings, and took a motor to move the two canoes. We decided to make a base camp on an island and take day trips from the base to save on portaging several times over the rugged trails of the Indians and fur traders. We saw ducks diving for fish, melancholy loons calling for a mate, beavers building dams, and chipmunks stealing our loaves of bread. We took coloring books for six-years old, Diane, who was quickly bored with fishing until someone got a bite, or caught a fish.

While twelve-year old Jim had a rod and reel in his hand instead of his usual spear gun. On this trip we were allowed to bring night crawlers as bait but ran out of them in a couple of days. We found a stream full of crawfish and had as much fun catching this bait as the fish for our dinners. The fish also found crawfish to be much tastier than night crawlers. We called Jim's catch of a five pound Walleye his "Gee Whiz" fish for that is all he could say when he saw the size of his trophy. Unfortunately, it was the proverbial "one that got away" when he tried to land the fish in the canoe.

We knew we didn't have more than a half hour after cooking bacon to vacate the camp if we didn't want to meet a black bear rummaging through our camp site. The outfitter told us bears can smell bacon for miles. The winds were in our favor for we never met a bear, thank goodness.

From this experience and our two previous trips to the Minnesota/ Canada border we knew that Oscar Meyer produced a delicious canned pre-fried bacon. A pound of bacon fits into a can the equivalent of a large-sized tuna fish container. The bacon was pre-fried so most of the fat was gone.

Upon my return to St. Thomas I called the Oscar Meyer supplier in Puerto Rico and inquired about buying some of this canned product that didn't need refrigeration. My next phone call from the supplier advised me that there were sixty cases of pre-fried bacon on the dock awaiting my pickup. What would I ever do with over 700 pounds of bacon? I quickly gave a sample can to every charter boat cook figuring they would welcome not having to dispose of a cup of hot grease from a sailboat. The bacon was so successful with the cooks that we imported many more shipments of bacon. We soon became the King and Queen of Pre-Fried Bacon on the island until it was too much to handle and we gave away the business.

We returned home from Minnesota on time to midwife our Doberman, Heidi. She had ten puppies, but one was born dead. Dogs don't seem to have as much trouble giving birth as humans so we were happy the children had the opportunity to witness this miracle of new life. One of Heidi's puppies, Max, was sold to a contractor. The dog was scheduled to guard a warehouse in Tortola, British Virgin Islands where the contractor would soon be building. He paid for Max to attend Guard Dog Training School. Max was the only Doberman in the school's history to flunk out of the course. What an embarrassment to all Dobermans.

In fairness to Max we had the trainer come to Treetops. Despite the padding on his arms the trainer had to guard his neck for Max's eye turned green with anger when he lunged for the trainer. Either Max was really serious about guarding his own property or remembered the school too well. Whenever they tried to anger him at school he cowered and promptly peed on himself. He was a different dog when the trainer tried to enter our gate. The contractor returned Max and got his money back. We planned on keeping him to breed with his mother, at the advice of the Vet, but he was hit by a car in front of the house, crushing his pelvis area and rendering him sterile. But we kept him around anyway.

Treetops enjoyed many northern visitors with one family from Minnesota bringing a cooler packed with snowballs for our two island children to see and feel what they looked like. They were really ice balls for they had to stay in a freezer until departure time for the islands plus they were packed in dry ice. The Carson family was to spend a camping vacation at the St. John National Park. They were spending a couple of nights before and after the camping trip with us. Coming through Puerto Rico, however, their luggage was lost and the cooler with snowballs was stolen. I am sure the thief thought the cooler was filled with meat. Many people on the island travelled to the States to do their "power shopping" as I always called my trips to Florida. Imagine the thief's chagrin when he opened the cooler and found nothing but water.

My uncle Fred, who was then manager of the Eastern Airlines operation in Philadelphia, was visiting at the same time as the Bosuns on their camping vacation. Fred and his family often visited us while they had free travel on Eastern. When the cooler was stolen Fred took a lot of ribbing from all of us, especially when Jan Carson said she was going to make a claim against Eastern Airlines for the loss of the snowballs. Fred said, if she did, he would frame the letter and hang it in his office.

Because we were travelling a lot for business and made quite a few trips to the States for shopping we bought a lifetime membership in the Eastern Airlines Ionosphere Club, where you could rest in a quiet atmosphere and have drinks. We naively thought it was for our lifetime, not the airline's lifetime. We witnessed the end of Eastern Airlines and also saw the end of Pan Am Airlines to the islands. In 1970 we were horrified with the crash of a Trans-Caribbean plane into the hillside. One of the crew members moved quickly to paint out the Trans-Caribbean logo on the fuselage before the photographers arrived. It wasn't until an American Airlines, Boeing 727 plane crashed in 1976 with the death of 37 people on that flight, resulting in the island finally getting the money from Washington to extend the runway into the ocean. Making it a proper length where the pilots no longer got hazard duty pay for each landing in St. Thomas. The planes often ended up running into the Shell Gas Station at the end of the runway. We wondered why there were not more fires.

The island people were warm hearted and were prepared to help in any tragedy. After this crash there were long lines at the local hospital to donate blood but unfortunately those that died were burned in the fire when the plane struck the Shell gas station. Corpses did not need blood donations.

On another occasion, March 30, 1979, tragedy struck the cruise ship Angelina Laura. She mysteriously caught on fire at the dock when most of the passengers were already ashore shopping. The ship was forty years old and in need of refurbishing. The fire burned for days and the fire boats from Hess Oil on St. Croix pumped so much water into her trying to extinguish the fires in all the cabin spaces that she sunk at the dock.

An announcement went out on the radio that the passengers needed to be put into local homes. Before we could make the 30 minute trip to the ship all the guests were taken care of and placed in homes. After a week at the dock the food began to rot. The fish had a feast, calling in all the surrounding sea life to join them in the Charlotte Amalie harbor for this bonanza. It was broadcast after the fire that she would go to China to be dismantled for steel scraps. Strangely the Angelina Laura went down in the middle of the Pacific Ocean on her way westward.

Diane began her education at the Montessori school and was thrilled to be going to school until a classmate cut off her long blond hair on one side of her head. She soon tackled him, sat on the boy and proceeded to cut his hair off. The teacher called me in for a conference to tame this three year old rebel. After that incident she wanted to go to Antilles School, where the "big kids" went.

I had planned on using the Calvert system to teach Jimmy while we sailed. When he was in second grade the nuns wanted him to repeat second grade. At that time he was diagnosed with having the education problem called dyslexia. Educators were just learning of the disability. There were no special education teachers on St. Thomas so the V.I. Education Department hired teachers from Eagle Hill Academy in Massachusetts to train tutors for the island. About one hundred students began the course and only about seventy graduated. I quickly joined the class to learn more of this problem that affects so many children, mostly boys. I had to quit my job with Public Health for they would not give me the time off to take the course because they really needed a Parasitologist. For about three years after graduating I, along with others, tried to be hired by the Education Dept. to use our new skill, but not one person from the class was hired.

I had heard of an experienced tutor being hired by some affluent business owners and was able to get Jimmy in a class of four students. He thrived in the small class situation, or on a one-on-one basis, but would eventually have to return to a normal class. Even though the classes at Antilles had only fifteen students he continued to have difficulty reading. At Antilles, a private school started by disgruntled parents, classes were often held outdoors at the picnic tables or under the shade of the large trees, while sitting on the grass.

Jimmy was found to reverse the first syllable of most words but with proper training he would be able to overcome his disability. When he was only fourteen years old we had to send him to Gables Academy, a school specializing in children with learning disabilities on the campus of the Florida Air Academy in Ft. Lauderdale, Florida as a boarding student. Sending Jimmy to a stateside private education school was a burden on our wallets. The only saving grace was that all expenses were tax deductible.

During summer vacations the children were usually in the camp run by Antilles school. They thrived in the camp during the summer of

1974 with Diane bringing home a first place ribbon in archery. Jimmy won his Junior Life Saving Certificate and came home with a large trophy for the best all-round camper for the entire school. He couldn't get his shirts buttoned for a couple of weeks afterwards.

It was in 1974 that the Fountain Valley Massacre occurred on St. Croix, forty miles south of St. Thomas. The nation heard about the murders that happened at the golf course but did not hear that the criminals are all serving eight consecutive life sentences in prisons in the States, or that some blacks were killed along with the whites. People did not hear that it was really a drug related crime involving Eastern Airlines and the transshipment of drugs. Miami played up this scenario endlessly trying to pull tourists away from the islands.

In mid-August, with a pilot friend aboard, Dan Scott, we flew Jimmy to St. Vincent in a four passenger Cherokee. The boy was invited to sail back island-hopping aboard the Walterson's new sailboat, Zulu Warrior. He would be keeping their daughter, Maria, company. Reluctantly the Waltersons gave up Mandoo when she leaked badly despite a fiberglass skin laid over the wooden hull. Ida would have to stand in the companionway with her fingers under her nose to indicate to Captain Don at the helm that the bilge water was just below the floorboards.

Our family enjoyed many sails on the schooner, Mandoo, where Don would have people sit in a bosun's chair dangling over the water. In a stiff breeze, he could dunk the chair or have it swing above the water depending on whether he sailed into or away from the wind. They often told the hapless rider that this game is also known as "shark trolling".

We were always looking for new areas to expand Water Management as business slowed down due to the Fountain Valley publicity. Jay and I took a mini-vacation to Mullet Bay Resort on the Dutch side of St. Maarten. We were given a contract on our first visit after explaining what we were able to accomplish for the Resort.

Mullet consists of almost 700 condominiums, an eighteen-hole golf course, beaches, good restaurants, and a casino for night time entertainment. We went every month and I golfed while Jay worked. The rooms, either a one or two bedroom condo, were complimentary as well as the food. We were given a vehicle to drive so we could explore the island. The island is half French, half Dutch.

The French gendarmes will not answer in English when asked for directions, even when they can speak the language. The markets are priced in guilders, francs and dollars. The canned snails purchased on the French side were one of the only saving graces from that side of the island.

The atmosphere in the Mullet Bay Casino is so much better than in San Juan, where the dealers or bar maids never crack a smile nor serve a free drink to the gamblers. Smartly, drinks are served to gamblers in St. Maarten. We were on a first name basis with the dealers and if we took too long to add up our cards at the black jack tables they would pass us up and say,

"You don't want a card."

There is always a government official sitting at the entrance of the casino to prevent locals from spending their hard earned money. But it was alright for the tourists to spend their cash.

One must keep a sense of humor living on a small island in a third world atmosphere. Its laugh or cry, you chose. A friend, Nick, went to the driver's licensing department to have his picture taken for his license. The power went out so Nick was told to return the next day for the photo. In the meantime the power came back on and when he returned the next day he was handed a license with a picture of an empty chair instead of his face. This is the photo Nick carries in his wallet to this day.

I had always had a secret desire to fly a plane so I talked Jay into taking flying lessons. It was not too difficult to convince him that it would be so much easier to fly our own plane instead of waiting for the "milk run" island plane. And, of course, he thought it would be wise for me to learn to land the plane in case something happened to him. I, naturally, thought he had an excellent idea, so proceeded to start my lessons as well.

Jay got his pilot's license in February of 1975, after flying to Puerto Rico to take the written exam. By July I had soloed, after causing my instructor to have strange facial tics in his jaw. In the islands our cross country flights are over water making us much more comfortable than flying over land, where if we go down it could take out innocent people on the ground. The legs of our cross country flights must be 100 miles or more.

St. Maarten is less than 100 miles east of St. Thomas so I had to fly to Guadeloupe to make my landing. I remember the tower telling me not to land at the beginning of the runway but to fly over it until I see the terminal. The runway is so long on that particular island to accommodate the large planes from France that I would hold up traffic if I landed early and had to taxi to the terminal. My other solos were touch-and-go landings at Isla Grande Airport in old San Juan and one at Humacao on the east end of Puerto Rico. This flight took me over El Yunque Mountain, the highest on the island, always covered with a rain cloud.

Vieques, an island off the east coast of Puerto Rico, has a Navy base. The island north of Vieques is known as Culebra. The two islands are used for bombing practice by the U.S. Navy. At times other Navies join the U.S. for war games in the area. When the bombing or war games are going on the area becomes "hot" or restricted, adding a little spice to our flight planning. We can hear the bombings at times on St. Thomas, making us thankful that we don't live on the other two islands.

Because of Jimmy's high expenses in a boarding school in Florida we put Diane in a public school this year and moved our office from our home into Power Products, across the street from Yacht Haven Hotel & Marina, so I could earn some money running both offices. Jan & Joris Renz, the owner of Power Products, sold generators, refrigerator holding plates, and any other type of equipment for boats and yachts.

Jan arrived in St. Thomas on a 55 ft. Alden ketch in 1952. He settled into island life as a sailor, pilot and later founded Power

Products in 1965. Jan was known as a first-rate aviator, but he was also known as a "fly by the seat of the pants" pilot. He was a tall man, over six feet, curly haired, mustached, round faced and husky.

As a pilot Jan has logged thousands of miles flying single engine planes across open seas from island to island throughout the Caribbean. He often took the seats out to deliver engines to desperate owners down islands or to rescue ancient cannons washed up on remote beaches. Jan has—on two separate but well known occasions "gone swimming".

He had built a homemade two-seater gyrocopter where, to get it flying, he had to stand in the plane and frantically spin the blades overhead until the motor started. The plane meanwhile was pulled by a boat until he could rise above the water. He was flying this homemade plane in 1976 at Antigua Sailing Week with a photographer in the passenger seat. He was over Shirley Heights when a down-draft sucked him into the path of a forest of oncoming masts. Jan tried to pull out but the plane stalled and dropped into the offshore swells.

"I was shook up" admits Jan.

"The plane was amphibious, but not upside down."

But his first "swim" was much more serious. It was February, 1976 when a 1500 foot wave hit his Cessna twin engine plane, "or the altimeter was off", he stated. His plane crashed fifteen miles short of the St. Thomas Airport, west of Sail Rock.

CHAPTER 22

"St Thomas Tower, this is Cessna November One Eight One Uniform, fifteen miles west of St. Thomas, inbound for a landing."

As Jan reported his position on the radio, I noted the time, 9:03 p.m., and placed a mark on the chart indicating that we were just west of Sail Rock, about half way between Culebra and St. Thomas, Virgin Islands.

"Not bad," I remarked to Jan, "for an estimated time of arrival of 9:08 p.m.

By flashlight I took a last quick glance at the instruments. All seemed well. We were at 1500 feet, starting our descent into the St. Thomas airport. Airspeed, 150 mph. I figured we should land in about five minutes.

Although the strobe lights at the end of the runway were visible, we could not yet differentiate the white runway markers. *Probably too far from the airport*, we thought. There was a slight haze in the night-sky which imparted an unusual glow to the lights, but nothing looked out of the ordinary. I glanced down and saw no boats plying the dark water. No moving lights in the sky blemished the velvety black canvas spread before our eyes. The moon, in its first quarter, would not be rising until morning. I noticed the white light identifying Sail Rock just below and to our right. Then a strange sound, momentarily. A slight splash of water seemed to be lapping the bottom of the plane. Impossible! We must be tired, I thought.

"What the h—!" exclaimed Jan. He didn't get to finish his sentence. The next instant brought sudden tremendous impact. Bouncing. Jolting. More bouncing.

"My God! We hit something!" I shouted over the noise. I was choking on my heart in my throat. I felt the strain of the seat belt as I was thrown forward. My head hit the instrument panel. A heavy weight was on my back. The steering yoke crushed into my chest. Multi-colored lights flashed through my vision as if my brain was electrically discharging. Then a full view of brilliant red washed away the colored stars.

"The red must be my blood rushing out of my eyes!"

"I must be dying." A moment or two more of conscious thoughts and it will all be over. *So this is what it's like,* I told myself. In these last thoughts of life I wondered how we could have been so far off our course as to hit the dark west end of St. Thomas. But water was coming into the cockpit. Perhaps there was a mid-air collision—but no other planes were visible.

"Everybody out!" shouted Jan.

His outburst brought me to my senses.

"I didn't die in the impact after all. I must still be alive."

But now I was engulfed in sea water. Jan's shout made me reach for the window latch and, at the same time, Dave's foot, kicking out the window, smashed my right hand. I realized the water would soon be over my head. There was a small air pocket above me. I strained to sit taller. I could hear Jan and Hal struggling to get out of the left window of the plane.

My mind screamed orders.

"Open the door! The plane is sinking and you're going down with it. You'll never reach the surface. It's too late. But you must try!"

I was amazed that I was not even trying to breathe under water during this eternity. How can I last so long under water? I can't even dive into a pool without coming up with a nose full. I forced the door open at last. There was total silence. My heart skipped a beat and my thoughts raced on again. *The others are gone! I'm alone!* I pushed away to leave the plane. *But which way is the surface? Did the plane turn over in the crash?* I could feel my body moving again, making a last attempt to get out, to let the sea water buoy me up to the surface.

Damn! I forgot the seat belt. Unhook it! Thank God! Free at last, of this belt that's trying to trap me in a watery grave. Vaguely, I heard Jan shout,

"Where's Dolly?" My head struck the wing in the rush to get out of the sinking plane. My hands probed to find the edge of the wing and I immediately broke through the surface screaming,

"I'm here. I'm here."

I was surprised that the surface was only a couple of feet above me. I must have only imagined that the aircraft was sinking so rapidly to unrecoverable depths. It had not flipped over on its back, as expected, when a high-wing plane hits the water at such a velocity.

I could see Hal some thirty feet away on the port side of the wreck. Dave was by my side and asked me to hold his suit jacket while he attempted to dive into the cabin for survival gear. He directed me to the tail and told me to hang on and catch my breath.

"Where's the raft?" yelled Jan.

"Under the seat," the men answered in unison. Jan dove and came up quickly, empty-handed.

"I can't find it."

"Try under the back seat."

He dove again and disappeared under the ghostly white wings that began to sink below the surface. It could not have been more than a minute or two, at the most, since we hit the water, and November One Eight One Uniform was already reaching for her grave under the sea.

Sharp pains gripped my chest as I gulped air too deeply. Salt mist seared my throat. The euphoria of finding myself alive was quickly squelched with the realization that Jan was still under water. Dave was forward, floating over the cabin roof, but seemed to be mesmerized by the entire scene. He could not summon the courage to dive after Jan into what looked like a hell hole. In the commotion I lost Dave's coat that he asked me to hold for him.

The wings were almost beyond sight. No Jan. It was far too long. My God, I prayed, please have him come up. Jan surfaced just as I felt a tug on the tail and had to let go. His lungs were about to burst but he knew he had to get the second raft out. He literally tore the metal fascia of the rear seat with his bare hands, producing unwanted blood. On impact he also hit the parking brake with his left leg and that was bleeding too. Hank had leaned forward to tell the pilot he saw water and hit his face on the pilot's seat. His eye was bleeding.

We didn't need all this blood to attract the denizens of the sea. The plane slid down to its final resting place, in eighty fathoms of water. Jan, with a triumphant grin inflated the one two-man raft that had to save four souls.

It was a cold February, the coldest St. Thomas had ever experienced. The seas were six to eight feet high. I could smell blood. But the high seas should keep the sharks away. Everyone thought of sharks but no one spoke of this menace of the sea. And I had just seen the movie, "Jaws" a month ago.

The date was February 25th. It was less than four weeks after I had had surgery to remove abdominal tumors, which, thankfully, were non-malignant. Due to Jimmy's high special education tuition I had taken the job of business management for Jan Renz's Company, Power Products.

Two years before, in 1974, Jan had a large yacht skip out owing him over $40,000. Both Jan and his wife, Jordis, were physically sick over the treachery. His business was failing; no suppliers would provide credit to his company. On my way to the hospital in January Jan asked me to swing by Onan Generators in Minneapolis to re-establish credit and explain what happened to Power Products. After Onan, I called on Perkins Engines in Farmington, Michigan to set up a meeting at the Miami Boat Show to pick up the distributorship for Jan's British, Virgin Islands affiliated company, Parts and Power, Ltd., run by Dave Mavin, who was also on this flight.

Hank Willy was the mechanic working in St. Thomas for Power Products. Jan wanted him along on the trip to convince Perkins that we had a capable mechanic working with us. Hal had worked for NASA, lost his job, and had just ended his third failed marriage.

I was still a student pilot so I sat in the copilot's seat to assist on the navigation. Hank was behind Jan and Dave was sitting behind me. He had just used the "bottle" and was not belted in when the crash occurred. This was the heavy weight I felt on my back at impact.

A high-winged plane like a Cessna usually flips on her back when she hits the water. We must have skipped like a stone tossed across the water, sheared off the fixed landing gear, then slowly settled into the water, still facing St. Thomas. We figured we were fifteen miles short of the runway. And, as Jan said to the reporter

"A 1500 foot wave hit us". Translation: the pilot misread the altimeter by 1500 feet. No wonder the lights at the ball field on Culebra looked so low as we passed them.

Since all four of us were sailors, we knew we had to kick due west or the southeast to northwest current would take us into the open Atlantic Ocean. Our chances for rescue would be even slimmer than now. We also knew that there were many small islands east of Culebra. We only had to reach one of these islands and we would survive.

Because of my recent surgery I sat in the raft, held onto Hal's belt with my left hand, Dave's belt with my right hand. Jan, was holding on to the rear of the raft behind me, kicking with all his might to the west. This was the beginning of a long night of trembling from the cold water. We shivered, so hard sometimes that it seemed our bones would break. I learned from the doctor later on that the body is designed to shiver to keep the blood flowing. I had lost my glasses and shoes in the crash, plus broke a tooth at impact or from the intense trembling.

We were in the water a short time when Hal pleaded with me to let him go. He was not a survivor. Dave got sick from drinking too much sea water and laid across the bow to throw up. He and Jan took turns on the bow while I concentrated on holding on to Hal. How was

I going to keep these three men awake and living through the night? Dave was so cold from my loss of his jacket and the thin cotton shirt he was wearing that he was almost catatonic. I finally held him against my body to keep him warm. I talked, sang, and prayed for hours.

"But I am an atheist", Jan said.

"You pray, anyway", I ordered.

After an hour in the water, we saw a Coast Guard helicopter searching for us. One of the men had a luminous watch so we knew the time. The chopper was forming an ever decreasing grid design. It was so tempting to swim over to the search light and wave our arms. We thought of the Antilles Air Boat that went down two weeks before, where the only survivors were the ones that stuck together.

When one of the men would shout:

"Chopper's coming!" they would have to point me in the right direction so I could help wave. We waved until we thought our arms would break or fall off. Without my glasses, I am somewhat blind, so they needed to tell me where to look. The chopper actually passed over us five times. Around midnight they called off the search. We were alone on this vast ocean. We had to fend for ourselves.

Then around 2:00 a.m. the raft started to soften. Would we make it to safety on a small rock island? About 4:00 a.m., after seven hours in the frigid water, we could hear waves breaking on rocks. We had to approach from the leeward side of the island, then risk being raked over a sharp coral reef rather than land on the windward side and be smashed by the waves against the rocks.

Jan put his feet down and touched bottom near the island. Hal was told to stand up but he said,

"Jan is taller than I am".

We had to drag this quitter up onto the shore. Dave came out of his stupor and helped to get us all ashore. We had landed on an island inhabited only by nesting Booby birds, which were not happy to share their island with us.

We managed to collapse in utter exhaustion just ten feet above the waves in a hollowed out rock covered with bird guano, the droppings often sold for fertilizer. Here was this 45 year old woman marooned on a tropical island with three men. A dream comes true! Yet our only concern was survival. We knew once on land we were safe. We needed only to wait for the sun the next day to dry and warm us. There were plenty of eggs in the nests, pockets of water lying in rock hollows, barrel cactus for more fluids, and berries on the cacti to sustain us, though no one was hungry. My denim suit was not a proper choice for swimming in the ocean. It was heavy and never dried from the salt water. Jan's wool sweater was really the most proper attire for swimming in clothes. It could be rung out and worn again for some warmth.

We huddled against each other for body heat and tried to sleep until morning light. The Boobies birds, however, screeched and attacked us until dawn. Hal begged me to take his contacts out of his bleeding eye but I said no. My hands, while waterlogged, were filthy. He also told me that he could not last another night, even though we were safely on an island. Hal's life must have been full of failure. He was willing to give up so easily. He was grey-haired and at least ten years older than the rest of us, who were all in our forties. He was almost as tall as Jan but not as fit or possessed of the joie de vivre Jan had. Dave was small in stature, had reddish-blond hair, clean-shaven, nice looking, and did not have much meat on his bones. He suffered the most from the cold.

We were on a tiny rock island with attacking Boobies, east of Culebra. Jan scoured the island and found only a short 2" x 4" piece of wood. He proposed using it as a paddle, take the life raft, and try to reach Culebra for help. We talked him out of that folly, insisting that the flimsy piece of wood would not counteract the current.

The sun never shone the next day. We had one rain squall after another with winds gusting to 30 or 40 knots, this was gale force. The waves were now fifteen footers. We never dried out or stopped shivering. I shivered so much that I thought my bones would break or I might chip a tooth or two.

Jay thought it was a great opportunity for me to take this trip. I could also visit Jimmy at Gable's Academy. The man got Diane off to school, gathered me and Dave Mavin, who stayed overnight at our house because of the early morning departure, and drove us to Jan's four-seater, high-performance Cessna 185. He picked up Hal at Power Products. Hal was living on a boat at the marina across the street. A last minute inspection was made of the plane, baggage stored, food and drinks placed within easy reach, and rescue gear located in accessible spaces. The morning was a little cloudy with clear patches to the north and south of the cloud cover. Jay kissed me goodbye, warned Jan to be careful and to be sure to file a flight plan. Jay warned that he would start a search if he didn't get a phone call by 2:00 p.m. Jan said to give him seven hours for the flight to Ft. Lauderdale before starting to worry.

He watched the heavy plane take off using less than 800 feet of the runway, climb out of the eastern pass with at least 400 feet of altitude turn south then west to Puerto Rico. Departure was at 8:00 a.m. They should arrive in Ft. Lauderdale by 3:00 p.m.

The rest of the day was uneventful. He came home early to be there for Diane, who was doing her homework when he arrived home. They missed Mommy at dinner but Jay assured her that Mommy would be home the next night and everything would be back to normal. Diane placed a note at her Mom's place at the table saying "Welcome home, Traveler". At about 4:00 p.m. Jay called San Juan Tower and asked them to contact Miami regarding our plane. He learned that we had just landed safely in Ft. Lauderdale.

The flight north to Miami was uneventful until we reached the "Bermuda Triangle". There truly is something mysterious about this area, which extends from Bermuda, to Puerto Rico, to the southern tip of Florida. We were enjoying the views over the Bahamas Islands when suddenly the instrument needles all went berserk. Jan concentrated on keeping the plane flying straight and level. We were suddenly enveloped in clouds. We couldn't trust our instruments or the feel of gravity on our bodies. Jan stared at the attitude indicator to keep the plane level. Don't dive, or climb and stall out. It was a frightening experience that gave us all a healthy respect for the "Triangle". We welcomed the sight of the smokestacks at the Ft. Lauderdale airport, happy to leave the "Triangle" behind.

The meeting with Perkins Engines was successful. The distributorship was obtained for Parts and Power. We headed back to St. Thomas out of the Ft. Lauderdale Airport in a rain squall, not getting clearance until about 11:00 a.m. We stopped in Providenciales in the Caicos Islands for fuel. It was an hour or so before we could find anyone to sell us fuel at the closed airport, although it was only 4:00 p.m. on a Wednesday during the high season of February. This would make our arrival on St. Thomas after dark. Jan was not instrument rated for night landings.

We headed southwest over the Bahamas into more cloud cover capping the higher islands of Dominican Republic/Haiti, and Puerto Rico. We climbed through a hole in the clouds over San Juan until I noticed that we were at 12,000 feet.

"Jan, we have to go down. You can't be this high without oxygen."

He turned east and we found another hole. We spiraled through it and came out of the clouds over the El Conquistador Hotel on the east end of Puerto Rico. Just another fifty miles and we will be home.

Jay left Diane asleep at home and went to the Airport to drive us home at our expected arrival time. He reached the Tower right after our inbound transmission. An American Airlines jumbo jet was late leaving New York and interrupted our message. The Tower forgot about us, turning their attention to the Jumbo Jet. There were many more people on the full jet. Jay pleaded with the Controller to start a search but received the reply that a phone search to nearby airports is not required until one hour after the scheduled arrival time. The Controller would not even play back our transmission for a frantic and worried man until the tower was closed at 11:00 p.m. I doubt that Jay got much sleep that night for he had no more luck when he stopped at the Coast Guard Cutter on the city dock.

Despite the bad weather the next day, Thursday, February 26, 1976, there were five planes, three helicopters, and several boats searching for us. Visibility was only one mile. The Tower allocated a private channel for the planes to communicate. Jay was in no shape to pilot a plane but when searching for people extra pairs of eyes are always needed. He spotted some wreckage in the open Atlantic and was close to losing hope.

He sent Diane to school in the morning not suspecting a thing about our missing plane. Friends picked her up after school and took care of her. I learned later how many people were concerned and prayed for all of us. Some even claimed they knew we were safe on a small island—we just had to be found.

The Coast Guard helicopter spotted us at 1:00 p.m. The young man caught a glimpse of the yellow raft out of the corner of his eye. Jan waved the raft whenever a chopper flew over us. Now that the Chopper spotted us they circled overhead and jettisoned fuel in order to pick up four people. We could smell the fuel being dumped. We were so excited to be found but had no idea the next experience would be another harrowing one.

We were standing on a flat spot near the edge of a cliff with a sheer drop to the high waves below. It was the only flat area to rest a basket. The basket was lowered from the hovering chopper, Jan reached up to grab the metal basket but it was hauled up immediately and he was waved away. You can easily be electrocuted by the whirling rotors. Being lifted in a swaying basket is an unwanted thrill, but there was no choice. Ladies first, the men all chimed together, so I had the first ride skyward praying that the cable was a strong one. I couldn't help hugging and kissing my savior when I reached the plane.

There was a crowd of well-wishers at the St. Thomas Airport to greet the helicopter when we landed including a very teary-eyed, choked up Jay. We were not supposed to survive such a crash, the aviators told us. We were quickly wrapped in blankets and rushed to the hospital. I had a black and blue imprint of the steering yoke on my chest, or blue boobs, I teased. I had loosened my ribs from the sternum but my hand was not broken.

Unbeknownst to us, our friends had arranged to have the Coast Guard crew return to St. Thomas for our Thanksgiving party. The raft that rescued the four of us looked mighty small floating in the tiny pool at Jan's home. The crew remarked that it was the first time that they ever celebrated with the people they rescued. One of the sailors stayed at our home, sleeping on the couch overnight. He startled our nine year old daughter, Diane, but she was accustomed to unexpected company at Treetops.

Both the survivors and the Coast Guard crew were thankful that we did not end up as just another case number.

CHAPTER 23

After this narrow escape from death in 1976 we knew the entire Greblick family needed a vacation. When the children finished school in 1977 we picked up Jim from Gables Academy, and took delivery of a Cadillac convertible that we found in a Miami newspaper. We were to deliver it to San Francisco. The owner said two weeks for the delivery. We pleaded for three, and started across the country. We left Florida the end of May and did not get the car to San Francisco for three weeks due to a delay in Texas waiting for parts for the broken down antique car. A desert dust storm had filled the car and passengers with red dust which damaged the engine.

We visited many friends along the way, some of whom had visited us on St. Thomas. We enjoyed seafood delicacies in the French Quarter of New Orleans, ate Texas steaks, attended a midnight show in Las Vegas where we sat so close to the stage that the lion's spit landed on our faces. Jay insisted the animals were not real, despite feeling the spittle. We stayed in cabins in the national parks, marveled at the Grand Canyon, Hoover Dam, hiked in Bryce and Zion, rode horses, walked down to the pits of the Carlsbad Caverns, steamed in the Arizona desert.

We drank Almaden wine in the vineyards of California, stood in awe under the giant Sequoias. We picnicked along clear mountain streams, visited with Indians in roadside stands, cooled off in the

Flagstaff night air. We gulped down steamed oysters and clams then feasted on abalone at Fisherman's Wharf in San Francisco.

When we appeared at his doorstep, the car owner was about to call the police to report the car stolen. After calming him down with the fact that we had to wait for parts in Texas, he didn't call the police. After this harrowing delivery we flew back to Florida and returned to our small island, which we appreciated even more after such a long trip.

I completed the written flight test and obtained my private pilot's license in July of 1977, the year following our crash into the sea. The instructors could not argue with me when I answered their question of what I would do if I had a sudden stall. I would land in the water near an island. There would be no fire to add to the problem. They passed me with flying colors. But I now knew that a night landing over water is an instrument approach. I made Jan, Jay, and George, another Power Products employee who was also a pilot, take instrument training with me.

To get this instrument rating we would need our own plane so we went into a partnership with Jan on a Cessna 172. We proceeded to buy all the instruments needed for this new rating. The only problem was that Jan had the plane most often.

Jim spent that summer working in our business with most of his time spent on the airplane. There were six coats of old paint to remove before it could be repainted. He grumbled but was happy to see his bank account grow each week.

Gables informed us that this would be Jimmy's last year of special education. He entered the seventh grade last year and now is in the ninth grade. With the expense of sending him to special education we took Diane out of Antilles private school and put her in a public school, but one of the best on the island. The bus picks her up and drops her off in front of Treetops, with free hot lunches included. But her school only goes through the sixth grade so she will be returning to Antilles for junior high and high school.

Because Power Products is so marine-oriented and constantly around boats, I reactivated a company Jon once had, Yacht Sales, Inc. People were always asking if I knew of someone interested in purchasing their boat. I not only sold boats but booked them for charter as well. The first boat I sold was a steel cargo boat tied up to the banana dock in St. Lucia. My buyer, being an instrument rated pilot, rented a Cessna 172 and off we flew to St. Lucia. My buyer and his partner wanted to convert this cargo boat into a repair shop, pulling up alongside the distressed yacht, and taking care of the problem.

Food was left on the galley table. The incoming cargo of Kotex pads and Tampaxes for their supermarket was held by the government in a large warehouse, awaiting payment. My buyer made the purchase and I am sure the government agents were happy to have the monstrosity removed from their pier.

Selling that cargo ship a few years later was even more interesting. The new buyer wanted to take the ship to Columbia for refurbishing, his attorney told us. He kept asking the owner how fast the ship could go. The large cargo holds that Burt converted into workshops would most likely be laden with a different cargo from Columbia. The transaction was to take place in Roadtown, Tortola, and a known tax haven. The new owner's attorney carried thousands in U.S.dollars needed to buy the ship. We learned later that an attorney does not have to declare the amount of money he is carrying across foreign borders. Due to their late arrival we had to stay overnight in Tortola along with the cash in hand. Coincidentally the attorney and his lady friend were staying in the same hotel.

I had visions of the new buyer's representatives crawling along the balcony, entering our rooms, knocking us out, and recouping the cash for the buyer who must have been a drug dealer. After a sleepless night, nothing happened. The local banks would not accept any more $100 or $50 dollar bills so we had to walk a few blocks to another bank that would accept the currency. I had my purse stuffed with more money than it had ever seen before. Burt's pockets also made him look much larger than normal.

The Yacht Sales provided other memorable moments; such as a doctor sending me monthly checks of $4,999.99. At that time if $5000 was transferred at one time the transfer had to be reported to the IRS. The doctor was sending checks from a Central America country until the yacht he wanted was paid in full.

Roadtown in 1977 did not even use numbered accounts as in Switzerland; all that was needed to open an account in this British Island was a signature. Rumor had it that Maureen O'Hara, the movie star, who bought Antilles Air Boats for her pilot husband, would make regular trips to Roadtown with suitcases full of cash. In later years the BVI made an agreement with the U.S. Internal Revenue Service to reveal accounts involving suspected criminal activities. A British Virgin Island Court might allow it, but in no circumstance can a person's background be revealed.

The sea trials for new buyers were much more exciting than showing condos or homes. The Tax Reform Act of 1986, designed to eliminate tax shelters, no longer allowed an owner of a yacht to deduct ten percent of the cost of his boat, after putting it into charter service. The Tax Law no longer provided buyers looking for yachts so I had to resort to some real estate sales, which were nowhere near as much fun as being a yacht broker.

In May of 1977 I was back in Detroit for a physical—modern medicine found another mass on my abdominal right side and I was scheduled to return in October to remove the mass. I didn't let them operate during the May visit since they had not yet invented a zipper for re-entry into the abdomen. With all the fancy space equipment you would think this would be feasible. During this visit I also planned on attending my 25th anniversary of my graduation from Marygrove College. Dad was 61 and Mom only 52 when they died so I was sure I would not live past 52 years myself. I had only six years left, I thought, so I had to quit flirting with death and make the most of those years. I had not been back to see my Alma Mater since graduation. It was time.

When you look the Grim Reaper in the eye you do take time to smell the roses. In October, through many prayers and positive thinking, with the help of Silva Mind Control classes, the doctors at Henry Ford Hospital could find no mass to remove. From Detroit I went on to Mayo Clinic in Minnesota to be sure there was no damage to the spine or sternum from the plane crash. Once the good doctors heard I was in a plane crash. Mayo treated me like I was a pariah and had contagious symptoms of the bubonic plague. They wanted no part of me when they heard of a plane crash. Nice gentlemen.

My employees in Yacht Sales included Kathy Sutton and her husband, John, who continued to sell yachts, while Kathy and I concentrated on booking charter yachts, where we could meet more people. Some yacht buyers wanted to moor their sailboat in front of their homes, like they can do in the waterways of Florida.

I happened to sell a fifty foot charter sailboat to a lady from California, Glenda Stout, who insisted that she wanted to moor her boat in front of her home. When she asked if I wanted the deposit in gold Krugerrands, I was ready to make plane reservations. Unfortunately her attorney in California talked her out of parting with her gold coins.

During these boom building years of the late 1970s Water Management was installing the sewage plant at Anchorage Condominiums on the east end of the island, next to the St. Thomas Yacht Club. I suggested to Glenda that she could join the yacht club and rent a mooring from the club. This was the closest we could come to tying her boat in front of her home. She said she would take over our spot in the waiting list of the condominiums. For our $500 deposit on a condo at Anchorage she paid us $40,000 to take our place. I was so thrilled in making two large sales that I asked her over for dinner that evening. When she walked through the gates of Treetops she was awed by the spaciousness of the house and asked if we wanted to sell it. In our flabbergasted moment we put a high price on the home. She said she wanted it. By this time we figured she had just escaped from the loony bin, but she wrote a check for $10,000 as a deposit on Treetops.

In 1978 we were still in the midst of a building boom. Many new hotels were in construction. This same year Jan broke our contract to run his company, most likely because my insurance company subrogated against him for my medical expenses. This lightened my workload with just Water Management and my new company of Dolly Greblick & Associates. I had to change the name from Yacht Sales due to the breakup. I was still selling yachts and occasionally real estate.

Kathy and I were quite flattered when the owner of one of the large real estate offices, David Jones of David Jones Real Estate, asked us out to lunch. To burst our bubble he announced that we were selling illegally, without a license, and asked us both to come and work for him.

With the break from Power Products I started my search for another space to operate Water Management. We rented the second floor of the Devcon offices in the countryside. Devcon, a concrete company, had many acres of land and was in the process of taking down a mountaintop for the rock they needed for the concrete. After a two year drought Jay looked into buying a drilling rig to find precious water on this tropical island.

Of course, the rains came soon after buying the drilling rig. Devcon also had a large maintenance area where we could park the rig and work on it. He bought a cable rig at first for a few thousand dollars we somehow scrapped together. We soon learned that this rig could not handle the hard, 40 million year old, Blue Bitch rock. We needed a costly rotary rig that ran into six figures. Off we went to the bank and the Small Business Administration to plead for money. We arranged for a two percent over prime loan but this is when prime interest rates were at 20 percent. There were times when the Greblicks went hungry in order to meet payroll.

The offices at Devcon consisted of three small private offices and a main room for a couple of secretary desks and a long counter space to establish an impressive laboratory. I remember testing the new girls by just asking them to type from Jay's handwritten notes. After some time fretting over the writing, one girl came up to me and said the job was just too hard for her.

Our good friend, Andy Harpin, the master builder of schooner sailboats from Cape Town, South Africa, used one of our small private offices for designing his next boat. Arthur was planning a bigger sailboat for a wealthy Argentinean businessman. He stayed at Treetops for several weeks after selling his 98 foot schooner, Antares. He became Uncle Andy to our children. The Antares was the third boat he built after two smaller sailboats, the Titch, which means "cabin boy", his nickname in his youth, and the Lorraine. All were built on the site of his truck hauling business in Cape Town. After the designing of the ships, he made a trip to the States to purchase a shipyard where he could build this boat. He always dreamed of building a much larger luxury charter schooner of 200 ft. that could handle 100 guests.

Andy was an adventurous man, a lonely one, but good looking, scrupulously honest, and full of tales of the sea which included whaling in Antarctica and swimming in the warm water of a caldera in Deception Bay. He single handed the Antares from Cape Town to the Virgin Islands, over 6000 miles, in forty days, the length of time it took him to reread the Bible again. Considering that this large ship had no pulleys to lift the boom or windlass for the anchor it was an amazing feat. To sail through a crowded harbor on the Antares with this master sailor on a 98 foot schooner was marvelous. He could wind his way through the anchorage, round up into the wind and drop the anchor. It was an experience not to be missed.

Along with our partners, Chase Manhattan Bank and the Small Business Administration, we bought, with the rotary drilling rig, a Smeal truck. The Smeal is a water well servicing truck that has a crane to lift or drop submersible pumps in deep wells. I was elected to drive the six wheel truck from St. Louis, MO to West Palm Beach, Fla. for fast delivery to St. Thomas. Jay equipped the truck with a CB radio, making me feel like a red hot road mama driving through the Ozarks countryside. The semis alerted me to any Smoky Bears ahead. Now I can add truck driver to my resume.

After pounding on the Blue Bitch rock for hours we sold the cable rig and bought a rotary. Despite the much higher cost, this rig cut through the Blue Bitch stone as if it was butter. There were many stories attached to this new rig. At one hotel we were trying to reach salt water less than fifty feet from the shoreline but after three attempts, did not find seawater. We were in solid rock. On another occasion at the request of the hotel management we were drilling on Water Island when an old-timer on the island announced we were drilling through a dump site where the U.S. Navy had buried nerve gas bombs. The rig was returned to St. Thomas hastily. In all cases the client picks the drilling site. We claimed to dig holes, not wells. We did not guarantee water.

Toward the end of the 1970s we were feeling the pain of high interest rates on an expensive drilling rig so Jay decided to take in a couple of partners to help financially. I became thoroughly disgusted with Jay's new partners, one from Chicago, Art Price, and the other from Hawaii, David Lester. They were living the high life on our hard-earned dollars, staying in the best hotels when they visited the island, holding expensive symposiums, (that they never paid for), upsetting our long established reputation.

We had an unexpected but good offer on Treetops, so I packed up and decided to move to Florida, leaving Jay to handle his new partners. Jim was tired of living with other families. I could now make a home for him and let Diane try the schools in Florida. We bought a duplex in Coral Springs. It had three bedrooms, two baths, plus laundry and family room on each side. I could rent out the other half and cover most of our expenses. But there was work to be done to prepare both sides for rental or living conditions. The entire building was painted inside and out, new curtains installed, both houses cleaned thoroughly.

I took a class in Creative Writing at the local public school facility for senior citizens in night school. I was young for the class but the professor, Bill Baxter, counted me a senior so I only had to pay $2.00 for a semester of classes. Bill had been an attorney in his working career and found when he retired at 70 years of age he was bored so he went to night classes at a local university to obtain a degree in creative writing, then proceeded to teach. He was in his nineties by the time he was my teacher. It was an interesting and exciting period for I had so many island stories to tell. I did learn that you cannot produce an entire book from one incident, such as the crash at sea so I always had intentions of writing our memoirs but time somehow slips by us during our busy lives.

I wanted to make use of my time during the day when the children were in school so I took a job with a sign company as an office manager but the more interesting job was working for a blind lawyer. I saw an ad in the Coral Springs paper requiring a "Gal Friday". When I called the attorney, Nick Cassas, I learned that he was totally blind because he lost everything he and his family had by investing in real estate. When disaster hits, the weakest part of his body failed, his eyes. When he became blind his wife divorced him; while his two teenage children had Social Security income because of his disability. His housekeeper/laundress hung his clothes in sets, pants, shirt and even socks pinned to the same hanger in his closet. When he made a drink for anyone he put his thumb in the glass to feel when the glass was full. I was to drive him to the store for shopping, eat in restaurants with him and take him to plays where we sat in the back row and I described the action on the stage. In unpacking the groceries I would place cans in certain areas of the pantry. He said he often had most interesting combinations of vegetables.

Nick's most thrilling adventure was when I took him to our golf course and let him drive the cart on the wide fairways. I directed him for hitting the ball, told him the approximate yardages to the flag, then handed him a club. He enjoyed putting on the green as well as the longer hits.

A blind person has free access to operator assistance and directory service. When we ate in a restaurant he told me to tell him where his food was located on the plate according to the clock, vegetables at 12:00 meat at 6:00, and so on. I learned to offer my elbow when there were obstacles in our path. This training helped considerably with my blind father-in-law. Dad, however, would not make use of the Library Services for the Blind with their multitudes of recorded books.

My job with Nick was to help him find tenants for his new shopping mall that he had bought years before. The market now seemed ready for another shopping center. And, of course, I read his mail, contracts and leases to him. Being of Greek descent his eyes had been dark brown in his youth but turned to bright blue when he became blind.

Diane entered Middle School in Coral Springs just as the public school system was beginning to bus students from the inner city of Detroit to the more affluent schools in the suburbs. Translation: black students were coming into all white schools. Neither group was happy about this situation. Having grown up on an island of 85% black she had no problem with the blacks, who consistently picked on the other students. She stood up to them and even made friends with several black girls.

One of the impressive things she said to me was that in the islands she could wear a skirt if she wanted to, or her jeans did not have to say Sassoon on them in order for her to fit in with the crowd. There were so many false facades in the States. The girls grew up way too fast, with no childhood or playtime. She said she could be herself in the islands.

It was April 1st when I came home from work and Jimmy told me his sister had been arrested. I didn't know whether to believe him or figure he was pulling an April Fool's joke on me. It seems Diane was caught by the owner of the concession store they walked past every day stealing candy bars. She said she was just the lookout. But all the children involved were arrested, taken to the local police station, where I had to pick her up. The police imposed an enduring lesson on the children. They had to wash police cars for several consecutive Saturdays. I couldn't resist taking embarrassing photographs of the entire group hard at work under the watchful eyes of a policeman.

CHAPTER 24

My twenty year career as a real estate broker resulted in many interesting experiences. I worked with local East Indian retailers that fancied themselves as developers. I found the land, hired construction personnel, established legal assistance, and then sold the condominiums. So many homes on the island were laden with history that it made research of the properties extremely interesting.

Kathy Sutton and I started out with David Jones Real Estate located in the Royal Dane Mall, downtown. I loved research and preferred the historic buildings in town, so I met most of the business owners of Charlotte Amalie. I learned to have tea and not rush into a business conversation when calling on the Indian owners, or not being surprised when listing an East Indian home and finding a closet or an entire room decorated as a prayer room. We learned to tolerate the smell of curry throughout the house.

We heard stories of many gods, of arranged marriages, and of Monday fastings. There were also stories of having to leave northern India when it became Pakistan, where, as Hindus, they could not live under Muslim rule, of young adults having to live at home until marriage, of careers decided for them by their parents.

I was invited to a wedding in Rye, New York by one of my Indian clients where there was a sit-down dinner for over 500 people. The canopy where the ceremony took place was sterling silver and the bride's sari had threads of gold and silver throughout the silk. It must have set the parent's pocketbook back by $20,000, we were told.

I worked with the Burger King Company that was trying to establish a location on St. Thomas. They did not succeed a few years earlier on St. Croix. The youth were not into hamburgers yet, but Kentucky Fried Chicken was a huge success. Burger King opened up on the waterfront where the tourists from the cruise ships could spot it and get their "Americana Fix".

When I took a developer from New York City to a local black architect and he asked "how much do the bribes cost here?" I could have crawled into a hole. Mike had been dealing with government agencies in New York where he told me it costs developers money just to move a piece of paper from one end of the desk to another.

Another developer, Harry Weston, built a large hotel, the Virgin Grand, on St. Thomas and duplicated it on St. John along with home sites. Harry was looking for another beach site on St. Thomas when, during our trek through the beachfront area from an adjoining property, we ran into a marijuana farm. We hoped that the farmers were not tending their plants while we were inspecting the land. We also found a cemetery with ancient grave markers at this undisturbed beach site. Harry never did buy the property because the site was on a north coast. The seas were crashing on the beach. It was not a good location for an upscale resort.

When John Armsted, developer of Mahogany Run golf course and condominiums, was starting a hotel on yet another beach property, Hull Bay, the bulldozers uncovered a 2,000 year old skeleton that was sent to the Smithsonian for carbon dating. I saw the female skeleton and even back then she had hands crippled hands with arthritis, like mine. John never had to build the hotel at Hull Bay for the government bought the site for $4,000,000 to preserve the Arawak Indian burial site. We often teased John that he could plant an old skeleton on any site for a fee. It made sense that on a steep rocky island the easiest place to bury the dead was in the sand of a beach area.

The David Jones manager was handling the Secret Harbor Hotel and Condominiums and made arrangements for his office to occupy the lobby desk with agents from his real estate office. One of my clients, Robert Ludlum, the author of thriller novels, almost bought two Secret Harbor condominiums from me. He claimed he had so many friends on the island that he would never find time to write his novels, so he reneged on the purchases. He did show me the house he once lived in with his wife, Mary, a Broadway actress, on a secluded mountain top. The swimming pool was a perfect circle for it once held a cannon installed by the Navy during the Second World War. The United States bought the islands from the Danes after World War I for $25 million after originally negotiating for $5 million. The roads on the island were built by the Navy prior to World War II. The Navy also installed cannons on the mountain tops, plus bunkers built into the hillsides to store ammunition. A submarine net was stretched across the harbor opening to keep German submarines out of the bay.

Fort Christian, overlooking the harbor, built in 1671, was named after a Danish King; the town of Charlotte Amalie was named after his wife. The fort was built to protect the residents from pirates and foreigners. Over the centuries it was used as a government house, prison, church, community center, police headquarters, and today the Virgin Islands Museum.

The town is overflowing with historic buildings dating to the 1600s, such as Bluebeard's Castle, now a hotel and time share. There is Blackbeard's Castle, where Edward Teach, the notorious English pirate kept his fair maidens locked in a tower while he was at sea, plundering. The Dutch Reformed Church is celebrating its 350th anniversary. Most of the students either attend the Anglican Church and school or St. Peter and Paul Cathedral and Catholic school. St. Thomas boasts the second oldest synagogue in the Western Hemisphere, with the longest continuous use under the American Flag. The seats, ark and bimah are all made of mahogany, the menorah dates to the 11th century and is thought to be Spanish, but the most unusual feature of this magnificent synagogue is the sand floor believed to commemorate the

Israelite journey through the desert. The less lofty buildings consist of the Pott Rum Distillery on St. Thomas, where cooking alcohol for the galley stove can be bought for less than a dollar a gallon. The excellent rum produced on St. Croix, is known as Cruzan Rum. On St. Thomas there was also a submarine base in the commercial port of Crown Bay with Water Island to the south to protect the sub base. Water Island had ponds of fresh water that was used by the pirates to replenish their ship's stores of water.

Today St. Thomas is known as the New York City of the Caribbean where natives come from every other island to earn big bucks. The St. Thomian wants a government job where the work is not too taxing but the down-islander will gladly take a job in the hotels or preferably as wait-staff in one of the busy restaurants and joyfully take several hundred dollars in tips to the bank every week.

The harbor of Charlotte Amalie is deep and well protected. We have seen as many as thirteen ships in the harbor, at anchor, or at the sub-base piers. These are the days you do not go downtown. The local cab driver declares only about $30 per week in tips. The local IRS office turns a blind eye on the practice, for more than likely; their relatives were driving the cabs.

I worked in the David Jones office for several years until the new owner wanted to cut back my commission split at the beginning of the year, back to a fifty-fifty split. I had earned him so much for him on my seventy-thirty split that I was inconsolably angry so another agent and I started our own office on the east end of St. Thomas. Donna Percy and I were both brokers long before our new owner, Bob Ortho, obtained his broker's license so we were free to leave.

This adventure lasted only a couple of years when we decided to flex our wings at Remax St. Thomas, Inc. located across from the cruise ships. Remax had a more favorable commission structure where you pay all your expenses but keep all the commission. You had to be quite self-confident in your ability to sell real estate.

For years we had been able to tell our buyers that property values on the island was appreciating at the rate of ten percent per year and that we had not had a hurricane hit the islands in fifty years. I often chased buyers to the airport and signed offers on the fender of the car. Purchases were usually influenced by the swaying palm trees, balmy nights, and too many pina coladas.

One incident stands out in my memory at Remax. I was on floor duty and took a call where the native fellow said I was supposed to show him an apartment. I never showed apartments to rent.

"Donna, call the police on another line. I think this is the guy that attacked Grace."

Donna called the police and she was immediately connected to the detective handling Grace's case.

"Keep him on the line", the detective told Donna.

"Set up an appointment for tomorrow, then come down to the police station afterwards".

I had never worked with rentals so I suspected this caller immediately. Just a few days prior to this call another agent, Grace, had been showing a young black man an apartment for rent. He attacked Grace with a knife. She fought back and almost lost her sight. Grace was not the only agent he had attacked.

The detective at the station said he would like to set up a sting to catch this violent man. I told him I would go along with the ruse. I was to meet this man the next day in the same parking lot of the church on the east end of St. Thomas where Grace had met him. The detective said they would have police available to apprehend him.

Of course, my husband, Jay, was not happy with my agreement to play the Ginny Pig. He said he would be there to defend me.

"Don't worry, Jay. The police said they would be there too", I replied.

"I still don't like it", he said.

Donna said she would be in the car with me and another agent, Mary, and her husband will also be in the area to watch. At the time I was driving a large black Mazda that we thought might be more conspicuous than Donna's beige Camry, a more common car. She would be crouched down on the floor in the back seat and would put a beach towel over herself to hide from the perpetrator. We nervously drove to the parking lot of the church at the allotted time.

"Don't turn off the engine so we can get away in a hurry", Donna demanded.

"Here he comes, from behind the school building. Thank goodness, school is not in session." I remarked.

The slender black man sauntered up to the car with his full head of dreadlocks peeking out from under a multi-colored knit cap, jeans, and a T-shirt bearing Bob Marley's picture. He reached for the handle and tried to open the locked passenger door, while I motioned for him to come around to the driver's side of the car, where I had the window cracked a mere two inches.

"Now, what do we do?" I asked Donna.

When the young man reached the driver's door I said

"Wait here a minute, I'll be right back."

He must have thought I had a screw loose as I raced out of the parking lot and down the street toward the shopping mall.

"Where are the police? And Jay? And Mary and her husband?"

No one was around. We fulfilled our end of the sting, we met the man. Then Donna saw several policemen emerge from the church grounds and bushes across the street. The detective later told us that the young man had an eight inch knife on him when he was arrested. Who knows what he would have done had I actually shown him an empty apartment.

I had to testify in court at his trial. I endured his cold, piercing stares, thankful that he was handcuffed and a police officer stood nearby. The judge commended me on the brave job I had done. Not many people are willing to help the police as I had, he advised. The island grapevine later divulged that he was out of jail. His mother had provided the bail money. This gave me another compelling reason to move to Florida and leave island life behind. This madman was not in jail.

$\mathcal{C}$HAPTER 25

Our first trip to Europe was in 1980 for a Water Conference in Amsterdam where we could write off the expenses of the trip. Being in business for yourself had to have some compensation for the risks involved as one island Internal Revenue Service man told me. The IRS in St. Thomas was eons behind the times. One audit required me to prove that my children were U.S. citizens and living on U.S. soil, another time I had to show that I changed my name when I got married. Immigration did not want to allow me to enter the British Virgin Island when they saw that my maiden name was different than my married name.

We were amazed when we saw the Red Light District in Amsterdam, for legalized prostitution. Women were sitting in the windows of their rooms displaying their bodies to entice the men. There were sex shops, peep shows, and a sex museum in this cosmopolitan town.

A trip down the Amstel River displayed the narrow buildings in this crowded city, including the narrow first McDonalds in Europe. It seemed to be only twenty feet wide but several stories in height. Most of the homes appeared to be of the same dimensions with one house just two meters wide, but several stories high. Transportation in this large, but very bicycle-friendly city was bicycles of every type, mostly old and well used. Driving a car in the city center is discouraged.

We visited the famous Diamond Center to watch experts cut and polish these gifts from Mother Nature. We marveled at the talent of Rembrandt at the Rijksmuseum, dedicated to the artist, We admired his Night Watch masterpiece. These were special events for first time visitors to Europe.

After travelling so many hours, we chose to experience only one other country. We figured we could only absorb the culture, language and currency of one country at a time. After the water conference in Amsterdam, we chose Portugal for it was noted to us by our well-travelled partners in Water Management that Portugal was still a bargain.

From Amsterdam we flew to Lisbon and rented a car to tour the country looking for the purple legs of people stamping the grapes by foot. Alas the ancient ways of crushing grapes by dancing accompanied by singing has given way to machines and the hand woven baskets for carrying the grapes are now replaced with plastic bags. Progress has changed everything. Now the farmers haul their grapes to a cooperative where the product depends on the supply.

We tasted the wines of the various regions and enjoyed their local foods, wine caves, Moorish castles, forts, and royal palaces. We were the first guests of a new hotel opening outside of Lisbon. In the dining room we were surrounded by tuxedoed waiters doting on our every move. The restaurants were always interesting as we knew no Portuguese, but sign language worked. We saw our first olive groves and cork oaks, stayed in a Pousada de Portugal that was previously a convent. We slept in a nun's cell where Jay had to bend down to enter the room. It must have belonged to a short nun. The Pousadas are usually in palaces, castles and manors but we were travelling in 1980 long before the country was developed for tourism. We had a prolonged stay at what was once the king's hunting palace in Bucaco, surrounded by trim gardens and hunting forests.

We witnesses the bravado of young men teasing the bulls running lose in barricaded streets and the greater bravery of the seafaring men in the fishing village of Nazare on the east coast of Portugal exposed to the Atlantic Ocean. This village is without a natural harbor and before the men can begin their fishing they must launch their heavy boats into breaking waves each morning then reverse the process at sunset. So many men are lost at sea that the entire village seemed to be dressed in black. Portugal is indeed a poor but proud little country that had established the first and most long-lived global empire in the world.

While in Coral Springs I answered an ad for a "girl Friday" to drive around Neal Castle, a man that I soon learned was an attorney who lost his sight from the stress of overinvesting in real estate. It was most interesting learning to work with a blind man. I learned that his laundress pinned an entire outfit together for him on a hanger so he was always well-dressed. I learned that you tell him where his food is located on his plate according to the clock. In other words, his veggies were at six, meat (I often cut it for him) was at twelve, etc. He had to trust cashiers to give him the correct change. He folded the various denominations in different ways and placed then in several compartments in his wallet. When he made a drink for you he discretely put his thumb in the glass so he could tell when it was full. He was given directory assistance at no charge by the telephone company. His children got social security benefits.

I often took him to plays where we sat in the back row so I could tell him quietly what was happening on the stage. He and I will always remember when I took him golfing and let him drive the cart on the wide fairways. He was ecstatic. I told him the distance, handed him the club he needed and advised him on the greens how far he was from the hole and pointed him in the right direction.

I figured with Jay's Dad's vision going this experience will come in handy. But Dad is a crusty old man and did not take kindly to new directions from anyone.

$\mathcal{C}$HAPTER 26

In 1981 Diane and I moved back to St. Thomas to try island living again. Jim stayed in Coral Springs to learn to live on his own without family around. Diane went back to Antilles School as a freshman. She told me she enjoys the small size of the classes on the island compared to the mega-sized classes in the States. She also said she can be herself on the island. If she wants to wear a dress or her jeans that don't say Sassoon on them, it's ok. Nobody teases her. The girls do not paint themselves up with different color make up each day. Their glow is a natural one, pink cheeks, suntans, and freckles, with a sparkle in their eyes that emanates from joy and friendship. They often have classes outdoors or eat their lunches at picnic tables scattered around the campus under Flamboyant, sea grape trees, or coconut palms. In Florida there were 2,000 students in the 6th, 7th, and 8th grades, while at Antilles there are 300 students in all the grades, from kindergarten through twelfth.

During this year we also sold our company, Water Management, to Polymetrics of San Jose, California, a manufacturer of reverse osmosis equipment (fresh water from the sea via filters). Jay was relieved of the financial and managerial responsibility so he could now concentrate on sales and engineering, his forte. I was coaxed into returning to the office to straighten out the confusion of two years of lackadaisical secretarial help and to consolidate the files of two companies into one.

The sad news of this period was the accidental death of our dear friend, Andy Harpin, on December 9th. He was hit by a car on a dark secondary road in Portsmouth, Rhode Island, while taking his usual evening stroll around 10:00 p.m. Unfortunately, Andy was wearing dark clothing and the driver did not see him in time to stop. No charges were pressed because the driver of the Volkswagen Beetle that killed him was the sheriff's son. Andy was not a small man and we were all surprised that a VW Beetle could kill him. Speed must have been a factor in his death but who can prove anything.

Andy must have had our information in his pocket for we got a call from the sheriff's office that night giving us the tragic news. When we received the call I started projecting my thoughts to Capetown, South Africa to have his partner, Norbert, call me. I had a vital message to relay to him. I often did this with Andy and he would always call a day or so later.

The man was a sailor beyond measure. He built several ships in Capetown, South Africa; all were gaff-rigged schooners. The first sailboat was Titch, a 60 foot schooner, (which means cabin boy, his nickname as a child), the second was Lorraine, a 72 footer, (named for his wife of short duration) and his final ship was Antares, a 98 footer. She was launched in Capetown in 1976. The Antares was given her name at midnight on the night she was transported from her building site to the sea. Her namesake star was directly overhead, and is the 15th brightest star in the skies. The Lorraine was chartered by Walt Disney for his film on the green turtles late in the 1960s.

I think every live-aboard boat had two or three baby turtles being raised on their decks in tubs, hoping one of their turtles might be the star of the movie.

The Harpins were not a wealthy family and often went without necessities. He had two brothers and two sisters but his short marriage produced no children. As a young boy, Andy frequently sat on the hills above Capetown watching the sailing ships come into port, dreaming the impossible dream of someday having his very own boat. The soft touch of a hand on his shoulder and the words of a wise teacher, recognizing the boy's desires, had said to him,

"Son, if you really want one of those ships in the harbor you will have it if you work hard enough toward that goal".

Andy remembered to invite his wise old teacher on the maiden voyage of the Antares to bear witness to the results of his inspirational words. He would sail his ships to the American Virgin Islands where he sold them after some time in the charter business. He would send some of the money home to avoid suspicion and stashed the rest in Tortola that didn't even have numbered accounts as they do in Switzerland. You only needed your signature to identify you. With his death the sailing world had lost a man devoted to bringing the romance of the gaff-rigged schooner to the forefront. His knowledge and skills will be sorely missed.

He often told us stories of whaling trips to Antarctica, swimming in a warm pool of water on that continent; taking young cadets on his ships to learn about schooners and to acquire their sea legs in the rough waves around Capetown. He had designed the steel hull for the Jessica, a three-masted 203 foot schooner for the king of Spain.

He single handed the Antares to St. Thomas. The journey took forty days, enough time for him to reread the bible. He was a self-made man that commanded respect, albeit a lonely, gentle man with a South African accent and very proper manners. His unpretentious clothing belied his actual material fortune.

When he sold the Antares he asked if he could spend a few days with us at Treetops. At that time Water Management had the second floor of the Devcon building on the east end of St. Thomas so we had an extra office where he could concentrate on designing his dream ship, a 200 foot, 100 berth, training ship for his cadets in Capetown or it could be the Queen of the charter fleet on St. Thomas. He needed a family life and the Greblicks provided it with two children and two dogs. He finally grew restless and decided he had to scour the east coast for a marina he could purchase to build this ship. Of course the ship would be a schooner, as all of his ships were.

As a young man he recognized the need for trucks versus railroads in South Africa and was one of the first to haul cargo by truck. His 18 hour days on the road led to the failure of his short-lived marriage. He then filled his life with reaching that secret goal of designing a 200 foot ship. Today he leaves two large companies, one a transportation firm and the other heavy construction equipment. Because of the salt spray from the rough seas around Capetown the ground must be turned one meter or over three feet to reach the new sweet soil for the farmers.

He chose his partners wisely and was soon able to begin the construction of his first yacht and to revive his spirit with retreats at sea. His adventures included two whaling expeditions to the Antarctic, a voyage from Capetown to Australia aboard the windjammer, "Lawhill", a trip on the "Shenandoah" an engineless schooner, out of Vineyard Haven. He sailed aboard the "Bill of Rights" out of Newport, R.I., the "Harvey Gamage" of Connecticut and St. Thomas and to Nova Scotia aboard the Canadian government schooner, "Blue Nose". He crossed the Atlantic as guest of the Argentinian, Mr. Carlos, owner of the "America" replica and was aboard with the King and Queen of Spain as additional guests. He was versatile enough to mix with sailors at sea or royalty. He was full of tales to tell but was a very private person and slow to bare his soul or thoughts to anyone.

His clever self-steering vane-design allowed him to maneuver this vessel, once the sails were set, with a slight movement of the wrist. It was an amazing sight to see this 98 foot sailboat barrel through an anchorage full of boats, round up into the wind and drop sails and anchor almost simultaneously.

The Antares won an Antigua race with only Arthur aboard along with one petite, slightly clad girl as crew. They were pitted against crews of half dozen men or more. The losers claim the tiny bikini was part of the winning captain's plan.

He was a true man of the sea. His partner, Norbert, took his ashes home and scattered them back into the cold, grey sea of Capetown, where they belonged.

My Yacht Sale Co. introduced us to other remarkable people. One couple, Carl and Nora Bartley were extraordinary folks. Carl was born in the 19th century on the Texas/Mexico border and remembers

Pancho Villa riding through his village when he was a child. Carl rode onto his land with his mother in a covered wagon when the United States Homestead Act was giving freehold title of 160 acres west of the Mississippi River to anyone that would improve the land and live on it for five years. Carl built up his ranch to 6,000 acres and then fenced in the entire property. The property was also known as the Bar-X-Bar Ranch. His land was surrounded by National Forest so it seemed much larger. He knew all of his boundaries, even when they were constantly changing. He was a most unforgettable character, a man that taught himself animal husbandry, who was also an opera singer. He was a staunch Baptist but not averse to having a sip of wine in the kitchen out of view of the other Baptists. He had made three fortunes in his lifetime. The first one was taking his honey bees around the country and was the first person to put a honeycomb in the jar; the second was inventing the lock-log system of building a log cabin and obtaining a patent for the system; and the third was selling the timber from his ranch.

Initially he charged for fishing trout out of his stocked ponds. He always envisioned a system wherein he sold yearly memberships to fish or hunt on his land. Unfortunately his sons were not interested in continuing the ranch operation so he turned his fenced-in property into an elk hunting setup where the hunter was guaranteed an elk but he was always accompanied by a guide.

On our first visit to this mountain paradise he and his wife, Nora, took us up to 11,000 ft. elevation to picnic. As he and Nora bounded up the hillside for the last 1000 ft. or so, Carl insisted that we take it easy as we lived at sea level. They were used to this elevation. Carl was also the sheriff of his county. He was well into his nineties when we met him. He had been patrolling his property on horseback; his horse stepped in a hole and threw him, breaking his shoulder. As he lay in the hospital bed staring at the ceiling he decided that he must do more with his life so he bought a 51 ft. Morgan sailboat, Snowflake, that had started her life in Alaska, thus the name, but he found her in Miami. Snowflake was delivered to St. Thomas where he then turned her over to the Greblick family to watch over her but we had free use of the yacht for an entire summer, or until Carl decided to donate her to a university for a tax deduction.

He was ninety six when I rented a car for them on one of their visits to the island. Carl and Nora always stayed at our home when on St. Thomas. Knowing how car rental operations do not like to have elderly clients rent a car in Florida, I asked him what would happen if they refused to rent to him. He said he would just have to sue them. There was no tolerance for age discrimination with him. He must have had attorneys on retainer with all he was involved in.

Before we moved back to St. Thomas Diane, had her childhood friend, Carol, visit us in our duplex in Florida. It was such a pleasure to show Carol what life was like on the mainland. She had lived on a small island her entire life and had never seen a bridge, an escalator, super highways, an amusement park, or a roller coaster. I took the girls to Disney World, Sea World, Wet and Wild, and every other place Carol wanted to see. She also joined us on one of our trips to New Mexico to the Bartley ranch. Carl said the quarter horses were too fat and needed to be ridden for exercise. When the girls were astride the horses their legs stuck straight out because the girl's legs were not long enough to wrap around the horse's huge bellies.

On one occasion I walked along the trails from restful waterfalls while the girls rode the horses back to the lodge.

I came around a bend and ran smack into a coyote. I don't know which of us was more surprised or frightened. I stood absolutely still and after an eternity of staring at each other he ran off into the forest, much to my relief. We heard, and then saw, brown bears and black bears rummaging through Nora's garbage.

When the spotted owl was placed on the endangered species list, Carl cursed, then allowed the environmentalists to camp on his land and search for the owls. Once his area was declared free of the spotted owl nests he still cursed the tree huggers and went on about his business. He took us to a homestead cabin, filled with the smoke from cooking, where daylight peeked through spaces between the logs;

he showed us an old mine that produced radioactive material; pointed out sheets of mica to us. The silicate was once used as the peering-in windows on stoves because of the high heat tolerance of mica. It was also used as the isinglass windows of the first Ford automobiles.

When we first returned to St. Thomas we had to move from Jay's one bedroom apartment on the north coast to a two bedroom unit to provide a room for Diane. We were still overlooking the north coast across the road from a neighborhood grocery store and a small but popular restaurant.

I enjoyed the sale of yachts for it was much more glamorous than real estate but with the changing of the tax code in 1976 buyers became very scarce. An investor could no longer take ten percent of the cost of his new yacht as a tax credit when he put it into charter service yacht. I had to turn to real estate which was also exciting but not as much fun as going out on sea trials.

I remember the sale of a large cargo boat that a local handyman bought as a floating workshop. He had visions of pulling up alongside a yacht in distress, fixing the problem, so the captain could proceed with his charter. When Burt, the handyman, and I flew to St. Lucia to examine the boat it was like stepping aboard a ghost ship. Plates full of food were set on the table as if a plague had struck the ship and the crew abandoned her quickly. Perhaps pirates threw the crew overboard; or law enforcement learned of the ship smuggling contraband. We even imagined aliens swooping the crew into a UFO. The police told us the boat had a cargo of tampons now stored in a government warehouse but they had no explanation for the condition of the ship. Burt bought the ship and turned it into his floating workshop. He kept it for a few years and I got to sell her again. This time around it was as interesting as when we found the boat.

The new buyer of the steel hulled cargo ship wanted to know how fast she could travel, he planned to take her to Columbia to have her refitted in that country (and we figured he would load her with drug cargo as well). The deal was to be consummated in Road Town, Tortola, where we learned that attorneys can carry large amounts of cash for their buyers without declaring what or how much they were transporting. We had to spend the night on that island. Burt's room at the hotel and mine each had balconies and our rooms were next door to the buyers. The cash had changed hands and Burt was now in possession of all the monies. You could easily climb from one balcony to another in this hotel. I had visions of us being hit over the head or worse and the money repossessed from Burt. This was a big commission for me and it caused many sleepless hours. We walked the next morning from Burt's bank to mine with my purse bulging with $50 bills. The island had run out of $100 bills.

That same year the crazy lady, Gladys Short, who bought a fifty foot sailboat from me, our reservation on a prebuilt Anchorage condo, and our home, Treetops, fell behind on her payments. This was before I knew much about real estate. We sold Treetops to her on a 30 year mortgage at a low interest rate.

We took her to court, repossessed the house and resold it to her on a five year balloon at a much higher interest rate. After that ordeal I decided I had to learn more about the real estate business if we were going to sell real property, especially to flaky people.

Gladys turned out to be a slum landlord, turning my lower laundry area into an apartment. One tenant was conducting a photography business and using the tub in the kids' bathroom as a darkroom. He got so much water on the teak deck that the toilet was about to fall through to the lower apartment. It was sad to see a property so neglected by a careless landlord.

CHAPTER 27

The year was 1983. Jim was working at Palm Aire in Pompano Beach; Diane was a junior at Antilles, president of her class, and working weekends at a beach resort after spending the summer in Wyandotte, Michigan with the Magorski family. This clan came to visit us at least twice a year when Fred was manager of Eastern Airlines, and they got free travel. Diane got to know her cousins better, rode a bike to her heart's content, helped take care of a new grandbaby, and shopped at big malls. She also got to visit Frankenmuth for their famous chicken dinner.

As the economy in the States gained steam we saw many new hotels being built on the islands. I achieved my broker's license in this year and the two Greblicks narrowly escaped death once again.

We booked a guided trip to Japan with International Weekends. We had to fly to New York from the island, and then catch one of the two weekly flights to Japan via Korean Air Lines. We enjoyed a couple of shows in the Big Apple, at midnight we boarded flight 007 for Seoul, Korea. It was April 28, 1983, a Thursday. We stopped for fuel in Anchorage, Alaska, while enjoying a spectacular display of northern lights. When we reached South Korea there was a five hour layover in the city so Korean Airlines took us on a bus tour of their city. In a city of eight million people we did not see more than five or six scraps of paper or any litter on the streets. People were sweeping down the fronts of their buildings, which were sold by the footage on the street regardless of the depth. We almost booked the following flight, which was the one the Russians shot down over the Kamchatka Peninsula, losing all aboard. We flew over the same peninsula, for it was a direct route to Seoul. Obviously, it was not our time to meet our Maker, or those guardian angels were working overtime. I was asleep on the floor in business class, where KAL had moved the entire group of 30, when Jay lifted the shade on the window and saw cars and trucks below. The Russians denied the shooting at first and then said we sent a 747 as a spy plane. We were in Tokyo when we heard of the mistake and the loss of all persons aboard, including a Congressman. Many in our group did not want to return home on Korean Air but this was a Russian mistake not the airlines mistake. KAL was most accommodating to us. The stewardesses changed into long hand-embroidered gown to serve dinner, there was a cart of drinks left out for anyone to help themselves, service was impeccable and the food excellent.

I had pictures of the girls in their gowns and sent them to the president of Korean Air Lines but he wrote and advised that this was not the crew that was aboard the unfortunate plane, there was a change of crew and our girls were fine. We then flew on to the port of Osaka, a busy commercial center trading rice, creating the first modern futures exchange market in the world. In Osaka the Japanese tour board guides took us by luxury bus, replete with chandelier and coffee table in the rear to Kyoto, once the ancient capital of Japan. We spent five exciting days in Kyoto, visiting the first Shogun's palace with its secret rooms, hallways, moats and guard towers. The most interesting part of the palace was the specially designed floors that squeak even when walking in bare or padded feet. The floors prevented anyone from sneaking around the palace at night without being heard.

Kyoto is a lovely city surrounded by mountains, dotted with castles and palaces and Japanese gardens where men are constantly raking the stones into various patterns. We hit all the tourist attractions but enjoyed the food in the restaurants as opposed to the hotel dining room. We always chose to sit on the floor. We drank sake and beer, ate tempura, sashimi and some unrecognizable things but all delicious, while the Japanese patrons sat at regular tables. If we couldn't communicate what we wanted to the waiter we could always point to a wooden replica of the meal in the storefront window.

We took our shoes off at the Imperial palace, and anywhere else necessary. We enjoyed a samurai show at the castle where the movie Shogun was filmed, lit incense sticks at Buddhist temples where the gods reign over sad occasions such as death. At the Shinto Shrines the gods rule over happy times such as births and weddings. We bought fortune papers at the shrines and hung them on the trees if the fortune predicted something bad. We learned a few words in Japanese and bowed politely as all Japanese do. I learned that my five foot two inch height towered over most of the men.

From Kyoto we took the famous bullet train for an overnight trip to Tokyo. We were disappointed that we could not see Mt. Fuji as we passed it because of cloud cover. We walked the Ginza that is as brightly lit as Las Vegas, shopped in the alleyways and window shopped at the fancy department stores. Tokyo not only allowed crossings at the curbs with the traffic lights, as we do in the States, but they also allowed jaywalking on the diagonals. You had to run, however, to get across the wide streets on time. The people and cities are impeccably clean. No land is wasted. Rice paddies grow right up to large factory buildings. We wanted to rent a car and tour the countryside but in 1983 there were no English signs on the roadway just Japanese. If you hesitated at a corner to look at a map, two or three people would approach wanting to practice their English and asked if they can help.

Our tour then took us to Taipei, Taiwan for an overnight stay in that country. We were housed in an opulent hotel with velvet drapes and hand carved rosewood furniture. The visit was much too short for this kaleidoscopic city. I wanted to see the Chinese treasures in the National Museum but we were busy shopping for a computer. In Taiwan the Apple clones are known as "Pineapples", but there are also

Bananas and Oranges, all to the dismay of Apple, USA. We did get to the night street market where vendors sold from their curbside tables every assortment of food, fruit, and crafts. There were medicinal cures made from snakes and other unrecognizable objects. Incense permeated the air. There was everything imaginable, even some unimaginable.

Back home when we had to call technical support for our new Pineapple computer the company would just send us a new hard drive rather than spend time on the phone trying to solve our problem.

This incredible bargain of a tour, two weeks in the Orient with airfare from New York, all transportation included, was booked through International Weekends for $1250 per person. This tour would be ending with a week in Hong Kong. Unfortunately the company is no longer in existence or we might still be travelling with them. They did such a good job.

Our first impression of Hong Kong was about fifty miles of Main Street, St. Thomas. The idea was to shop for the best price and then try to find the store again that gave you that unbeatable price. It was almost impossible! Hong Kong is a teeming seaport, surrounded by mountains, crowded with high rise buildings, bright neon signs in Chinese, with a view of Kowloon, Hong Kong, Red China and the out islands. The ride on the tram to Victoria Peak takes only eight minutes. In its 100 year history there has never been an accident on the tram. The variety of restaurants and shops is mind boggling, and although merchants were complaining about their poor business every fourth car was a Mercedes. When we asked a waiter where they got their shrimp for their abundant dishes he advised, from Miami. Fortunately we had our sampan ride through the myriad of boats anchored in Aberdeen and enjoyed a meal at the famous Jumbo Floating Restaurant before a typhoon hit the area. Many offices were emptied and the employees sent home. I towered over the men rushing on the subway and across the Star Ferry, but this also meant that no clothing purchases would fit an American. We spent the time in the hotel on Kowloon playing bridge with other guests and then tried to sleep through the night with the crashing sounds of neon lights giving way to the 150 mile per hour winds. The buildings stood solid since their closeness doesn't allow much of a wind effect.

International Weekends did such a great job that we joined them the next year, 1984, for our second trip to Europe. This was now a chartered plane packed with more passengers heading for the Continent, where language is not such a barrier. We decided to only tour one country at a time, much easier on language, money exchange, learning the customs of the new country. We decided on Italy for this trip. For $900 per person, including airfare from Boston to Milan, plus all hotel rooms, ground transportation, and some meals, we couldn't beat the price.

Jim was still living in Coral Springs, Florida, working at Palm Aire condos; Diane was already a senior at Antilles, again president of her class and in the throes of college hunting. The school counselor at Antilles took seven seniors on a familiarization trip to ten colleges in ten days in October. It was the first trip to the States for some seniors and the first time for fall colors in New England for all of them. After they all caught colds when the temperature dipped into the thirties one night she started to consider warmer climates. We figured this was a good chance to get away so in September Jay and I had a delightful two weeks in Italy.

In April of 1984 Jay began his downward slide of losing his sight. It started with detached retinas in both eyes, which was sudden and unexpected. He had no blow to the head or accident, just an inherited eye weakness from his Dad. Over the Easter school holidays we had moved into a three bedroom rental condo overlooking the harbor and Jay noticed a black crescent at the bottom of his vision, which was the retina detaching at the top. He was on a plane to Miami and the Bascom Palmer Eye Institute on the Tuesday after Easter and they operated in an emergency situation on Wednesday. The hospital did not let him retrieve his suitcase from his rental car. He had to call friends, the Smiths, to bring his bag from the car. I reached him as they were ready to take him to the operating room.

We were so impressed with the job that International Weekends did on the trip to Japan that we booked a two week vacation with them again in 1984 but this time to Europe. We flew to Boston where we were to start our trip to Italy. We rented a car and drove to Merrimack, New Hampshire to see the magnificent Budweiser Clydesdale horses. These huge horses are strong, weight about a ton, have beautiful coloring, and live for about twenty years. Our homes should be as clean as was their barn, no odor, no droppings, each with an attendant groomsman.

Flying to Europe can't compare to the half-filled plane to Seoul, where we could stretch out, and be treated like royalty by the attendants. This charter plane to Europe was crammed full with Americans. Milan is a bustling metropolis with large department stores, an extravagant glass galleria or shopping mall, and the Duomo, a cathedral. It seems like every town has a Duomo. The one in Milan has over two hundred white marble statues in its pinnacles. We would have loved to hear a concert or see an opera in the world-renowned, magnificent, opera house, La Scala, but we were there in the daytime. We saw Leonardo daVinci's Last Supper, under restoration for many years now, and the pictures of the miracle that spared the painting during World War II when the rest of the building was rubble from bombings—yet this wall stood. Leonardo started this painting at the end of the 15th century. It was the back wall of a dining hall in a monastery with the kitchen located behind the wall. The monks feared that the heat of the kitchen would damage the painting but it was more the artist's selection of methods that deteriorated the painting quickly plus abuse over the centuries.

It was a pleasure to be bussed everywhere in comfort where both could enjoy the view not just the passenger. We lunched in Verona where we saw the famous balcony featured in the beloved Shakespearian play, Romeo and Juliet. Then visited the first century Arena of pink marble, seating 25,000, still in use today because if its perfect acoustics.

Our next stop was incredible Venice, with its labyrinth of canals and very narrow streets. The city stretches across 117 islands. One can only marvel at the ingenuity of building a city in a marshy area, where the only mode of transportation is by boat. Early historians agree that the original population of Venice consisted of refugees from surrounding Roman cities. You expect a masked and cloaked figure to greet you around each corner. It is difficult to describe St. Mark's Square, with the romance of stringed instruments playing waltzes, with no amplification, under the stars, the hundreds of pigeons, or the Doge's Palace with its wealth of gilded rooms, altars, statues, where democracy reigned in the twelfth century. In the thirteenth century, The Republic of Venice, fearing fire and destruction of the mostly wooden buildings in the city tore down all the foundries in the city, forcing the glassblowers to center on the island of Murano. Over the years the craftsmen became so skilled that they became the elite of society. They could wear swords, were immune from prosecution from the Venetian state, and found their daughters married into the most affluent families, in exchange the craftsman were not allowed to leave the Republic.

We went on to the peace and silence of Assisi, an ancient walled city with St. Francis' little wooden chapel within the walls of the basilica, a truly holy place. You felt you could commune with the animals and flowers in this lovely spot on earth, just as the Saint did long ago. The gentle Saint born in Assisi founded the order of Franciscan monks. He is remembered as a lover of nature, even by non-Christians, with his preaching to a flock of birds becoming a legend of his life.

Our Italian/English guide excitedly told our group of a jousting contest that was taking place in a neighboring town of Foligno. We took the most adventurous of our crowd onto a local train and enjoyed one of the most memorable moments of our trip to Italy. It was the town's annual jousting festival. Ten exceptional horsemen from surrounding counties, dressed in seventeenth century costumes of velvet breeches, ruffled collars, white wigs of long locks, capes, and plumed hats, vied for their lady's hand. Each lady had a full court of knaves and ladies-in-waiting, all in velvet of different colors for each court. What a colorful spectacle and a thrilling exhibition of riding skill. The knights must ride a timed, figure eight course at full gallop and remove three decreasing size rings from a statues extended arm with their eight foot jousting pole. After the competition each court served seventeenth century food in the courtyards of various homes. It was a most delightful highlight of our trip with some serendipity thrown in.

From Assisi we went on to Naples, or Napoli, as the Italians say. There is no reason for anyone to go to Naples. We were warned of the mob of boys, no more than eight or nine years old, that are sure to surround you, distract you and then rob you. One merchant pointed at the square in Jay's pocket figuring it was a wallet and warned us that we would quickly lose it. The front desk alerted us that we had to walk in a group to dinner just a block from the dirty hotel. Drivers to the restaurant had to pay "protection money" to the crowd of boys to watch their car—most likely to keep the hoodlums from stealing everything not anchored down. We watched in awe as a nun, dressed in her black habit, glibly stepped off the curb and nonchalantly crossed the street completely ignoring the many lanes of traffic going helter-skelter in this busy metropolis. She must have figured she had someone very powerful watching over her.

When we visited the incredible Blue Grotto on the island of Capri the guide told us it obtains its special color from radioactivity plus the angle of the light entering the Grotto. It was quite different from the phosphorescence we know in the Caribbean waters. We had to lay flat in the rowboats as we entered the Grotto, a large sea water cave of immense size holding many rowboats. It was a surreal experience. In ancient times the waters of the Blue Grotto were thought to have mystical powers that included healing and prolonging youth.

The bus took us next to the ruins of Pompeii. This town was a bustling Roman city five centuries before Christ but in 79 AD Pompeii and its sister city, Herculaneum, were buried under 60 feet of ash from the eruption of Mount Vesuvius, looming nearby. The city was accidentally rediscovered in 1599. Herculaneum was not rediscovered for two more centuries when workmen were digging for the foundation of a summer palace for the king of Naples. How beautiful Pompeii must have been in its day with the main square paved in white marble and the buildings marble facaded. The population of wealthy Romans that vacationed in this resort city was about 25,000. It was a favorite city of Roman Emperors. Shops lined the streets filled with the finest silks and jewelry of the known world. We marveled at the castings of people where you could see and almost feel their agony in death. They seem to be stopped in their tracks, writhing in pain. We blushed at the suggestive statues used in the breeding rooms that were meant to entice the slaves to have sex and breed more slaves. The brick streets were rutted from the chariot wheels, and the pipes bringing water from the aquaducts to the home were taxed according to size so the homes had minimal size pipes and then gathered at the Baths for hygiene. Easily malleable lead was used to supply the water. The lead pipes were later believed to be one of the reasons for the Fall of the Roman Empire.

Then, at last, Rome, the Eternal City, where weeks are necessary to explore this fascinating ancient city, built on seven hills and located on the Tiber River. The history of this capital and most populous city of Italy spans over two and a half thousand years. We walked the Appian Way under the pines of Rome and could hear the faint echoes of Roman legions marching back to the Eternal City. The Appian Way was built by the Romans in 312 BC. It was one of the earliest and strategically most important roads. The Roman army to be successful needed good roads for easy access and supply from Rome. They became master of road construction and eventually roads led to every part of the Empire. In the catacombs we felt engulfed by the ghosts of thousands of early Christians buried there. We heard their screams and in the immense Coliseum could hear the roar of lions. The ruins are located just east of the Roman Forum. The building has been damaged by earthquakes and stone robbers. One wonders how this colossal structure was built in the first century without the benefit of cranes and heavy equipment. You could sit for hours in the ruins of the Palatine Hill and imagine the Senators debating in the Roman Senate, the most enduring institutions of the Empire.

One cannot be in Rome without a tour of the Vatican, seat of the Roman Catholic Church, home to the Pope, and keeper of the priceless art treasures of the Church in the Basilica and the Museum. A full day can hardly touch the highlights even with a private guide. An elderly gentleman approached us to ask if we needed someone to explain the wonders of the Basilica and Museum. His English was so impeccable that we couldn't resist hiring him. This guide obtained for me a rosary supposedly blessed by the Pope. He told us to just tell the guards that we were celebrating our anniversary. In this most holy place of Christendom we were telling a little fib. We could also have seen the Pope if he hadn't inconsiderately been out of the country. St. Peters's Basilica, the most majestic building in the world, can hold three St. Patrick's Cathedrals of New York City, end on end inside the structure plus 150,000 people. The floor was marked with the distances that the major cathedrals of the world would reach.

In one of the side altars stood Michelangelo's Pieta. I can't find the words to describe the beauty of this work of his. At the time we were in Rome we could see her without a glass encasement. A deranged person some years later defaced her and she has since been encased to protect her.

This Basilica is the burial site of St. Peter and many other Popes have been interred here as well. The most famous feature of this massive church is the double dome, also designed and built by Michelangelo. We climbed the narrowing stairs between the two domes to a roof area that delivered a full view of the Vatican Square. And then we enjoyed the Sistine Chapel painted by this same artist and other great Renaissance artists of the time. The Chapel is also the site of the Papal Conclave, where a new Pope is elected.

Before returning home from Rome we also visited Florence and the magnificent statue of David, sculpted by Michelangelo. The two days we had in Florence was just not enough time to explore this city. The craftsmanship of the jewelers demanded admiration, especially with prices much lower than in the States. A good example of serendipity was a list of places to see in Italy that I obtained from a salesman that I met at the desk of Secret Harbor when we were selling condos at the beach property. This man traveled often to Italy purchasing leather goods for his store. He told us about a restaurant that had wonderful food. We entered through the beaded curtain and sat at the picnic tables along with locals that asked us how we ever found their particular favorite hiding place. It was not a tourist attraction. We just hope, if and when we return to Florence that we can find it again and that it still exists. So much changes over the years.

CHAPTER 28

The following year, 1985, Jay was busy keeping his water treatment consultation business going while also building a vacation villa that we named Sand Dollar because it was the only home on St. Thomas that had a beautiful sand beach. Sand Dollar was located on the world-famous Magen's Bay. I tell everyone that asks how we managed to build such a magnificent villa—that we sold the kids and bought the beach. We procrastinated for as long as the building permit allowed, three years, before we had the nerve to go to our bank for a construction loan. The project was on-the-job training for Jay although he did supervise the building of Treetops a few years earlier.

We were just in the cistern stage when, during a very wet season; a large boulder rolled down the steep hill and broke the cistern wall. On this island, by law, everyone must build ten gallons of storage capacity for every square foot of roof area. The law specified fifteen gallons is required if there is an apartment. Because of this law our business, Water Management, was kept busy with the testing of the drinking water collected from our roofs. Often birds liked to warm themselves on the roofs so we became experts in handling our most precious commodity on the island, water. The luxuries like wine and liquor were inexpensive but necessities, like water and electricity, cost us dearly.

Sand Dollar had 27,000 gallons of storage capacity. Sort of like a basement full of water. The law also stated that no bathroom could be located over the cistern in case of pipe leaks. The cistern was usually situated under the living room. Island houses always faced the view so they were entered in the rear, and in an ideally built home, the view was visible from the entranceway. When you ran out of water you could always have it trucked to the site and pumped into the cistern. The cost was about six cents a gallon so most toilets had a sign over them that read: "On this island in the sun, we don't flush for number one."

Sand Dollar, with its special beach, was to be a vacation villa that would be rented out by the week. It was not going to be a Bed and Breakfast because I said I would not be getting up and making breakfasts for anyone. They could make their own meals. We rented the house by the week, providing the TV, furnishings, spices, kitchenware, barbeque, but no groceries. Each bedroom in this villa would need its own bathroom. We added a deck and an outdoor shower to the two master bedrooms at the top level. The house was built on a 45 degree slope so it had to be stepped down the hill with the main area consisting of two levels. The two master bedrooms were at the entrance door, a third bedroom, with its own bathroom, was on the living level that had the kitchen, dining area, half bath and laundry room. There was also a one bedroom apartment on the lowest level, just a few steps away from the pool with a gazebo to hide from the sun. The 76 wooden steps leading down to the beach had to be built by hand with the men carrying the concrete for the supporting pillars down the hill in buckets.

Building a large home on a small island leads to many frustrations, just as in planning a special dinner for guests. The island might be completely out of a necessary ingredient, and it was up to the cook to find a proper substitution. The same was true in construction. The lumber yards might be out of 2x4s one week or even worse the dregs were always sent to the islands. We had to inspect each piece of lumber and often had to special order. We frequently had to fly to the States and do a "power shopping" trip. There was an earlier time when, during my two years of living in the States, I could find a needed item, buy a plane ticket to the islands, which was good for a year, check the cargo in at curbside, make a reservation and then call Jay to let him know the flight I was booked on, so he could pick up the cargo from the baggage carousel on the island. But then we had a cruise ship high-jacking where a passenger was killed. That ended our free dinners and shows aboard the cruise ships. We once could slip the maître d'a twenty dollar bill and proceed to dinner and the Vegas style show. The ships then became very safety conscious, or at least they had an excuse to stop all visitors. Then several planes were redirected to other countries by terrorists or madmen, which brought a screeching halt to our easy cargo shipping plan.

Jim was still living in Coral Springs with his two roommates during this year and Diane, having graduated from Antilles school, again as president of her class, was invited to spend the summer in Geneva, Switzerland with a friend that had come to Antilles school to polish up her English. Clair wanted to become a travel agent. In Europe they must be fluent in several languages. Dad and I thought it was a great chance for her to be immersed in other cultures of the world.

In October she spent time in the south of France visiting Mrs. Hartman in St. Tropez, France. Mrs. Hartman had been a substitute teacher of French at Antilles and made the classes so interesting to the students that Diane wanted to go to school in France. When her visit in St. Tropez was over Mrs. Hartman drove her to Nice, helped her settle into an apartment with another student, Nicole, and made sure she was enrolled in the University of Nice, to begin her studies in linguistics for the February term.

The two girls learned to live on their own with some assistance from their Moms and Dads. They learned that France has many cheeses but not a good cheddar, that they had to walk to town every day to buy their fresh bread and produce, that their refrigerator did not hold much food, and lastly to turn off the lights to keep their expenses down. The two girls hitchhiked all over Europe and including sneaking onto the Eurail trains. Mom would have worried if she had known about this mode of transportation.

In early April Muammar Gadhafi of Libya was blamed for the bombing of a discotheque in West Berlin frequented by the U.S. military. The bombing killed two soldiers and injured more than 230 people including dozens of military personnel. After diplomatic efforts failed, President Ronald Reagan ordered the attack on Tripoli, with the help of the Royal Air Force of Great Britain. Gadhafi retaliated with the bombing of Pan Am flight 103 from Heathrow in London to JFK in New York. That incident killed all passengers, crew and some residents in Lockerbie, Scotland in 1988. This was a good example of how wars begin or can escalate.

It was June when Jay and I decided to visit Diane in Nice right after the United States bombed Tripoli. We were very uncomfortable with the landing in Nice where soldiers paraded up and down the terminal with machine guns casually slung over their shoulders. It reminded us of Venezuela where very young men, actually boys, carried similar lethal weapons.

We rented a car and drove throughout the eastern half of France, having no idea that the country was as large as Texas. We drove one night to Monte Carlo where the Rolls Royce limos were lined up, drivers twiddling their thumbs until they could pick up their sheiks. We marveled at the high stakes in the casino. It was easy for one to forget the value of the chips that were usually $25,000 each.

We saw the Grand Canyon area of France, toured perfume factories and medieval villages, tasted wine in the Caves of Bordeaux, toured chateaus in the Loire Valley, rode to the top of the Eiffel Tower, and marveled at the Versailles' opulence. We enjoyed the Louvre although the Mona Lisa was a disappointment but not the Venus de Milo. We people-watched on the Champs Elysee while drinking eight dollar glasses of beer all the time marveling at the fortitude of the gendarmes trying to sort out traffic around the Arch de Triomphe. We were told that you could circle the Arch many times before working your way to the exterior circle to exit.

We ate too much cheese and drank gallons of wine, reveled in fresh berries, and finally gorged on sausages and beer in Strassburg. Jay had to return to work so we took him to the airport in Paris while I stayed on for five more weeks with Diane. We felt like royalty overnighting at the d'Esclimont Castle, then stayed with relatives of Diane's Nice roommate in Solothurn, Switzerland. The Bogarts family had taken Diane and Nicolle to their cabin in the Alps during spring break and taught Diane to ski, as the mother and father were both ski instructors. She had seen her first snow while staying in Geneva at Chamonix, France. Chamonix is a picture postcard village with a river gushing through the town. Snow tickled our noses when we ascended the mountain on the chair lift even though it was June. Diane enjoyed her sojourn in France but she said the country, while lovely, was just too full of French people.

My mission was also to bring my daughter back home with me. She had become infatuated with her French instructor who was a Muslim from a small village in Morocco. I told my blue-eyed, blond Scandinavian daughter that she would not look good in a full length black burka with only her blue eyes showing and sitting on the dirt floor eating with her hands.

We quickly entrenched her in our duplex with Jim and Doris and promptly enrolled her in the Broward Community College. It was good to get her feet back on U.S. soil. She is taking Spanish and tutoring French but hasn't decided on a major. After living in France for eighteen months she certainly should be able to tutor French.

CHAPTER 29

The building of Sand Dollar was a major project that took all of our weekends and evenings for over three years while others in my real estate office enjoyed their leisure time at the beaches. We were teased often about working on this monstrosity without a free moment to ourselves. We were harassed relentlessly until we were able to finish the villa, furnish it, and were planning to obtain bookings at $4200 per week in the wintertime. Then the other realtors respected us.

We couldn't take any extended vacation trips while we worked on the house. However, we helped Jay's Dad celebrate his 92nd birthday in February; then in June we spent time at our time-share condo on the beach at Estero Island for a week of golfing. In September we were scheduled for laser eye surgery for Jay because his medication was not controlling the glaucoma pressure but when we arrived at the Bascom Palmer Eye Institute in Miami, his pressure was normal so he did not need the surgery. The next month, October, his Dad was scheduled for gallbladder surgery but suffered congestive heart failure when they were wheeling him into the operating room. We were on a plane within two hours and spent ten days with him. I slept on a cot in his room to help him through the nights. He recovered with flying colors, but I doubt I had anything to do with it.

We were able to sell the duplex in Coral Springs this year, 1988. Jim was working in Miami for a landscape maintenance company;

Diane was in school at the Art Institute in Ft. Lauderdale. She wanted to pursue a career in Interior Design until she learned that she would have to apprentice for five years before she could flex her own wings.

Coral Springs was too far west for either of them to drive so we were happy to sell the duplex that year despite the fact that it held many happy memories for us. It was from the duplex that I took a creative writing course from a gentleman in his nineties, Bill Baxter, who retired from his law profession at seventy years of age. Bill soon became bored staying home, and went back to school to learn how to teach creative writing. He was teaching a night class for senior citizens and accepted me in the class although I was only in my forties and did not qualify as a senior. The course was several weeks long and cost a total of $2.00.

This year was another boom year in real estate for the islands. Sales have been doing exceedingly well; in fact, we are running out of inventory. We have been able to tell customers that the prices are rising about 10% a year. Tourists are buying condos in the range of $200,000 to $400,000 with our average home running about $250,000. There has also been an explosion in new hotel construction which is keeping Jay very busy with his sewage plant installations. In addition he has the weekend job of finishing Sand Dollar. By late 1988 we were in the roof raising stage of the house and building retaining walls to hold the hill in place. Jay was reluctant to fill the pool with water. He was afraid it would slip down the hill when full.

The lot was so steep that I remember tying a rope around the waist of our gardener as he planted ground cover to keep the soil from ending up on the white sand beach. We always had help around to clean this large vacation villa and a gardener, Thomas, to plant. We did remember to sit down when we planted a coconut tree so it would not grow too tall, per a previous gardener's instruction. And by gosh, it always remained a short tree. There were banana trees at the sewage treatment plant near the overflow for they needed lots of water; cashew nut trees, gathered from shoots at Shibui Hotel or Little Dix Bay on Virgin Gorda. The trees were planted on the hillsides. It was so easy to start plants in the tropics. You could root them in water or merely stick them in the ground and they would grow profusely. Most of the ground cover, Wandering Jew, was picked from areas along the roadway where it seems to be an invasive plant, but spreads easily. It is also known as Purple Heart or Purple Queen for a more dignified name.

After selling the duplex we bought a two bedrooms, two baths, condominium for Diane to finish her education at the Art Institute. The condo was a shorter drive to school plus we wanted a place in Florida for our power shopping trips. The tri-rail train, a few blocks away from the condo, drops Jay off in Miami for a short walk to Bascom Palmer Eye Institute and the Veteran's Hospital. We passed up a three week booking for Sand Dollar over Christmas because both Jim and Diane will be with us for the holidays.

I was in Florida in September of 1989 to help Diane get the new condo ready for occupancy. We were busy shopping for furniture and were in the midst of tiling the floors when we heard that Hurricane Hugo would hit St. Croix. St. Thomas would feel the powerful northeast quadrant of this category 5 storm.

When prospective buyers asked about hurricanes the realtors were always able to say that a hurricane had not hit St. Thomas directly for over fifty years that is until 1989 when Hurricane Hugo plowed through the Leeward Islands leaving Montserrat and Guadeloupe in shambles then hit St. Croix, some thirty five miles to the south of St. Thomas. Hugo hit St Croix directly and went on to Puerto Rico and South Carolina. It was the costliest storm on record in the United States up to that date. In lives there were 50 fatalities and in dollars about $10 billion.

St. Croix lost thousands of power poles and St. Thomas, which was damaged almost as heavily, lost nearly as many. Several States sent entire power line crews along with their trucks to the islands to help our local power company establish electricity once again to the homes and businesses.

Living in a 3rd world country (I sometimes called it a 4th world) we were accustomed to regular power outages. After Hugo, however, we were without power for eight weeks. Our lives consisted of waiting in lines, at the gas stations to buy fuel, at the FEMA trucks to get water, or the grocery stores to buy ice or some canned goods. There were no phone lines either. Jay was able to stay in touch by climbing to the top of the Peterburg Hill to make a phone call to me in Florida. The local V.I. Telephone Company ran underwater cables from this location to Florida so he was able to call and tell me that he was alive and well and that it was imperative that I ship a small generator to St. Thomas. I ran to Home Depot and had them immediately send a 6-KW generator to Riviera Beach. The Albert Walters Construction Co. had a ship each week leaving from that port with hotel supplies.

I was able to return to St. Thomas about a week later when the airport finally opened. Upon landing I thought the island looked like a nuclear bomb had hit it. There were no leaves on the trees. Only the center shoots of the coconut trees were green, which meant they would live. The island worried about the loss of the hummingbird population. One wonders where all the birds hide during a storm.

We began our eight week ordeal of waiting in lines, bathing in cold water on the pool deck with a hose run from the cistern outflow (the pool deck was below the cistern so we had running water). We could dip a bucket of water directly from the cistern to flush the toilet. Our cooking was done on the outdoor propane grill, we read by candlelight, slept on air mattresses with our noses to the screens so we could get a breath of fresh air, and then woke up at first light to start the process all over again. With Jay in residence our apartment below suffered little damage. The apartment had drop-down canvas awnings to keep out the rain. There were no windows in the sitting area of the apartment; none were needed in the perfect climate of St. Thomas. Hourly, he had to risk being blown down the steep hill, to retie the awnings. They were banging so hard against the concrete that I was surprised they weren't in shreds. The storm lasted for hours with the wind blowing the tops of the waves into spindrift that disappeared into the haze.

You could not see the mile across the bay. Jay said the noise was like standing next to a jet engine. There were winds of 140 mph and gusts up to 240 mph.

Our power line crews were making great progress until October when an earthquake devastated San Francisco. Many FEMA men and line crews were called to help a much larger city than Charlotte Amalie. We were lucky to have a generator that operated a few lights and the refrigerator, but no fans—it felt like an eternity.

The year ended on an upbeat note for we had both Jim and Diane spending the Christmas holidays with us for 1988. It had been many years since we had all been together for the holidays, seven years since Jim has been on St. Thomas.

CHAPTER 30

We lived on construction power in the apartment for several years while building the villa but once Sand Dollar had its occupancy permit we unwisely rented the property long term to a couple who we thought were going to be good tenants. They had a five year old son so we figured they would be a stable couple and with us living on the premises there would be no late night parties. Kiki, his significant other, told us Yosef had so much clout that he could literally move the markets. He would buy large blocks of stock in a failing company and then sue the administrators for mismanagement. The only thing this couple taught us was how expensive it can be for legal fees.

We figured that against this dynamo we needed a good lawyer so we hired an attorney who had just left the bench, figuring he knew his law. After about $10,000 in legal fees, Hank finally repossessed our home on May 31st, 1990. Yosef had the gall to change the combination locks on the built-in safe in the floor of the master bedroom. A gardener we had clearing the property, knew the layout of the house and with a couple of assistants tried to break into the safe, unsuccessfully. Yosef never told us, the owners, about changing the combination. It took another locksmith and another fee to admit us into our own safe.

The Feinsteins' callousness became evident when the couple down the road, who had lost the roof on their home, asked to stay at Sand

Dollar, which was a more substantial building. They had two small children in tow when they asked the Feinsteins. Our tenants gave them an emphatic NO. I had sold Carl and Laura Downey the home they resided in but it was not built out of concrete and block like Jay had built Sand Dollar.

Yosef then sued us for not being able to provide power to his rented home. Of course, the entire island was without power, even the hospital. Hugo had hit on September 17th; a few months after the Feinsteins occupied the villa. We decided after the lawsuit to never rent out the vacation villa long term again. We would take only weekly bookings, and certainly not to sleazeballs like Yosef. However, I still worked with the man after the lawsuit for he also bought a large piece of vacant land on Peterborg, known as Little Magen's Bay. The two acres of land, with its own beach like at Sand Dollar, was close to magnificent Magen's Bay. Magen's had been voted by National Geographic as one of the ten most beautiful beaches in the world. The previous owners of Little Magen's Bay, however, were in jail so the sale couldn't finalize until they were sentenced and the U.S. government possessed the land for it was purchased with drug money. This sale was very large commissions for me for brokers were getting 10% on vacant land sales. The property sold for $3,000,000, which presented no problem for Yosef.

After the purchase of this property my boss had invited the Feinsteins to an after-work party over the holidays. Yosef arrived decked out in a tuxedo and Kiki in a floor-length, low cut gown. Everyone asked if they were the entertainment for the evening. The rest of us were all in casual work clothes.

I have met many an odd couple with hotel operations, real estate sales, and villa rentals. The diamond merchant from New York was so typically Jewish; he had the curly locks and black hat and clothes of a typical Hasidic rabbi. I could not reach him from sundown on Friday until the Sabbath for he was not allowed to pick up a telephone or even push the buttons on the elevators. Some hotels have the elevators programmed to stop at every floor to accommodate their Jewish guests.

This man was considering buying a large building on Main Street and turning it into a diamond cutting display and sales area. It would have succeeded for there are millions of tourists filling up the cruise ships calling in the harbor at St. Thomas.

There was also a young girl who owned an Inn in New England. She almost bought a local hotel with an adjoining residence, the famous Blackbeard's Castle, until her attorney stopped her. He couldn't believe she would pay so much for a small piece of property on a tiny island. She reneged after we visited her spacious Inn on acres of land. We were trying to convince her to proceed with the purchase, but her attorney won.

Our first short term rental of Sand Dollar was a wedding on the pool deck. The bride's Daddy had oil wells in Texas so the younger sister of the bride said she also wanted to marry at Sand Dollar when her time came. We worried along with the parents when the minister who was to perform the ceremony had trouble finding the villa. He arrived an hour late to the dismay of the grandparents, all dressed up and baking in the tropical sun.

Many guests rebook year after year. We watched the children growing up, many sleeping in dresser drawers the first year they come as tiny babies. We had two families book every Christmas until their teenage boys wanted more activity, read girls. They then went to South Beach in Miami for the boys' sake. We saw two gay fellows come back many times. We enjoyed a couple from Russia who operated the McDonald's and Baskin Robbins in Moscow. There were attorneys involved in the Savings and Loan fiasco, and Saudi Arabians coming in white bourkhas after the Gulf War. Jay was to never look at them lest he see an exposed ankle or knee. The women must have gone swimming in full dress, although these were tropical weight and filmy bourkhas. The poor things could not go to their villa on the Red Sea because of the war nor did they choose their apartment in London. They came to Sand Dollar but we would never have them again. They were accustomed to having servants wait on them. We found diapers thrown down the hill from the pool deck. They asked us if they could butcher a lamb on the premises. After an emphatic NO they settled on a goat from a farmer on the east end of the island. It was probably one that wandered the roads eating everything in sight for the guests offered a plate to us and, while tasty, it was very chewy and inedible, in our opinion. These Arabs came to us through a well-publicized Canadian broker. While they were told to use a credit card to make phone calls, they used the entire damage deposit on two phone calls to Saudi Arabia. Then we had trouble collecting the deposit from the broker.

The villa was earning her keep so in March of 1990 we took a family vacation to visit the Bogarts in Switzerland. It would be Diane's third occasion in Europe but Jim's first experience with snow, where he could actually make a snowball rather than see it on a distant mountain top. At the last minute Jay could not get away from his job of installing a treatment plant at the new Elysian Hotel so I was the only one who got to appreciate the children on the trip. I enjoyed the panic on Jim's face for it was his first time on skis but he did quite well, considering. I took many movies and marveled at his sister taking him on the advanced slopes in Arosa, a popular Swiss resort. He did arrive at the bottom in one piece, in spite of his sister. We drove to St. Tropez one day just to say we were there. There was nothing more delightful, however, than to ski downhill from the door of the Bogarts' chalet in the Alps; then when tired ski back to the cabin from the top of the hills.

We learned that an Alp, to the Swiss, is really the grassy meadow high in the mountains where cheese is made. Each farmer receives cheese according to how much milk his cows produce. The whey is then given to the pigs so both animals are kept at an Alp. We learned that we could just bury the beer bottles in the snow outside the back door, that you don't read and dilly-dally on the cold seat in the unheated room of the toilet, that it was glorious to open your eyes every morning to the Piz Beverin mountain towering over the chalet with its crown of snow, that it was really warm on the glassed-in back porch, and that a feather bed was indeed warm and cozy, once the feathers absorbed your body heat.

Swiss law does not allow any new structures to be built in the Alps so this cabin will stay in the family for generations. People are taking barns, feeding stations, any type of building and converting it to a livable structure. Henrietta's husband, Evert, is what we would call a Ranger. He must find any wounded deer and bring it in, thus the Bogarts eat only venison that he has hunted or rescued. Every male citizen in the country is in the Armed Services and must report yearly for duty and training, plus have a rifle at home. The Swiss are totally prepared for any emergency, but with the world's treasures hidden in their bank coffers they don't anticipate emergencies. The canton (state) even provides firewood along the roadsides for anyone to take home. Each young man, when he reaches his eighteenth birthday and completed high school, must serve two years in the military. At that time he is given a rifle, taught how to use it, and must keep it at his home.

In April Jay was scheduled for cataract surgery so we went to Bascom Palmer Eye Institute again. Due to his detached retinas some years before, Dr Hodapp's assistant said that it was the worst operation she had ever seen, with the vitreous solution coming out of the eyeball.

The end of May we repossessed Sand Dollar agreeing that we would never rent the villa out again long-term. We had learned our lesson, an expensive one. In November I attended the National Realtors Convention in New Orleans having a chance to visit with Harry and Leslie Fick, whom we met in the Bahamas and were our financial angels. They lent us the money to build Treetops, our first home on St. Thomas.

The end of the year had two joyous occasions. Diane graduated from the Art Institute in Ft. Lauderdale. She did very well in her studies, and is looking forward to some full time work before she possibly continues with any further studies. Jim called and told us that he was marrying Sally Harvey and that they were pregnant already.

We were elated. When Jim was a baby at his foster mother's home he cried so hard that he crushed a testacle. We were told at the time that he might not be able to produce progeny and if there was a problem psychologically then an aluminum gonad could be inserted. Marrying during the holidays gave us the opportunity to visit with the Greblicks in St. Petersburg at the same time. It was Sally's second marriage but Jim's first. Sally, who was also an adopted child, had the large wedding with all the trimmings when she married her high school sweetheart against her parent's wishes.

Sand Dollar's first short-term rental was a wedding. Daddy had oil wells in Texas so the bride's younger sister said she also wanted to marry at Sand Dollar when her time came.

$\mathcal{C}$HAPTER 31

The following year, 1992, Jay and I flew off to Switzerland for a week of skiing after some twenty five years away from the sport. The Bogarts graciously let us use their chalet in the Alps, where you can literally ski from the cabin doorsteps. We had a wonderful time but on the last day of skiing, the weather warmed up, the snow got wet and heavy, my binder did not release and I fell. I could hear the bone twist and snap. A ski patroller immediately placed his skis into an x slightly uphill to warn the other skiers. I was taken down the slope on a sled with two patrollers controlling my descent, put in an ambulance and carted off to the hospital in Tschappina, a small town with a population of only 150 souls. It was a town near a ski area where the doctors know how to handle broken bones. The only problem was that it was in the German speaking part of Switzerland, and I knew no German. There were only a few people in the hospital that could speak any English. The doctors always found someone who could translate for me.

There are four languages spoken in Switzerland, German, Italian, French and Romanish, depending on what nation borders the various parts of Switzerland. There is no such thing as a Swiss written language; you speak either German, Italian or French. In Tschappina, however, Romanish and Portuguese are the second and third languages.

My experience in this German speaking hospital was most interesting. The breakfasts consisted of European styles with meat, cheese, course bread, and always delicious yoghurt. I remember lifting the metal cover on one dinner and finding a ham hock adorned with so much fat that I could not even look at the hock, much less taste it. The church choir always came around on Sundays and serenaded the patients after church. Of course, they were all German songs. This was such a nice treat for the patients.

Once I could handle the stairs with my crutches I could come home. I left in nine days with just an ace bandage wrapped around the broken bone. The break was a torsion twist and I was advised by the Swiss doctors to have the plate removed after 18 months, or so. Henrietta picked me up from the hospital and drove me to her son's apartment in Zurich. I had a tough time climbing the many stairs to his upstairs apartment. She then drove me to the airport for my return from Zurich.

I arrived home just on time to welcome son Jim, his new wife, Sally, and her parents, the Harveys, who came to see how the other half of the family lives. We were invited to spend the day at the Virgin Grand Hotel in St. John with the owners/builders of the hotel, Harry and Sarah Walters. They treated us to dinner after an afternoon of using the large hotel pool or their smaller condo pool. I believe the day impressed the Harveys, but they didn't say anything about it. I remember but never mentioned to the Harvey's that when the hotel had its grand opening, I had too many champagne glasses with strawberries. It must have been a hangover from the strawberries, or I am told it is the bubbles in the champagne that give you such a headache.

Our greatest blessing and joy in 1991 was becoming grandparents. Jim and Sally had a son, Jimmy, whom we try to see as often as possible. We were scheduled to be in Florida for the Christmas holidays but we were booked on Panam and it died. It reminded us of buying a lifetime membership in Eastern's Ionosphere Club. Then Eastern died.

In June of this year Jay had his first hand surgery for dupuytrins contracture. Dupuytrins is a disease that hardens the palm of the hand and curves the fingers toward the palm. In 1991 they cut the palm open and allowed it to heal from the inside outward. The palm had to be washed every day with peroxide. It was an awful sight to behold. He also required extensive therapy to straighten the fingers. He was able to stay in our condo at the Anchorage for Diane had moved to her friend's home to help Carol Williams, her island friend, care for her dying mother. Jay was able to walk the mile to the Tri-Rail to see his hand surgeon at the Vet's hospital in Miami, while I returned home to mind the store.

I was still on crutches in April when I wrote to our close friends from Ethyl Corporation days and said it was time to have another Pinochle Club meeting. I invited Cathy and Greg Heffelfinger and Jack and Laurie Oldenkamp, chemists that worked with us back in the 1950s. Cathy and Greg were the youngest in the group and met and married in those days. Jack and Laurie were the couple that had nine living children. They brought along their newly widowed sister-in-law, Jerry, who had married Jack's brother. There were so many good memories of parties shared with these friends. It had been twenty years since we had seen them, their kids had all grown up, and our aches and pains had started to set in. Little did I realize that I would be starting a tradition that would extend for years to come!

While the Pinochle Club was visiting we had a day booking for a wedding on the beach. The bride and groom arrived in a limousine that remained on the upper road for our driveway was too steep for such a long vehicle. It would hang up in the middle and be teetering precariously. Jay and I were witnesses for the ceremony on the beach. The couple then said we were welcome to use their limo while they relaxed and enjoyed Sand Dollar. We hiked to the limo and told Felix, the driver, to take us to the "Udder Delite" stand at the dairy for milk shakes.

When we were not riding in a luxurious limousine we piled into the back of Jay's pickup truck, on foam cushions to ease the bumps from the pot holes, and went down to see the Carnival Village and Parade in town. Pickups were a popular mode of transportation to haul work crews around the island. Jay and I had belonged to a Parade Troupe for many years and while Jay served drinks with a friend, Peter Leffelman, from a float set up as a bar, Lilly, Peter's wife, and I always danced down the streets, to the point where we got blisters on our feet. We enjoyed the bustle of every meeting as the end of April approached. Often the gatherings were "Eatin' Meetin's", where the ladies brought tasty island pot-luck dishes. Carnival was always held the last week of April and was the largest event after the Rio Carnival. The troupes took pride in making their own costumes and always hoped to win the coveted first prize. The judges sat on a balcony at the Grand Hotel overlooking the Post Office Square, in the middle of town. The Village, located in the parking lot next to Fort Christian, had hundreds of colorful booths where you could taste the delicacies of the Caribbean until you can no longer stuff johnny cakes, pates, chicken wings or callaloo, (spinach soup), into your stomach.

1991 was a bad year for college students to find work in Interior Design. Not one student in Diane's class has the promise of a job. The teachers did not alert the students that a five year apprenticeship is required to work in this field. By 1992 she was out of school for two years and still having trouble finding work in that field.

In February we were in Florida for our perpetual shopping trip for Sand Dollar and getting acquainted with our grandson, Jimmy. He, of course, is the most handsome, the smartest, the most delightful child, as everyone's grandchildren are to the grandparents. We enjoyed walking the few blocks and taking him to the Big Park where he could show off all his newly acquired skills. May found us in Tucson for our second annual Pinochle Club Reunion, where the Oldenkamps had moved. We even played a little pinochle at the weeklong festivities of good food, great company, a week of laughter and reminiscing. We enjoyed their new home, watched the sunset over the mountains, hiked the canyons, explored the Sequoia desert, picnicked on the mountaintop.

Sand Dollar was experiencing a good year. We now had repeat guests coming back for the third and fourth time. We have had composers, executives, oil brokers, ranchers, honeymooners, bridal couples married poolside or on the beach, babies, many children, friends, doctors, lawyers, but still no Indian Chiefs as yet, except for the Saudi sheiks and their harems, whom we would never book again. Jay had to hibernate for the week and not cast his eyes upon their women. Because of this they could swim only at night, most likely in the nude.

In September we spent another week in Florida then headed north to visit Garth and Doris Thomas in Connecticut and to see the wonders of Mother Nature with her spectacular changing of colors. It had been many years since we saw her display. Doris was also in real estate sales and when they bid higher than the listed price for a condominium at the Anchorage in St. Thomas I was amazed when they got the condo for the listing was with another office and they also had a cash buyer. The Thomases won the bid, however. We had to drive up to Vermont to see any color change, enjoying a night with Garth's parents and sampling pure maple syrup from this state. The crisp, dry weather convinced us that the cold climate was not for us anymore. Our blood was too thin after so many years in the tropics.

I brought a collection of colored leaves, various weeds, swamp grass, cattails home with me. I would have been placed in a funny jacket if anyone else besides our hosts had seen me ironing the treasures between sheets of wax paper to preserve them. This was Doris' suggestion, despite smoking up her home for a long time.

1992 and 1993 were poor years for the real estate market in St. Thomas, ever since Hurricane Hugo hit St. Croix in 1989. In 1993 Diane finally found a job in Interior Design with Home Depot. During October she transferred with the company to a new store in Reno, Nevada. It was a big change for her after flat Florida. Jim and Sally were busy raising Jimmy, now 2.5 years old and talking up a storm, and sending Jim back to Kaiser Academy to become an x-ray technician. He is going to school full time and working part time.

We are so proud of him for he is excelling in school after having such a hard time with his dyslexia. It now seems like little Jimmy will also have a learning problem.

Most of our off-island journeys were to visit family but we did get to Seattle to stay with Dave Scott, who sailed with us to the Bahamas before he went into the military service and the Gregs, whom we met in the Bahamas, at their new home in the San Juan Islands. Wendell took Jay out salmon fishing in such heavy fog that they found the fish with a fish finder and their way home via the marked buoys along with a GPS and a map.

The Gregs took us to see the spectacular Butchart Sunken Gardens on Vancouver Island. Mr. Butchart began making Portland cement in 1888. He came to the west coast because of the rich limestone deposits necessary for cement production. When the quarry was exhausted in 1909 Mrs. Butchart began building the Sunken Gardens. The gardens have since been designated a national historic site of Canada. The Gardens have become a popular tourist attraction for Vancouver Island.

CHAPTER 32

The following year, 1994, brought many changes to the Greblick family. The real estate market seemed to be turning around but mostly with local people trying to secure a piece of the rock. A few larger homes sold. We even had an offer on Sand Dollar but it was too low to consider. We became the typical seller that doesn't accept the first offer and then never ends up with another offer as good as the first.

We tried an even exchange of Sand Dollar for a three bedroom condo in Lake Tahoe, but it was hardly an even exchange. We had to buy some kitchen items like placemats and towels whereas at Sand Dollar we furnish the entire villa, down to the spices. But we had fun with the two couples we invited to spend the week with us, the Heffelfingers and the Oldenkamps. On the same trip we had a chance to visit Diane and the family she was rooming with. In June we were back in Florida to help baby Jimmy celebrate his 3rd birthday. In September we were off to visit the Bartleys on their ranch in the Sangre de Cristo Mountains. This time around Carl had Norwegian fjord horses that are smaller than normal but a strong horse breed. Their temperament is as friendly as a pet dog. They come running from the pastures to be petted, or better still, fed. The Bar-X-Bar ranch is surrounded by a million acres of National Forest so we love to spend time at the ranch while the Bartleys miss the Caribbean, they say, and will be visiting us in October.

Over the Labor Day weekend Diane surprised us and drove the 3000 miles from Reno to Ft. Lauderdale in three days. I don't know what the real fire was but she used the excuse that she missed her family and friends. She is back in the condo that we bought for her to attend the Art Institute. In the meantime Jim and Sally moved north to Vero Beach with Sally's job. Jim was working in a Ft. Pearce hospital handling two double shifts on the weekends so he could babysit Jimmy during the week while Sally tended to her moneyed clients.

Over Thanksgiving we had illustrious guests staying at Sand Dollar. Jay came into my office one day at Remax and said the Vice President wanted to stay at Sand Dollar. My response was the Vice President of what? When he said the United States I fell off my chair. It seems that a lawyer on Vice-President Gore's staff had spent a vacation on St. Thomas. The Gores wanted to try something different rather than going back to the family farm in Carthage, Tennessee. They would only be at Sand Dollar from Wednesday to Sunday. We began a week of inquiries and investigations of us and our backgrounds. We were asked for our social security numbers, our birthdates, and our children's social security numbers and their birthdates, before their Attorney Rob Lang committed to the short stay at Sand Dollar. I heard from Tipper's social secretary that she wanted to rent a convertible for their four children. I advised against it. I also said the stretch limousine they wanted to ship down would not be able to handle our steep driveway. Following the investigations into our background, we had a week of physical inspection of the building itself including opening the safe and cistern covers. Jay was required to lock his registered pistol in the safe during their visit. We were surprised at how thorough the building inspection was. There were motion detection sensors installed on the spotlights that lit up the stairs leading to the beach. I suppose the agents had to worry about access from the water. Doctor Abbott's house next door was rented as the command center for the Vice President. For the privacy of the Gore family we had to leave the premises and spend the four days at the Frenchman's Reef Hotel.

On a tropical island you can wait for weeks to have a telephone installed. In this case we had one in three days with the lines run across the roof—it would be so easy to cut the lines and deny the Vice President access to the world.

Every restaurant we suggested was inspected as well as an escape route planned for the family. I am sure the chefs were inspected with a secret service agent watching the chef in the kitchen during the preparation of the meals. We surmised that only about 40 secret service agents travel with the Vice President or the First Lady. The country can only protect the President with so much more security, even when he lands for a few minutes.

We met the lead agent, Cathy Mackenzie, who was on the Vice President's detail. She had been trained as a policewoman, has trained other police forces, and now has been transferred to Europe, where she is in charge of a large area of Europe. We have kept in touch with Cathy through the years via emails. There are some people you meet that you feel you have known forever.

I wrote the following note for the Gore family and left it on the kitchen counter for them:

November 22, 1994
Dear Vice President Gore and Family:
We are pleased and honored that you have chosen our villa, SAND DOLLAR, to celebrate this Thanksgiving holiday. We hope you will enjoy our special retreat as much as our other guests, some now returning for their 5th and 6th visit.

Perhaps you will come back to relax to the sound of Magen's Bay waves lapping the shore; marvel at the glorious sunsets reflecting on the water; fall asleep to the chirp of the tree frogs or awake to the morning call of the doves or thrushes. The banana quits (our yellow breasted "national bird") will demand your attention if their sugar bowl or water bath is empty.

The hummingbirds will whiz by your ears to ask you to refill their feeder. Resident iguanas will ignore you when they come to feast on the hibiscus flowers at the pool deck. Don't be surprised if they drink at the pool or dive in for a swim from the tourist tree (the one that is always "red and peeling").

You will see butterflies swarming the blossoming trees and even exploring the house. Sadly, some will die because they cannot find their way out again. Please pick them up otherwise a battalion of ants will marck in to carry them away—or any morsel of food dropped on the counters or floor. Beware of the thrushes who will fly right into the kitchen to test any fruit or steel the meat from your sandwich.

Watch the water for turtles, sting rays, schools of monnows, tarpon and pelicans diving for supper in the late afternoon. Feed the small tropical fish at the rock outcroppings with bread that you must take down to the water in a zip loc bag so it doesn't fall apart before you reach their home. In the rocks look for the puffer fish who swells up like a porcupine when you startle him. Swim out to the coral heads and you will see sea cucumbers, giant slugs, creeping along the sand bottom in twenty feet of water. Occasionally you might even spot a grouper or, if lucky a sea biscuit. Stand waist deep in the water and dig your toes in the sand a couple of inches and you will find sand dollars, mostly in the late afternoon. They are brown when alive and turn white when bleached in the sun or Chlorox water. They make charming Christmas decorations when hung on the tree with red ribbon. Sand dollars must be transported carefully wrapped as they are very fragile. They can be strengthened with several coats of Elmer's glue.

Don't miss the milk shakes at Udder Delite (great name), the ice cream stand at the St. Thomas Dairy. They are famous for they use real liquor—a rum raisin shake actually has rum in it.

If you have any questions, need advice, or directions, please do not hesitate to call us at 774-9164. Enjoy your stay. We look forward to welcoming you back to Sand Dollar in the future and would appreciate it if you signed our guest book upon your departure. We understand you are here on vacation but would like very much to meet you and bid you goodbye, if at all possible.

Our best regards,
<u>Dolly and Jay Greblick</u>

And for their son, Albert, we left the following note:

Dear Albert,

Since we will not be here during your visit we would like to ask a special favor of you. Would you please feed our banana quits and hummingbirds? The quits are given sugar and water. I have left a plastic container of sugar with a scoop in it and an extra bag of sugar in the lower level near the feeder. If you need to open the extra bag be sure to keep the container and bag closed tightly or the ants will invade.

You might have to wask their dishes out when the sugar cades or the dish looks dirty and the water turns oily from their feathers. The water jug can be filled at the kitchen sink. They need water as much as the sugar.

I am also leaving sugar water in a quart jar for the hummers.

Thank you for taking care of our pets. We appreciate it and I am sure the birds will too.

Have a wonderful vacation.

<u>Mr. and Mrs. Greblick</u>

We did meet the Gores when Air Force 2 was leaving the island. Tipper said she wanted to come back to Sand Dollar and that she found the privacy she was looking for. She also said that Al was finally relaxing but it was already time to leave. I asked Rob to send a family picture to us and he did. The secret service agents swept down the runway before Air Force 2 was allowed to land, perhaps looking for debris like a bomb.

And when their first grandchild arrived I knitted a blanket for the baby and sent it to Tipper for her new offspring.

CHAPTER 33

The next year, 1995, Jay and I celebrated our 40th anniversary with a trip to New Zealand. We went in March, the beginning of their autumn season so we started in their cooler climate of the South Island and headed to their tropical North Island, wisely, for it started to snow as soon as we left the South Island. The flight was extremely long, more so, because we were using frequent flyer miles and had to overshoot our goal and spend a night in Sydney, Australia, then back track four hours of flight time to reach Christchurch, New Zealand. We happened to reach Sydney the night of their large gay celebration. There were over 350,000 gays from around the world participating in this parade/carnival. Not something we were interested in seeing. We had to stay quite a distance out of Sydney because of this gala event and as usual our cab fare out to the motel was quite different than the cab fare into the city. We did get to see the famous Opera House, the downtown wharf scene, the sidewalk entertainers and heard the haunting aborigine horns.

From St. Thomas, it took us the better part of a week to travel to and from New Zealand so we had little time to linger in any one spot. We opted not to rent their famous campers as friends had just returned from New Zealand and advised us that we would be much more comfortable staying in the reasonably priced motels, almost all with kitchens, However, it is perfectly safe to pull off the road and spend the night.

The roads are mainly two lanes, many just gravel so we were glad that we spent the extra money for windshield protection insurance as we had some pits in the windshield when we turned the car back in. The bridges on the road are only one lane wide so a traffic light is installed at each end of the bridge telling us who had the right of way to cross. If you saw a dozen cars in a day's drive it was a traffic jam.

The country is so diverse, friendly, interesting, uncrowded, super-clean and inexpensive—a great vacation destination. In this country there are only three million people and sixty million sheep. We were disappointed to see a Kentucky Fried Chicken and a Taco Bell restaurant in the most remote areas of the island. We enjoyed the farm raised venison more than the lamb. The stores have the same variety as we have in our supermarket but different brand names. At liquor stores you can bring your own bottle to fill with wine or liquor for a fraction of the price of bottles spirits. Bottles must be very scarce on these remote islands.

We traversed the southern island across the dry plains of Canterbury to the west Tasmanian Sea coastline, spent a day at the Doubtful Sound fjord. It was a spectacular sight and less touristy than Milford Sound. Before climbing on a bus for a trip to an underground power plant we had a llama spit at us across from the motel we had spent the night in. He was not a friendly creature. The underground power plant furnished electricity for an aluminum plant far to the south end of the island. Later on a boat trip on the Sound the captain edged the boat to where we could merely reach out and get a cupful of water from the pristine waterfalls.

We visited Queenstown, capital of bungee jumping. As senior citizens we could have jumped free (about $80.00 U.S. per jump) but with my spinal fusion and Jay's eye problems we passed on the bungee jumping, or at least that was our excuse. We did watch a 73 year old woman leap from the 120 foot high bridge. The attendants ask you if you want to be dunked in the river below or not so they adjust the ropes accordingly. This was not the daring bridge which we are told was 300 feet high for seasoned jumpers and further inland. It was not located near a main highway.

We headed north across the snow covered peaks of the Southern Alps, along the rugged west coast to the Hans Josef glacier, then through the stone fruit region of peaches, plums and apricots. We tasted wine at several vineyards of the northern area of the South Island. Highway One continues on to the ferry boat that carries you to the north island along with your car. Even passenger trains boarded the large ferry boats.

We met a couple on the train that could immigrate to New Zealand only because their only daughter married a New Zealander, otherwise they would not be able to relocate to the islands. We had tried when we first got married, to experience this different country but we were not accepted, even with our scientific background. We could only invest in the island but not having the required cash necessary, we gave up the idea of moving to New Zealand.

We did not linger in large cities such as Wellington but went right on to the thermal region of Rotarua, where we visited Maori villages that put on a show with the frightening faces of the Indians who stuck out their tongues to scare their enemies. We walked on wooden boardwalks over moonscape-looking parks with bubbling cauldrons of melted rock and hissing fissures of sulfurous steam emanating from cracks in the cliffs. We enjoyed a Hangi feast where all the food is steamed over natural hot springs, slept in a motel near the hot springs where the motel piped the steaming water into their spa tub. We attended a farm show to see the great variety of sheep and watch the indispensable sheep dogs at work, saw how they rounded up the strays and walked on the backs of the sheep pack. We also saw the immense Kaori trees rivaling our Sequoias. We then spent the remaining time in the tropics of the North Island, so similar to our climate at home. The journey ended too soon and we left Auckland for our long flight home.

June 17th was soon upon us, the wedding day for Diane to Robert Sussman, brother of her childhood friend, Stacy. They re-met at Stacy's wedding the previous October. Diane and Richard had a lovely, traditional church wedding at our cathedral with the reception being held at Sand Dollar. Preparations were typically hectic, exciting, yet enjoyable to see the family together. The bride and groom honeymooned on a sailboat cruise through our Virgin Islands. Later they resided at Fort Knox in Kentucky where Richard was stationed. He was soon retiring as a Major from the Army.

We no sooner saw the newlyweds off when on June 28th, on our grandson Jimmy's fourth birthday, we had a propane tanker truck delivering gas to us roll over one and three quarters time from our upper driveway. The truck landed on its side, just a few feet from our upper bedrooms. We had guests in the house which Jay awoke in a panic and rushed them out of the house, before the truck exploded. It was an all day ordeal with every fireman, rescue worker, Army Corps of Engineers and even the governor, deciding how to safely remove the explosive gas and the truck from our property. There were water and fire trucks plus several ambulances standing by. Ten firemen continuously sprayed water on the disabled truck to avoid sparks. The propane was eventually bubbled through our swimming pool via long hoses. Two backhoes finally righted the crippled truck and pushed/pulled it off our site. The fire department later requested a copy of my video for training purposes.

On September 1st we headed back to Tucson for our annual Pinochle Club reunion but this time we spent little time in Tucson, which was over 100 degrees. We enjoyed Jack and Laurie's vacation home in the mountains of Pinetop, four hours north of Tucson and many degrees cooler. From Pinetop we made a side trip to Meteor Crater and the Grand Canyon where we overnighted so that Jack, Laurie, Jay and I could take the mule trip down the canyon. The other four opted to explore the park on tram and foot around the Lodge. The first few hairpin turns looking down sheer 1000 foot cliffs caused a few palpitations but after the wrangler assured us that the mules were not suicidal we relaxed and enjoyed the spectacular journey. It was an all-day ride and we have very sore backsides and walked funny for a couple of days when we got off the mules but it was a worthwhile trip.

We vowed never to travel away from St. Thomas during hurricane season again for Hurricane Marilyn hit our island while we were riding the mules down the canyon trail. Unlike Hurricane Hugo Jay was not home to tend to the home fires so we did not know what was left of our home. We were able to fly in on Tuesday, the third day after the storm. We had trouble finding a ride home and walked the last quarter mile down our entrance road for a power pole was lying across the road. We pulled our carry-ons down the bumpy road, managed to get around the downed pole and were thrilled to see the roof still on the house. Fortunately, Jay had built Sand Dollar like a fortress. We had minor damage compared to the devastation that we saw throughout the island. We lost half our rain gutters in the storm. These were important because the roof is our water supply. It is rainwater that we catch on the roof and store in the cistern.

We both contracted giardia from drinking the contaminated water and after two courses of antibiotics we learned from a general practitioner in Florida that we only needed to take pepto-bismol for a couple of weeks to rid us of the giardia. In fact, it is a good idea to take the Pepto-bismol as a preventative whenever travelling to other countries.

We were without ice on the island the first week after the hurricane, then spent hours in line waiting to buy gas, ice, food, even phone calls. Without electricity we operated on a small generator that kept our refrigerator cold. A generator that I had sent down six years earlier when Hurricane Hugo hit St. Croix, amazingly it was exactly six years to the day that the hurricanes occurred, September 17th.

We then bit the bullet and ordered a twenty kilowatt generator that could run the entire house, to keep our guests coming. We ran the 20 KW generator only nine days when we were hooked up to real power on November 20th, eight and a half weeks without power after the storm and eight weeks ahead of schedule. Miraculously, our apartment phone was hooked up on November 22ⁿᵈ then shortly afterwards we received a call from Tipper Gore's office inquiring how we were and how Sand Dollar fared through the hurricane. The winds were much more than the official 130 miles per hour reported, with the storm breeding many tornadoes. We had a home on Skyline Drive that was called the "front door house" for that was all that was left of the home. We don't anticipate cable TV for several more months and are awaiting a new satellite that will reach our area so we can buy an eighteen inch dish. In the meantime my business has picked up selling damaged homes to stateside contractors and speculators.

With our department stores damaged and the lack of inventory this will be a quiet Christmas season, but we welcome the rest. We can remember when high seas broke the chains holding the cargo containers dropping several containers off the cargo ships into the sea. Christmas was very lean that year. We improvised trees for the holidays from century plants that could not be brought into the house because of termites. The children had homemade toys. Other Christmases, when we had expensive trees imported by the grocery stores I remember picking up the balsam needles that fell off the trees and making pillows stuffed with the needles. You could crush the pillows and get the smell of balsam needles whenever you felt like smelling the woods or pines of the forest. The destruction on the island after Marilyn often brought tears.

CHAPTER 34

The following year, 1996, ended with an even more illustrious family visiting Sand Dollar. President Clinton, Hillary and Chelsea came to stay for a few days at the villa. We thought there was so much preparation for the Vice President but for the President it is a magnitude of several degrees higher. We learned that Air Force One alone takes over sixty men to handle the plane and each man has a separate room at our largest and most expensive hotel, the Frenchman's Reef. About 250 secret service men travel with the President plus his staff (his doctor, cooks, political staff, personal aides) etc.

We were told that the Secret Service can only protect one person as completely as this operation. Large palm trees were lined up along the pool deck for privacy and heavy metal bullet proof steel plates were placed outside of the palms. The local Coast Guard guarded the water approach to the house. The lead team installed lighting where the steps to the ocean might have darker spots.

My 37th annual newsletter was not sent out until January, 1997, because we wanted to tell everyone we had the honor of the Clintons staying at Sand Dollar. On December 13th we received a call from the same White House staff attorney, who was our initial contact when the Vice President, Al Gore, and his family vacationed with us in November, 1994. He said we would be hearing from a lady named Kelly in ten minutes. The call never came and we wondered over the weekend who would be thinking about St. Thomas from the White House. We do know that the Gores said they would like to come back, they enjoyed Sand Dollar so much. It was Tuesday, the 17th when Kelly called stating she was from the First Lady's staff, was on island and would be at our home within a half hour to look over the house. We were flabbergasted that the First Family was considering our home. She arrived in the Governor's chauffeured limo with the Governor's aide, police escort and all. She had looked at several homes on St. John, St. Croix and even a backup home in Florida but once she saw Sand Dollar she said this was it.

There was just one big problem-we had been booked for the holidays for several months. For the first time we agreed to a group of six adults and five children. More than the house holds comfortably but the Gabbers, from Madison, WI, assured us that they could all fit in. Jay kept saying no, that the sewage plant couldn't handle that number, but John Gabber asked to speak to me, knowing that I would give in. John likes to tell the story of my asking them to leave the house early because we had a chance to host the most powerful man in the world. He says I fed them hors d'oevres and wine before I asked them to leave early. He said he thought I had just escaped from the looney bin. They had had a rough trip arriving on the island (one couple came from Germany) so we were happy when they agreed to leave early. They were upset at first but then agreed, plus they booked for the next holiday season again for another two weeks.

In the meantime, our Governor said we had to get the Gabbers out of the house. He didn't say who would cover the cost if the families sued us. He also told us that we had to compliment the President. We said we would only if the local government paid us the balance of $53,000+ that they owed us for chlorine delivered to Public Works.

Every restaurant that we suggested had to be investigated, and an escape route planned for the First Family. They ended up eating at Zorba's, a Greek restaurant in town, and a shack next to the Renaissance (previously Stouffers, and before that the Virgin Grand). The party was hosted by our Governor but financed by the Marriot hotel and ATT. We all got to meet the President and First Family privately for a short visit and photos, before they went into the crowd. They were both very personable and genuinely interested in meeting people. Virgin Islanders cannot vote for the President, so even though they didn't have a vote coming from anyone in the crowd they acted like we were all special to them, including the waiters, bartenders, and musicians.

I didn't get our annual newsletter out until January because of the excitement of hosting the President of the United States, the most powerful man in the world. Secret Service agents told us it is very unusual that we had both the Vice President and the President stay at the same home. When the President travels there are at least 250 agents that protect him, even if he stops for a few minutes, the same preparations must go on. We were not supposed to broadcast where the Clintons were staying but our Governor announced his arrival as early as December 23rd. He was coming on January 1st to the 5th. Then the guessing game began as to where they were staying. This was a vacation so only sixty press people were on the island from all the major networks, CNN, Reuters, etc. The Associated Press tried to find us for several days but never succeeded. But our neighbors knew where he was staying when Public Works planted bougainvillea, crotons and palm trees along our approach roads that stopped at our driveway. Armored Suburbans were flown in for the family but many other sports vehicles with Washington plates lined our street, which was totally closed off. Via Grenadines, being a circular road did not restrict anyone living west of us.

At the reception Saturday night Hillary gave me a big hug and said she really liked the house and would like to come back. I suggested we swap houses next time and she said that was a great idea. I told her it didn't have to be the big house, the country one, Camp David, would do.

We were all surprised at how much better they look in person than their photos. Secret Service men confirmed that it was most unusual to get both the President and Vice President at the same house, the two top guns of the world. The Gores had recommended Sand Dollar to the Clintons so I wrote a thank you note to Tipper. We also invited the attorney, Rob Lang, to be our guest. He started the whole excitement. What can top this one? The Pope is coming to Cuba in 1998 so I invited him to stay at Sand Dollar. I received an answer from the Vatican's Secretary of State. The Pope is not coming to Sand Dollar, but he sent us his blessings.

There was a great deal of positive press and we hope the islands will benefit from it for we need a lift after the hurricane Marilyn. The First Family arrived after dark on January 1, relaxed all day at the villa on their first day and on the second sailed and snorkeled to Magen's beach in the morning. On the third day and fourth day Bill golfed at Mahogany Run in the afternoon. I can picture Navy Seals accompanying these two snorkelers to Magen's beach, while a destroyer or two held off any terrorists.

Many local merchants donated food to the Clintons but only items that were factory wrapped would be allowed in the house. Even our cistern water that we drank all the time was not considered safe for the top dog.

This same year in February we also celebrated Jay's Dad's 100th birthday and returned to Florida in April to bury him. In May our Pinochle Club met in Richmond, VA with an overnight trip to Washington, D.C. Our entire group, four couples, had a tour of the White House. In July we attended a pig roast in Ohio at the Roth farm. We shot off potatoes from a potato launcher denting the top of the silo, harvested an entire field of garlic, picked tomatoes, blackberried and raspberries until our stomachs ached, fished for walleyes on Lake Erie, and then braided all the garlic the next day.

Throughout 1996 we hosted several friends, the Thomases from Connecticut, The Roths from New York and Ohio, the Ficks from Louisiana and Montana, and the Ottos from Dayton, Ohio. We spent a weekend with the Ottos for some R & R at their rental house on the island of Anguilla, north of St. Maarten.

We traveled back to Florida and the Bascomb Palmer Eye Institute for the many operations and checkups Jay needed for his eyes. Dad had glaucoma that led to his blindness because he didn't take care of it. Glaucoma is an insipid disease because there are no symptoms until after the damage is done to the optic nerve. We became very aware of Dad's problem and figured his son might have the same difficulties as he aged.

We had to travel back to St, Thomas on Jay's birthday, the 29th, to get ready for the President's visit. We had a rough time flying home, getting bumped in San Juan for we couldn't tell anyone why we were so eager to reach our home. We did get to see our son, Jim, our fast growing grandson, Jimmy, now five years old, and Jim's wife, Sally. She moved with her job to Vero Beach, FL where there is much more money in Vero Beach than in Ft. Lauderdale. She handled monies for several wealthy clients for the banks. They rented at first then bought a two story house. We visited them whenever we were in Florida.

CHAPTER 35

On November 13th of 1997 we received a phone call from the White House telling us that the Clintons wanted to return to Sand Dollar for four days starting January 1st as they did last year. Unbeknownst to us, John Gabber had offered the time to the Clintons again but didn't tell us so we had to check with them before we allowed it. John, who owned a lens manufacturing plant for eyeglasses, had sent new glasses to the President after seeing him with outdated reading glasses on TV and, at the same time, offered them the last days of their vacation again at Sand Dollar. They never really expected him to take them up on the offer.

In the meantime the Clintons added to their family with Buddy, the golden retriever. The White House asked if they could bring Buddy with them and while Jay kept saying NO to them they asked for me again and I said ok as long as Buddy didn't mess in the house. Can you imagine a Secret Service agent having to follow Buddy around and picking up after him? This was another example of well spent taxpayer's dollars. The dog had his first swim in the warm Caribbean waters of Magen's Bay in front of Sand Dollar. After they returned to the White House I cross stitched a picture of Buddy and sent it to Bill Clinton.

The most difficult thing for us was that we were asked not to tell anyone that the President was returning to Sand Dollar. We had spent Thanksgiving with our family instead of our usual Christmas visit.

We were sworn to secrecy, were told we couldn't tell anyone about this truly amazing experience—that we were hosting the Clintons a second time at our vacation villa. It must mean they truly found it restful, interesting, and enjoyable.

We dutifully kept the secret about the return visit but when we stepped off the plane in St. Thomas the first person to greet us was the reservation manager from the Frenchman's Reef hotel. He asked us if the President was returning to our home. He said the Secret Service Agency had called that very day and asked if they had 250 rooms available. Fortunately, our tourist season wanes right after Christmas so I am sure the Reef was able to accommodate the President, and all the agents that travel with him. It's a very small island. So the secret was out, we then told our family.

The incredible preparations began on December 26th with the Advance Team coming to set up the communication and command center but this time the installation was made as a permanent one. A bridge was built between our Sand Dollar and Dr. Abbott's house so that the personnel didn't have to climb the doctor's steep driveway or ours. The bridge was on a level with our main house and the doctor's apartment level below his house, which was the command/security center. His apartment was similar to the apartment where we lived below the main house. The entire operation would not have worked so well if they could not use his house as the communication and security center. We figured with the permanent bridge he was going to come back for the third time but he was busy in Washington with the impeachment hearings the next January. The hearings were led by a man; Newt Gingrich that should not have thrown any stones himself for his life was no example of innocence.

The Secret Service this time installed one inch plates of bullet proof steel that the President could duck behind in case someone across Magen's Bay wanted to do him in. We did find bullets on our deck when the Frenchies shot bullets over the bay when one of their policemen was killed on duty and a memorial service was held for the deceased on the hills across the bay. The neighbors across the bay suddenly bought telescopes so they could watch the President and his family. What a pity that there is no privacy for this family or any other that seeks a political life.

But the excitement didn't end with the return trip of the President. On December 10th the White House called again to invite us, our family and our guests, all 11 of the Gabbers, to attend a Christmas party at the White House on December 21st. The invitation came from Bill and Hillary Clinton. We were thrilled and immediately made whirlwind arrangements for us, Jim, Sally, grandson Jimmy, and Diane, newly divorced from her husband, Robert Snyder.

When Jimmy was asked by his class what he did over the Christmas vacation and he told them that he went to the White House for a party, the teacher and classmates didn't believe him until he brought the pictures in to school, showing him standing in front of ore the President with the President's hands on Jimmy's shoulders.

After passing through very tight security it was like stepping into a fairyland. Because someone in the Gabber plant had not faxed all the social security numbers to the White House for their investigation there was a problem with the admittance of our guests, the Gabber family. Jay came to their rescue and stayed with them until they were finally admitted.

There were large Christmas trees everywhere you looked. There were trees made from live roses, Marines guarded the long entrance hall. They were decked out in full dress uniforms, and looked so colorful. On the regular tours of the White House most of the areas are blocked off but we could wander everywhere, sit anywhere and dance in the East Room.

When I asked a waiter if they every ran out of shrimp, an item on the buffet table while I waited for a refill. He said

"We never run out of shrimp. I think we raise them in the basement".

I asked a person standing next to me in the reception line how he knew the President. He said

"I am his first cousin".

When we reached the reception line where we had a photo shoot with the first family Hillary jumped out of line, threw her arms around me and said

"I am so happy you came".

The reception line was in the lower part of the White House where the various china sets that each First Lady picked out was displayed all the way back to Mrs. Washington. Even the washroom had fancy towels that we couldn't help but take a few home for souvenirs. But most of the souvenirs were left at Sand Dollar, like plastic glasses with the Presidents seal on them, or a jigsaw puzzle that he worked on.

Anything sent by merchants on the island to the house for the President's use had to be factory wrapped. One local merchant sent a fifty pound bag of dog food for Buddy. As if that poor puppy could eat that much, especially in five days.

I think it was because the President of the United States came back to Sand Dollar that the Gabbers became interested in buying Sand Dollar. They could see the potential in advertising that both of the most powerful men in the world liked our vacation villa. We spent the days at the Frenchman's Reef negotiating a sale of the villa.

We had had the villa on the market for some time but as all Sellers do, we didn't accept the first offer because it was too low but we knew that the Gabbers had the money to purchase the home. We sold our villa to them for $800,000, paid off our mortgage on the house, then lived comfortably on the 7 percent interest, or $42,000 per year on the $600,000 first mortgage we held on the property. We sold it to them on a three year balloon, meaning that it was due in three years, with the option of renewing it again in three years. John wanted to pay 6 percent interest and we said 8 percent so we compromised at 7 percent, with a $200,000 down payment. John's brother, Ted Gabber was also on the deed as well as John's wife, Ursa.

We agreed to stay on to manage the villa for them. Then they proceeded to change Sand Dollar completely. They hired artists to paint murals all over the walls, closed in the patio that we enjoyed so much where guests could watch the sea life and even some nudies on the beach from the open arches. They hired a carpenter to build doors that fit all the curves so that the entire house could be air conditioned. The Gabbers were not water oriented people so they had no interest in the water activities, but the main focus was on the television and comfort while watching the boob tube.

They kept the villa only four years and sold it for $2,010,000 to one of their guests, but they had altered it so much that we figured that they spent about $300,000 on the renovations. That same year that the Gabbers bought Sand Dollar they also bought a home for another $800,000 in Madison, Wisconsin, where they are from, and having gotten estimates to remodel that were too much to build what they wanted, tore the house down and began to build a German castle. The castle included gargoyles on the parapets and a Rathskeller in the basement where the guest's quarters are located, next to their fitness room. Across Lake Mendota from this mansion you can enjoy the view of the capital of Wisconsin at night and must pass the governor's mansion whenever you go to the castle.

We have known the Gabbers for many years, and helped Ursa celebrate her big 50th birthday before the castle was built. Ted's wife died young so Ursa was the only female in the family that became both Auntie and Mom, to his two girls. Ted has a manufacturing plant that makes park benches and bike racks for various cities.

We have spent a couple of Thanksgiving dinners with this family we like so much enjoying their feast of turkey grilled on the barbeque by John. They have two girls, Jolie and Jacque so we were there to help them celebrate their birthdays only a day apart on November 26th and 27th, respectively, all at Thanksgiving time.

John and Ursa have a German shepherd dog, Misha that is interesting to watch. She can go out on their expansive front lawn by merely pushing the door handle down and exiting the house but when she wants to come in she must push the handle down on the exterior and pull the door toward her, backing up in the meantime on the narrow stoop that also held the barbeque. We watched her arthritis become so bad that we had to help her up the stairs to reach the main level of the house. Misha liked to sleep on the cool basement floor next to our bedroom, all the while having the guests think that she was there to guard them.

She still got all excited when she went to the dog park for her daily walks. It could have been that she also saw all of her friends there . . .

$\mathcal{C}$HAPTER 36

Ursa Gabber is from a small village in Germany, Neuenrade, of approximately 9000 souls. We joined the Gabbers for a parade to help them celebrate Schutzenfest. A marksman's shooting contest that is part of the culture of Switzerland and Germany.

The first time we went to Germany the local papers proudly stated that the three men, Jay, John and Ted, were the only Americans in the parade.

We met the Gabbers in late July of 1998 to help them celebrate Schutzenfest in Neuenrade. There were many tents set up in people's back yards during the festival so family and friends could join in for singing, drinking and a good time with many schnapps bottles downed with beer chasers. There was a daytime area where the marksmen could display their skills and onlookers could get beer and brats off the grill. A massive beer tent was set up in town within walking distance where many polkas were danced. The oompah bands were tireless.

Ursa's brother, Walter, and his wife, Helen, were elected the king and queen of the following year's festival. So at the invitation of the king and queen we promised to return the next year so we could proudly sit at their table. The following year did not produce near the publicity as the first year did.

We managed to get a room at a hotel in town but the bells of the Lutheran church next door awakened us each morning, almost throwing us out of bed.

We enjoyed meeting Ursa's mother and father. He had been a fighter pilot during our war against Germany. He was shot down over France and said a farmer nursed him back to health and released him back to his squadron.

The parents had a large home that Walter added on to for his family. Then John bought the entire house so his family could use the upper unit whenever they were in Germany. John and Ursa's girls became quite proficient in German having learned it from their grandparents.

Helen, Walter's wife had trouble conceiving. She went through several in vitro attempts which the German state paid for, and finally had twins. Unfortunately, Helen had a drinking problem and died prematurely leaving Walter to spoil the twins. It was a blessing that he had added on to his parents home so he had family support for his children.

The entire village of Neuenrade is only a few blocks long so we walked everywhere. Because John and Ursa could not pick us up at the airport we flew in to Darmstadt where Andrea and Wolfgang Dinglemann picked us up at the airport. They showed us their shoe stores that were thriving, and then treated us to a lunch at an outdoor beer garden in Darmstadt. They ordered and enjoyed a dish that looked like raw bacon to us. We cut off the fat and ate only what looked like the meat. At their home, Wolfgang showed us the bomb shelter they used during the war was nearly completely destroyed by the Allies. The bomb shelter is now a wine cellar. John and Ursa picked us up at the Dinglemann's and drove us to Neuenrade. After the Schutzenfest Andrea drove us to Tschapinna where we spent a couple more weeks with Evert and Henrietta Bogart; except Evert was doing his work in the woods chasing wounded deer with his hunting dog, Britta, and bringing them in from the woods. Switzerland also places firewood along the roadways for anyone to pick up for the winter season. Public

Works cuts up fallen trees in the forest, so nothing is wasted for the frugal Swiss.

Ida Walterson from St. Thomas joined us for a vacation in Tschapinna. Ida, however, had a problem with her heel so had trouble keeping up with us as we hiked miles through the Alps in this interesting summertime area. Henrietta took us to an Alp nearby where we learned that the farmer receives wheels of cheese depending on how much milk his cows contribute to the process. From the cheese making the pigs are fed the dregs of the milk to cheese production.

Other news of this year was that we listed and sold quickly the two bedroom condo we bought for Diane to attend the Art Institute. In its place we found a 3 bedroom, 2.5 bath condo at Palm Aire Country Club, which has five golf courses, a spa, and 10,000 units with over 50 swimming pools. I enjoyed the golfing for we played on a different one of the four regulation size golf courses each week. Then everyone that golfed went to lunch at the main dining room after playing the game.

We picked a unit on the top floor of our building, ten stories high and often walked up the stairs, just for the exercise. The noise from the air-conditioners on the roof could often be heard when the windows were open. The entire area is very Jewish so we learned of Hanukah, lox, salmon salad, great rye breads, and famous Reuben sandwiches along with crocks of dill pickles and sauerkraut on the tables. There were many Jews in our building, most from the New York area. We met many interesting people, especially when I became President of the association and we reroofed our building. The owners believed in an escrow account so that helped defray expenses of our new roof. We were even invited to a Seder at one couple's home, and various memorial funeral services that were held a year after the deceased left our planet. Jews must be buried in twenty four hours, so a memorial is held a year later.

We had been in small quarters for so long that we relished all the space in the condo. The previous owner of the Palm Aire condo was an ex-attorney who was obviously very wealthy from the quality of the furniture he left in the unit. He had died in his 90s so his children were in their fifties and sixties and did not want anything left in the condominium.

Directly below our unit was the executive course, which was less than a regulation golf course, so we often took our son and grandson out to play in the late afternoon. Many times we had to run indoors because of sudden showers and lightning. You do not want to be on a golf course during any lightning, especially with a golf club in your hand. In fact, the sirens often would blare and alert people to get inside.

We had lasted only one year in managing Sand Dollar for the Gabbers. When Jay began to fall and could no longer tell if he needed a Phillips or a regular screwdriver, we had to make a move. We closed one chapter and opened another.

CHAPTER 37

The following year 1999 changed our lives forever. We left St. Thomas where we had lived for 33 years and moved to our condo in Pompano Beach. When many people asked us why we moved from the idyllic island life (that they desired), we said for easier living. We no longer had to take our trash to bins on the road; the paper was delivered to your doorstep, the power stayed on throughout the day and night, there were grocery stores everywhere stocked with fresh produce and canned goods galore.

We flew to Brussels that summer with Bob and Fiona Smith, rented a car and drove through Holland with a stop in Almsmeer, which the Smiths had visited previously. We had to overnight at a Bed and Breakfast in the village to get to the auction house early. Millions of flowers are auctioned to buyers in the early morning. In the super large warehouse you walk on catwalks over a profusion of colors. Workers bring in a cart at a time to the buyers seated in an amphitheater. They bid on the flowers, are sold, and shipped out to destinations all over the world by 2:00 p.m.

We drove on to Denmark to visit Peter and Betty Kaufmann, the delightful couple we met when sailing with Don and Ida Walterson on Zulu Warrior. In Denmark we sailed on the Danes beautiful sailboat that Don single handed to the Caribbean. Bob and I took a very short dip in the cold North Sea. We marveled at the modern designs in

Denmark, rode on their sons motorcycle, took a drive to Copenhagen topping off the drive with a fine dinner at Tivoli Gardens. The van we drove to Copenhagen was broken into, almost hijacked, to be sent across the Baltic Sea to Poland where there is a big market for vans. They are used as taxis, we presume.

From Denmark we drove to Darmstadt to revisit friends Andrea and Wolfgang Dinglemann then on to Neuenrade to celebrate Schutzenfest with the Gabbers, now owners of Sand Dollar. We there at the king and queen's invitation for a week of fun parades, beer, bratwurst, oompah music and more beer but the Smiths were with us this time, and they enjoyed the festivities also.

It was our turn to host our annual Ethyl/Pinochle Club reunion and since we no longer owned Sand Dollar, we rented a four bedroom home in Maggie Valley, NC for a month. We had our week of Ethyl reunion which included a week of cards, board games, a trip to the Indian casino, a clogging show, and a visit to the Biltmore Estate in Asheville. From this rental house we spent a day driving to Knoxville, TN where my cousin Greg and Betty Kapolka live. Greg is a Chemistry Professor at the University in Knoxville and travels the world lecturing.

In the fall we flew to Madison, WI to help Ursa celebrate her 50th birthday even though the weather was too chilly for us thin-blooded island expatriates. After the party we bused to Milwaukee to visit Jay's cousins, Mary and Steve Bostic. It was Mary who was told by her doctors that she only had about a year to live, more than forty years ago. She has had a lifetime of misery, pain, and operations, but utter support from her husband, Steve. In the end they determined that she had a tick bite and Lime's disease all these years. When Steve acquired diabetes and his kidneys shut down it was an employee from his machine shop that donated a kidney to him. Steve earned his halo over the years taking care of Mary and arranging for a nurse in his building to care for her when we visited them. Later he made arrangements for her to be placed in a nursing home upon his demise. He has since passed away.

CHAPTER 38

Moving into a condominium was an easy decision. We could travel as much as we wished without worrying about the yard or maintenance of any kind. Palm Aire has 6,000 units, 53 swimming pools on property, a two block walk to a large supermarket, drug store, Blockbuster, beauty shop and restaurants. There are 119 apartments in our ten-story building. We are on the top floor, which is okay when the windows are not open to hear the air-conditioners on the roof. We have a great view of the golf courses to the west and a night view to the east toward the ocean and beachside skyscrapers, just five miles away.

But I wasn't happy with the President of the Board so I ran for the office and became the President of the Homeowners Association. We met many interesting and lovely people while on the Board of Directors. Most of the residents were from the New York area and of Jewish decent. We were invited to a Seder, and a funeral memorial service, which was held on the anniversary of the person's demise since a Jew must be buried within 24 hours. We learned to eat Reubens at a local restaurant that had a crock of dill pickles and sauerkraut on each table, savor a cheaper salmon spread to take the place of expensive lox (smoked salmon), to relish bagels with the salmon spread, learn to make Matzo but not enjoy it, and drink Manishewitz wine. We even learned to talk back to the large Jewish population of the association, no longer cowering under their bluntness.

During my tenure as the President, we undertook the reroofing of the condo complex. The roof was about twenty years old and in need of a new rooftop. This was a much bigger job than expected but fortunately the Jews did believe in a reserve fund. The roof cost over $200,000 and we had the money to undergo this project. There were some leaks that reached all the way down to the first floor. A real problem but all residents were very thoughtful and helpful. However, we moved out of the condo because Jay got tired of taking complaints from the residents.

Palm Aire was a great place to live for golfers. There were four regulation courses and one executive course. The ladies league used a different one of the four each week. So there was no monotony during the playing season. We took guests, Jim and his son, Jimmy, on the executive course for there was no charge for that sub-standard course. We went late in the afternoon but always had to come indoors when we saw the first lightning and it always stormed in the summer in the afternoon.

One lady that was a good golfer was 96 and still going strong. I only wish I could look as good as she does and keep playing that well when I reach that age.

In the fall of this year of 2000 we took a cruise with the Smiths who traveled with us to Europe the year before. We were on the Tropicale, a Carnival ship. The weather was so rough that people with staterooms in the bow had to sleep on the floor of the main lobby. We were in the stern and didn't have it so bumpy. Our first stop was in Key West. How it has changed from the sleepy village it was back in 1966 where we walked to various restaurants to taste their Key Lime pies. We stopped in Grand Cayman, Cozumel and Belize. Because the Smiths were with us and were well versed in travelling, we avoided the high priced tours from the cruise ship, took a cab to the boats that took us out to the sandbar where the rays are located. The rays are so accustomed to being fed by humans that you hold a squid in the palm of your hand and the rays swoop down and grab it out of your palm. I was holding my hand out to feed a smaller ray in front of me when a larger one nudged my back to remind me that he was behind me, and he wanted a squid also.

We do miss St. Thomas' ideal climate, powdery sand beaches, crystal clear water, incredible colors of the Caribbean Sea and sunsets, and the slower pace of island life. Here Florida's roads are crowded. The drivers on the interstate are crazy but real estate is booming and prices are rising. I thought running hotels in St. Thomas were tough but this tops it, by far. When the stock market took a nosedive real estate became hot. Our condos now selling the day they are listed at much higher prices than what we paid three years ago. Great for sellers but what will replace it?

Besides the condo dealings I sit on the Marine Advisory Board for our city of Pompano Beach but that meets only once a month so is not as demanding as the Presidency of our condominium association. On the Advisory Board we decide which of the many canals in Pompano needed to be dredged out and made sure that no house blocked the view of the canal from another house.

Our summer heat escape was a nine week driving trip that covered almost 11,000 miles in our new Avalon automobile. Our trips for the past thirty years or so were mainly for family affairs, power-shopping trips to Florida for Sand Dollar, or to far off foreign countries. We had not seen much of our great country since living in the islands. We visited family and friends in Florida, Ohio, Illinois, Minnesota, Montana, Arizona, New Mexico and Texas. We spent a few days in our national parks, Mt. Rushmore, Yellowstone, and Glacier, Bryce and Zion. Visited the Crazy Horse monument in construction that will dwarf Mt. Rushmore when completed. We particularly enjoyed the Canadian Rockies and their parks, Banff, Lake Louise and Jasper. They are truly majestic mountains. We drove below snow-covered mountains, walked on glaciers in the ice fields, and hiked mountain trails, enjoyed peaches that were ripening in September in the stone country of Canada. We planned our drive through Utah to be in Salt Lake City on Sunday morning to hear the Mormon Tabernacle Choir take their radio performance. We visited their new conference center that seats 22,000 people and their incredible genealogy library. We visited eleven different homes along the way that made our trip most enjoyable. It was an easy adventure for we would drive for a day or so and then stop with family and friends for a few days only. Visitors start to smell like fish after three days we are told so we carefully departed within the allotted time.

$\mathcal{C}$HAPTER 39

Our annual Christmas Newsletter was sent early to all because we left Broward County and moved to central Florida. We are awaiting the completion of a new house being built for us. Our job on this, the fourth home we have built is to supervise only. The labor is being left to the younger folks. The swiftness of the sale of our condo surprised us, not giving us a chance to say goodbye to many of the friends we mat at Palm Aire. We sold the condo in a weeks' time so we started packing in July, left for a three week trip to China from August 11 to September 1, then finished packing and moving on September 13th.

CHINA WITH UNIWORLD, 8/11/02-9/1/02

China was planning on flooding the Yangtze River and we wanted to see it before it was flooded. Our cost for the trip for the two of us was $9134 which included airfare, all meals, five flights in China, six nights on a Yangtze River cruise ship, a Grand Canal river cruise, all ground transportation, 16 nights in five star hotels, two acrobat performances, and of course trips to various factories to entice us to purchase silk, embroidery, jade, jewelry and souvenirs at greatly reduced prices.

China is not just a country on the other side of the globe, it is another world. It is slightly smaller than the United States and covers several time zones yet the entire country stays on one time, Beijing time. The population in 2002 was 1.3 billion people with the majority living in the eastern half of the country. The population is still growing due to greater life expectancy despite their "one child" strict rule. Couples lost social benefits and even their jobs if they had more than one child. This has led to another problem of more ageing dependents for each person at work. The elderly were always cared for by their children but with only one child the burden will be overwhelming. Girls are usually given up for adoption, boys are preferred and with doting parents and two sets of grandparents the boys are called "little emperors".

For centuries China has stood as a leading civilization, outpacing the rest of the world in arts and sciences. But in the first half of the twentieth century China was beset by major famines, civil unrest, military defeats and foreign occupation. After World War II, the Communists under Mao Zedong established a dictatorship that, while ensuring China's Sovereignty imposed strict controls over everyday life and cost the lives of tens of millions of people. After 1978, his successor Deng Xiaoping, gradually introduced market-oriented reforms and decentralized economic decisions making. Today our various guides are were allowed to tell us that Mao had set their country back at least twenty to thirty years.

We arrived in Beijing directly from Chicago, two hours late, but the same time as our watches, just twelve hours different.

The Beijing airport was very modern with granite floors, large lobbies and moving sidewalks. Immigration and Customs was quick and friendly. The airport ladies room was our introduction to eastern/western toilets. There was a hole in the floor for the eastern women who learned to squat as children and the regular toilets for us wimpy westerners. I would have made out on the eastern toilets if they only had grap bars on the walls to pull myself up. Toilet paper was supplied only in the most touristy places and then only a few squares at a time, so you learned to walk with wads of paper taken from our fine hotel rooms.

BEIJING

We were met at the baggage area by our Chinese guild, Frank Qi (Chi), who was to remain with us for the majority of the trip. He was once a pediatrician but left the profession for he said it was too depressing. Healthy second children and girls were often disposed of. Porters took care of our luggage throughout the trip. Clean buses of around 40 person capacity transported us on all our land trips. Our group consisted of only seventeen persons.

From the airport we were taken to Yilong Hotel for our first Chinese dinner. The dinners, and lunches, were always served at round tables with large lazy susans that held a multitude of various dishes. There were salads of cold cucumbers in a vinaigrette sauce or other cold vegetables. No tossed salads like we have at home. The soups came last, were too bland, plus we were always too full to try the soups. Dessert was usually watermelon, sometimes there were small cakes. The Chinese seldom eat dessert, accounting for their small size. There were always chopsticks unless we asked for forks. We always asked for extra serving spoons also so no one was double dipping. For drinks we had a choice of a glass of beer, soda, or bottled water and always tea, most often jasmine—no sugar or cream was offered. Any additional drinks were at your own expense but cheap, a large one-liter bottle of beer was only 16 Yuan. The Yuan exchange was approximately 8.3 Yuan to the U.S. dollar so the beer was about $2.00. The entrees included fish dishes, usually carp, which was too bony for us; a couple of times shrimp, always chicken, pork, sometimes beef, and many vegetable dishes. The flavors varied depending on the area we were visiting with a definite change to spicy when we were in Sichuan. The meals were plentiful and delicious but we did get tired of Chinese after a couple dozen lunches and dinners of the same fare.

Our first three nights in China were in the Kempinski Hotel in Beijing. Beijing is the capital of China, has a population of thirteen million, is huge in size, 6500 square miles and flat, a blessing for the many cycling commuters. The Kempinski is a plush five-star hotel with doormen dressed in classy uniforms with pillbox hats, white gloves; women staff were in satin, sleek, high-neck embroidered uniforms just like the old Hollywood movie depictions. Guests are furnished with thick terry robes, slippers, fancy toiletries and souvenir jester's heads on the pillow following the turndown night service.

TIANANMEN SQUARE

Had a poor night's sleep. Our body clocks were still confused? The incredible breakfasts offered at the Kempinski were Western, European and Asian fare, fresh fruits, anything your heart might desire. We boarded our air-conditioned bus at 8:30 a.m. for Tiananmen Square. The common entrance is through the south gate near a memorial hall, which contains the embalmed body of Mao Zedong. Mao's body, flag-draped in a crystal sarcophagus, is raised each day from a subterranean freezer so the multitudes of visitors can troop past in. The smog is so bad, resulting in poor pictures. August is a holiday month for most Chinese, a poor time for foreign visitors.

FORBIDDEN CITY

The Forbidden City, now known as the Palace Museum was so called because it was out of bounds to ordinary people for more than 500 years. Within the walls stand 800 structures, mostly built between 1406 and 1420. In the Forbidden City and other major cities, there are Drum and Bell Towers. The Drum Tower was used to mark the hours of the day and the Bell Tower was used to wake the city at 5 a.m. The city gates were opened and closed by these signals.

SUMMER PALACE

After a western lunch in a pub we were driven to the Summer Palace, ten miles northwest of the Forbidden City. Palace scarcely describes the 700 acres of landscaped park including a full-size marble ship sitting on the bottom of the lake at a dock where the Empress Dowager Cixi views the sunsets. It is said that funds intended to modernize the Chinese navy were used to create this earthly paradise, thus contributing to defeat by the Japanese. Cixi, a former concubine, had been the power behind the throne for forty years in the late 1800s. We had just 30 minutes to clean up before out drive to dinner and the Chinese Opera, which no one really appreciated for we were all exhausted. It was 90 to 95 degrees and humid. We crashed.

GREAT WALL OF CHINA

Had an early morning forty mile drive north of Beijing to the Great Wall at the Badaling Pass, the most accessible and must visited resulting in a vast encampment of souvenir stands and restaurants. The Great Wall, the world's most colossal construction, snakes through barren hills and along mountain ridges for more than 3000 miles. It's not just a single fortification but a whole system. Its origins date from 2500 years ago, when warring states began to build walls between their territories. The Qin (Chin) emperor united most of China by 221 BC then decreed that various sections be joined. The forced labor of millions became the method of construction through the ensuing centuries. The top of the wall is 20 ft. wide. It is awesome to see, to climb the steep steps of rock and bricks until you must rest. You catch your breath and ponder this unbelievable feat, the toll it took on the laborers, the many that died and the numerous bodies buried in the wall. It is the only man-made structure that can be seen from the International Space Station. We feel the Wall must be preserved for all humanity.

On our trip back to Beijing we were given a tour of a silk carpet factory. Young girls do the delicate work of tying the fine silk threads. The work is so delicate that their eyesight fails by the time they are forty years old. The amazing thing is that the carpets look different depending on what direction you are viewing the carpet.

Had only a short time to get ready for our farewell dinner in Beijing, Peking duck, which was not to our liking for it, had more fat than we were accustomed to. No limit on drinks, however.

SHANGHAI

Caught the first of five flights we would have in China. Frank always checked the group in, paid the departure taxes, and got the luggage weighed in as a group. Frank watched his flock carefully and made sure we got on the right plane. The terminals were clean, the people courteous. We found western toilets and plenty of paper in each terminal.

Shanghai has a population of over sixteen million and is the largest and is the most vibrant city in China. At the peak of the building boom in 1990s it is said that a quarter of the construction cranes in the world were at work in Shanghai. It was one of the first five Treaty Ports opened to foreign trade in the 1840s. Today there are awesome skyscrapers, many putting ours to shame. The elevated highways are only three years old with hanging flowerpots on the exterior walls. Greenery is everywhere. There are escalators climbing the hills to take the maids up to the houses they tend and then it reverses in the afternoon to bring them back to their residences in the city. We had such a different picture in our minds of what China would be like, barefoot peasants in rice paddies, Mao uniforms and shy natives. We haven't even seen a rice paddy as yet.

The five-star Shanghai Hilton is not as five-star as the Kempinski in Beijing but the breakfast buffets are fabulous. The days are always well planned; in fact, we had too much to do and got tired. The Shanghai Museum on the Bund was first, then the Children's Palace, where you students of dance and music perform for the tourists. The Yu Yuan Gardens was next. Being Saturday it was very crowded but there were no incidents or cause to fear the throngs of people. The Old Town was next where we had lunch in an air-conditioned Starbucks. There was an interesting elderly, toothless, Chinese man who spoke many languages trying his skills on the crowds. He was not panhandling, just trying out his language skills. That evening we couldn't face another Chinese dinner so joined two ladies for a western dinner at the hotel then took a cab and joined the group for a spectacular performance in a beautiful theatre by the Shanghai Acrobats.

TINGLI

Early morning trip to Tingli, a small town that retains its original Ming Dynasty style, 1368-1644. This town boasts a picturesque blend of ancient bridges, narrow streets, simple homes, and teahouses. Boats filled with tourists ply the waterways much like in Venice. An old fisherman in a rickety boat had his cormorants performing for the tourists. Usually night fishing birds, the cormorants are trained to dive for fish but cannot swallow the fish for their long neck is bound with a restricting. The bird coughs up the fish for the fisherman but is finally awarded with fish for all his work, he told us.

GRAND CANAL

In the afternoon we boarded a river boat for a welcome two hour ride up the Grand Canal. The Canal was built in 610 A.D. to facilitate traffic heading north and south. The major rivers in China run east and west so as early as the fifth century B.C. local rulers began to link lakes and rivers by way of canals. The 1100 mile Grand Canal remained in use until the 19th century, when rebellions disrupted canal traffic and prevented regular dredging to remove the silt carried by the major rivers. Railways and coastal shipping took over the canal's role. It is hoped eventually to reopen the entire length.

We saw many barges, some ramshackle, pass by loaded with bricks, sand, cement, rocks, dogs, bicycles, cooking stoves, potted plants and all with clotheslines full of laundry drying in the sun. We passed a couple of large goose farms along the edges of the canal with fenced areas in the water for the fowl to swim. There were also many farms growing mulberry bushes, the food needed for the silk worms.

GOVERNMENT SILK FACTORY

From the river boat we were taken to a government silk factory where we could see the entire silk process, from the worms chomping on the mulberry plants, the soring of the cocoons, the soaking and cleaning of the pupae, the unthreading of the fine thread and the spinning of the yarn. I even had a chance to pet a silk worm—it is as soft as the silk it produces. It was a government store so there was no dickering over price. Because the prices were 1/10th the Stateside price, I think everyone in our group bought a comforter and a silk duvet cover. Jay and I trusted the government store to ship our package home—it arrived one week after we got home via air express service.

SUZHOU

Suzhou, an ancient city with many canals, surrounded by a moat, known as a city of gardens, is located just 52 miles northwest of Shanghai. Marco Polo, in the 13th century told of its splendors and labeled it the "Venice of the East". The Sheraton Suzhou was a true maze, so we were given maps to find our rooms. This was the first hotel where we could drink the tap water for the hotel had their own reverse osmosis system. In all other hotels we were given a bottle of drinking water per day. In the heat of the shore excursions we often purchased more water or their delicious beer.

We had an early morning tour of the Humble Administrators Garden, which was not so humble. The lotus blossoms in bloom were at least 12 inches across. They were awesome. The next stop was most interesting to me, the Suzhou Embroidery Institute. Young girls perform this artistic "painting with thread", as I label the skill. The women go to school for 3 years after high school then apprentice for

6 years at the Institute. With a secret process they can embroider a double image on the same fine piece of silk.

We had lunch near the Shanghai airport before boarding our flight #2, where we flew west to Wuhan to board the ship for our Yangtze River cruise.

YANGTZE RIVER CRUISE

We were put on the Blue Whale ship and would be cruising the Middle Reaches of the Yangtze from Wuhan to Chongqing (Chonking). The Upper Reaches are unnavigable, dropping from the Tibet Plateau. The Yangtze has over 700 tributary rivers, washes 500-600 million tons of silt away each year. It is the longest river in China and the 3rd largest in the world by length, 3900 miles, and volume. It has an average depth of 7-10 meters and is 20-30 meters deep in the Three Gorges area. Water speed averages three meters per second. The Middle Reaches have a smoother current but is always under severe flood threat, which is one of the reasons for the Great Dam project. The dam will control flooding as well as provide clean power. There are many sharp curves that are one-way traffic, controlled by water authority officers in small buildings on the shore, who raise flags to indicate right-of-way to the ship's captain.

The staterooms were adequate on this Chinese cruise ship, we had twin beds, two chairs, two end tables, hanging locker, a luggage rack but no drawers so we had to live out of the suitcase. There was a refrigerator to keep our water cool. Breakfasts and lunches were served buffet style with some western choices for lunch which we all appreciated. Lovely young ladies dressed in flattering satin, high-necked, tight-fitting past suits served dinner.

We arrived in Yueyang mid-morning and disembarked for a shore excursion to the Song Dynasty Yueyang Tower. As we go further into the interior we see more squalor but the people are polite. They look but don't stare. No longer are western faces or currency, an unfamiliar sight. On day three of our cruise, from Yueyang to Yichang, 150 km., we sailed two of the three mystical Gorges. Xiling is the longest and grandest, 47 miles, the Wu Gorge followed with 3,000 foot cliffs and is on a scale equal to the Grand Canyon in the United States.

We arrived in Yichang mid afternoon and had to disembark again, for a smaller ship, the Victoria Pearl. The recent rains and flooding past the dam site made the passage too treacherous so ships were not allowed through this dangerous area. We changed ships via bouncing rusty, floating docks. At time two men wearing life jackets held a length of bamboo pole as a handrail for us. Small men, and even women, with a suitcase or two at each end of a pole balanced on their shoulders carried our heavy luggage along the same path to the bus.

GREAT DAM PROJECT

We were busses to the next ship via this mind boggling site. An entire city was built to house the 20,000 workers. This $20 billion project began in 1994, total completion is expected in 2009. Next July, 2003, the dam itself will be completed and the level of the Yangtze above the dam will rise 175 meters, displacing 2 million people. The Three Gorges will be submerged, leaving only their peaks as islets above water. Entire villages are built high up on the river slopes. Every brick that can be reused is saved. The native will receive a new unit in a high-rise building the size of the home they must leave. They must pay the difference for a larger unit.

LESSER GORGES

On the fourth day of our cruise, Yichang to Badong, 170 kms, we left the Pearl again to board motorized sampans to sail the Daning River through the Lesser (Three Little) Gorges. Wushan, where we were to board our sampans, will lose much of its waterfront when the dam is completed so relocation has begun. We had to walk from the waterfront to the sampans through a gauntlet of local children, trying to sell you something. Many are disfigured and limbless. They learned quickly how to gain sympathy from the tourists.

The Lesser Gorges have much clearer, green water compared to the brown, silt-filled Yangtze. The Ba tribe hung their coffins in caves on the 1500 foot cliffs in the Misty Gorge. On distant shores monkeys romp through the trees and squeal at us. After a late lunch on the Pearl we sailed through the last, the shortest, 8 kms, of the Three Gorges, the Qutang Gorge. The Yangtze is so muddy from recent heavy rains it is like sailing on a river of milk chocolate.

WANXIAN

Day five of our cruise was from Wushan to Wanxian. We were required to explore Wanxian, a small city of only 1.5 million people. We climbed what seemed like 100 steps from the dock to the bus. Wanxian is best known for its Mandarin Orange orchards and thriving silk-weaving industry. We were bussed to a street market with open stalls of clothing, souvenirs and food. Meat hung from hooks above the tables, fish jumped out of the water tanks and flopped on the streets, live chickens, ducks, pigeons and quail squawk for freedom. Children are everywhere hawking leis made out of jasmine flowers. No bicycles, too hilly. We were then treated to a great acrobat show in a cool theatre. We had the ships Chinese doctor give Jay an herbal prescription to help his gallstone problem; we could get it filled in Chongqing at an herb store.

CONGQING

After lunch we set sail for Chongqing, Victoria Cruises homeport. We have travelled 840 miles upriver from Wuhan. Five nights on the Yangtze was sufficient.

We were bused to the Chongqing Hilton, opened only three months ago, and more exquisite than anything we had experienced so far. The rooms were decorated in very expensive zebra and lace wood.

The rooms had a king size bed, feather pillows and comforter, a true five-star hotel with a 7-star bathroom.

Chongqing with its narrow stone lanes winding up and down the hills, thus no bicycles, cave dwellings, bridges, outdoor markets and misty pine-clad hills, is a step into a rich historic past. The town was opened as a treaty port in the late 19ᵗʰ century.

DAZU

After lunch we boarded a cool bus for a 2.5 hour trip to Dazu to explore more than 50,000 stone sculptures scattered through the area. Buddhist artists began the work in 892 A.D. and continued for more than 400 years. More importantly during our trip to Dazu we saw our first rice paddy with barefoot farmers in knee-high water wearing coolie hats. The true China. The highway we were traveling on was built in 1996 as two lanes in each direction. However, the farmers were drying their rice on the hot roadway usurping the two outside lanes. The rice drying went on for miles, reducing the new highway to two lanes.

On our return to the Hilton two girls showered us with rose pedals and offered cold, slushy orange or watermelon juice in bamboo cups.

With Frank translating, he took Jay to an upscale, impressive herb store near the hotel. Jay felt quite smug for he bragged that he got his three herb prescription filled for less than $10. The only problem was that each bag was a kilo, or 2.2 pounds. He was supposed to take one teaspoon of each herb to make a tea, but he doesn't drink tea. They would never let us back into the States with all this herb that looks like something many people smoke.

XI'AN

Sorry we had only one night in this fabulous hotel in Chongqing and to kill the time before our 6:00 p.m. flight, #3, to Xi'an we were bussed to the zoo to see two lethargic pandas coaxed into eating eucalyptus leaves for the tourists, an art museum, and a new condo project to show us what the government is doing for the middle class. No one was impressed with the quality of construction. So much is still not open to the locals. CNN news is available in the large hotels for the tourists but not for the locals. Our guide, Frank, stayed in the same hotels but did his room have TV? The one-hour flight north to Xi'an was crowded. Passengers are bussed to the planes parked on the tarmac. Construction cannot keep up with the demands of tourism.

In Xi'an we checked into the Shangri-la Golden Flower hotel, older and in need of refurbishing but the largest room we have had so far. Xi'an, an ancient city with a population of 6 million had been the capital to eleven dynasties. It was the eastern end of the Silk Road. From the city walls, wider than the twenty feet of the Great Wall, we were driven, in the early morning, to the 8th Wonder of the Ancient World, the Terracotta Warriors. In 1974 peasants were digging a well east of the Qin Emperor's tomb and stumbled on what was part of a great pottery army designed to accompany the Emperor in the afterlife. At a book signing in the souvenir store we met the farmers that discovered the Warriors. The Warriors are more than life-size, dating from the Qin (Chin) Empire, 2200 years ago. Emperor Qin unified China, began the Great Wall and as his power grew so did the plans for his tomb become more grandiose. By the time of his death in 210 B.C. a whole subterranean city had been built with another city on the surface. There were underground lakes of mercury and vast quantities of gold and jewels. When the Emperor was buried all his concubines who had no children were entombed along with him, and an artificial hill 378 feet high was built over the spot. You cannot fathom the immensity of this project from the pictures. There are more than 7,000 figures with hundreds of horses and chariots, not yet excavated. The warriors were not made in one piece but assembled from a solid lower half, a hollow torso and separate head. The warriors had been broken into many pieces when the Qin Dynasty was overthrown. Historians and archeologists are piecing them together, a daunting problem for the excavators. Visitors view them from raised walkways; the first sight of the pit is truly breathtaking. Only about 1000 warriors have been restored to date. The Emperor's tomb will not be opened until they are sure they can preserve the treasures from the exposure to air, pollution, and the breath of hundreds of thousands of visitors.

The afternoon was spent at the 7th century Big Wild Goose Pagoda, an active Buddhist temple. We were allowed to photograph the many Buddha statues, and purchase the monks' artwork. Had only 1.5 hours to rest after this most interesting day before being whisked off to an excellent dinner and cultural show of the Tang Dynasty that rivaled any Las Vegas production except these performers were fully dressed.

We visited a jade factory the final morning in Xi'an. The artwork is exquisite. Everyone bought a memento to treasure. The afternoon was filled with a visit to the Shanxi Museum. But we are getting "museumed out". We did enjoy the special dumpling lunch on our way the airport. Our next flight, #4, was south to Guilin. It was 8 p.m. before they stopped for dinner prior to checking into the Guilin Sheraton. We were just too tired and it was too late to appreciate the food.

GUILIN

Guilin's landscape has been the inspiration for Chinese artists and poets for centuries. Its mirror smooth rivers and tall pinnacles of rock eroded by rain bring great numbers of tourists to the area. Few historic buildings have survived since Guilin was bombed and then captured by the Japanese in 1944. The Sheraton is another beautiful hotel with glass elevators ascending a multi-storied lobby. It is on the banks of the Li River that meanders through the center of town.

LI RIVER CRUISE

We had an early morning departure for our 4.5 hour ride down the Li River from Guilin to Yangshuo on one of the many flat-bottomed, government-owned boats plying the river. The food aboard was just ok but the scenery was breathtaking. Each turn in the river revealed one spectacular scene after the other-of humped limestone peaks, fishermen aboard bamboo rafts, women laundering clothes along the edges, children splashing, farmers toiling in rice paddies, and grazing water buffalos. Wolfgang, our new friend from Chicago, had the nerve to purchase a glass of snake wine. There were dozens of snakes in the bottle. He and I had the nerve to taste this wine, not exciting but we survived. We had to bring a bottle home to startle our guests. with it. This cruise is one of the highlights of a trip to China.

At Yangshuo we boarded our bus back to Guilin, with a stop at a riverside village so we could shop at a street market. This is where I bought my lovely watercolor of the Li River for 50 Yuan's, or $6. It cost me more to frame the pictures.

We had some time before dinner so I coaxed Jay to join me along with 3 women to have a foot massage. Frank led us to a parlor across the street from the Sheraton. In a private room we settled into chaise lounges and five young ladies, with surprising strong hands, started our reflexology with a soak in warm herb water. Jay got nervous when they worked above the knee. We expected to work only on the feet but after the foot massage they sat us up on the footstools and gave us a back massage. It was a great, relaxing experience.

The next morning was free to enjoy the beauty of Guilin. I went for a before-breakfast walk with Joanne, our comedian, up Elephant Walk, on one of the rounded limestone hills on the bank of the Li River. There were hundreds of Chinese out at this time, walking, meditating, practicing Tai Chi, even ballroom dancing along the river's edge. We were the only non-Asians. They were practicing their English "hello" and we were practicing our "nihao" on them. Westerners could learn how to start each day from these ancient people.

After lunch we visited the Reed Flute Cave on the way to the airport for out 5th short southeastern and final flight in China from Guilin to Hong Kong. The Cave was full of stalactites, stalagmites and a huge Crystal Palace cavern but blunted by the souvenir shops at the entrance.

We were sorry that Frank Qi had to leave us at the Guilin airport. Even though he is a Chinese national he cannot travel to Hong Kong without a visa. The government does not want to have Hong Kong overrun with people from the mainland striving for better jobs.

HONG KONG

The Chep Lap Kok airport, extending into the harbor was quite impressive, but by the time we checked into the ultra-luxurious Mandarin Hotel in Hong Kong it was too late for us to consider a large dinner. The Mandarin is even more luxurious than the Kempinski in Beijing, although the Kempinski had larger rooms. Except for the great breakfast buffets at the hotel we were on our own in Hong Kong for lunch and dinner. We could finally get back to our normal eating habits. Often the fruit in the rooms, including edible orchids, sufficed for lunch.

Through a connected concourse we found Oliver's Deli across the street and bought vodka for only $17 versus $55 in Guilin. In Guilin we could not have found a liquor store on our own. Jay and I chose to ride the Star Ferry to Kowloon and back and were delighted that seniors ride free. We had visited Hong Kong in the 1980s and were amazed at how much more has been built in this city. All the night lights and new construction are blemished by the increased smog. The smog also resulted in poor pictures in many large cities of China necessitating the purchase of post cards.

Our early morning tour of the city began with a bus ride up Victoria Peak, then on to Repulse Bay for a harbor cruise of the colorful fisherman's village at Aberdeen. Next was a shopping stop at the famous Stanley Market. I bought two cashmere stoles at irresistible prices. Then back to the hotel to enjoy the fruit lunch before going out to dinner with Joanne and Sherry, our two comedians. We went to the Revolving 66 restaurant for we remember how elegant it was when we were here twenty some years ago. We closed the place after two and a half revolutions, two bottles of wine and much laughter. Many did not join us for it was now a buffet instead of full service. The buffet, however, was above average with shark fin soup, oysters, lobster, prime rib and many other western choices. It was their loss.

The next morning was free so everyone slept in then started to pack. In the afternoon a harbor cruise was scheduled around Hong Kong Island through the multitude of cargo ships being off or on loaded at anchor. Dock cannot handle the volume of trade in this busy port city.

At a farewell dinner the entire group met in the Mandarin Oriental's Vong Restaurant on the top floor for an excellent seafood dinner and to say our goodbyes. Our thirteen hours back to San Francisco was uneventful, with our three hour layover in a frigid San Francisco terminal resulted in coming home with colds after this busy but most memorable vacation.

*C*HAPTER 40

The next year, 2003, we moved into a beautiful home that we had built for us in the Deerbrooke Subdivision at 5522 Antler Trail, Lakeland, FL. We had bought two quarter acre lots for $25,000 each, figuring we would sell one, eventually. We had lived on a small island for 33 years so we did not need to be near the water any longer. We had taken a week's trip from Pompano Beach to Central Florida and driven as far north as Mount Dora, which was too touristy for us; we saw that in St. Thomas. Looked at Ocala; it was too isolated. Then spent a night in Winter Haven but it was too close to Disney with all their seasonal tourists. We settled on Lakeland. We had three criteria, high speed internet access, good medical facilities and airports nearby so we could travel. By choosing Lakeland we were between Tampa International, 35 miles and Orlando International, 50 miles.

We rented a single wide trailer at Highland Village, just a few miles from the home we had built for us so we could keep track of it daily. We could have everything we wanted in this house including a modem in the garage, three bedrooms downstairs with one being an office, two full baths downstairs including a spa tub in the master bedroom, a door to the back lanai, a loft with another full bath, a sewing room with wooden floors, two attics where we could have storage space without climbing up a folding stairway, the dining room and breakfast room, also with wooden floors, kitchen with all new appliances, a laundry room with washer, dryer, extra refrigerator, two car oversized garage with an exit door, open design where you can see into the main living room with decorative lights in the upper cove, a large screened porch in the rear, and a front porch. We did not want to bother with a pool, having that experience at Sand Dollar where a pool is a requirement for a rental vacation home. We chose to put the tile field in the back yard but later in driving by the house we saw the new owners had added a pool after moving the tile field to the side of the house. What fun I had picking out all the new appliances, finding an upholsterer in Lakeland to recover my sister-in-laws rater new sofa and my first easy chair for the master bedroom. She was moving at the same time into a facility in St. Petersburg where she can go from independent living to full nursing care when required.

I had spent a great effort in the landscaping of the property plus we had a professional put in a berm in the backyard and landscaped the berm. We sold the extra lot to a single lady that was a process server for an attorney's firm. Next door to us lived a young family with two small children. Across the street was a brother and sister living together, their mother had died before we found the place. The area was dotted with large live oak trees. So much was being developed in the vicinity. The entrance into the subdivision had a builder's model home on the first lot, this is how we found our builder who showed us his home nearby and, seeing his quality of work, we hired him immediately. We were cash buyers so he anticipated no problems from us, as long as he performed his end of the bargain.

CHAPTER 41

We were living in our new beautiful home in Deerbrooke. We told the builder to repair any damage while we were gone but we were leaving for a long-planned trip.

We had postponed our trip to Australia because we wanted to see the Yangtze River in China before it was raised and flooded by the Great Dam project. Now we could plan our trip "Down-Under". I had spent many hours on the Internet planning this long trip from August 31st to October 17th in 2004. We had hoped to go in March but we could not get frequent flyer miles seats until August. We had saved up our frequent flyer miles; I transferred the maximum allowed, 10,000 miles and had to purchase some miles for Jay, as I do most of the shopping. We were able to go first class on this long flight to the other side of the world. One leg from Los Angeles to Melbourne was in business class but upstairs so it was quiet. We started on a Tuesday, 8/31/04, crossed the International Date Line and landed in Melbourne on Friday, 9/3/04. Jenn Beck of Goway included Goway's VIP program because we choose upscale hotels. Jenn did a fantastic job for our entire trip. We were picked up by private car at the airport and transferred to the Park Hyatt, a five-star hotel.

MELBOURNE

We spent the first two nights at the Hyatt, reminding us of the fancy hotels on our trip to China. The hallways and our spacious room were paneled in dark mahogany. The lighting was ultra-modern. The marble bath had a spa tub with another wall TV over the tub. Down comforters and pillows adorned the king size bed, both much appreciated after our eighteen hour flight.

After a short nap we strolled around the hotel, the park, visited the cathedral and wandered down along the Yarra River. We hopped on a free trolley the city provided to the Queen Victoria Market. We again took the trolley to the Tramcar Restaurant where we were scheduled to dine at the first seating. We were early so we stopped for a drink at the Crown Casino near the Tramcar. Jay had a beer; I wanted a martini until I learned they were $12.00. I said never mind and took a sip of Jay's beer.

I was surprised and embarrassed when a tall, young, Aussie set down a martini in front of me. He had been sitting at the bar and overheard me. As we thanked him he told us he had just won $3500 at the casino and was sharing some of his winnings. What a pleasant greeting on our first night in a new country from an extraordinary goodwill ambassador.

The Tramcar was a unique and fabulous experience. These glossy traveling tramcar restaurants on wheels are the only ones in the world. The car was decorated in Victorian era burgundy velvet booths, fringed lamps and gold satin drapes. The Maitr'd made sure our glass was never empty. An exceptional evening, dining and drinking Australia's finest.

The next morning we had our first glitch in the trip: we missed the bus because we were not told that we had to be down on the street as the bus could not come up the narrow Hyatt driveway. The cabbie was upset because this was only a $5 fare after he waited in line for two hours. He asked for $8, we gave him $10 and planned on back charging Goway. He got us to the tour bus run by Australian Pacific

Tours for a city tour. We viewed cathedrals, parks, gardens, the Shrine of Remembrance war memorial and historic landmarks. It was the beginning of springtime in Australia with many spring flowers in bloom.

We were on our own for lunch. We settled on a local café downtown and found that the portions were as large as those served in the States. After lunch we boarded a different bus to be taken to Phillip Island National Park to see the world renowned "Little Penguin Parade". We stopped at Warrook Homestead for refreshments along the way and the Koala Conservation Center. At the Warrook Homestead we could pet and feed wallabies and kangaroos, both nocturnal animals and lethargic during daylight hours. I did have a fight with a wallaby that wanted my cone filled with seeds. He boxed me until I gave him the entire cone.

Before the penguin parade we were driven to the tip of Summerland Peninsula where we saw Australia's largest population of fur seals on the rocks at the The Nobbies along with thousands of shearwaters and muttonbirds, nesting here from September to April, when they return north to the Bering Strait in the Arctic.

At dusk we lined up along the elevated boardwalk at Summerland Beach where the little penguins emerge from the sea. The doll size penguins were called "fairy penguins" before the days of "political correctness". These flightless birds waddle a couple hundred yards up a steep hill to their burrows dug into the sand dunes where their young are waiting to be fed. No pictures were allowed as the flash would frighten the penguins but postcards are available. You must check under thwe car or bus before leaving the parking lot to avoid hitting a wee one that might be enjoying the engine warmth. We were in the southern hemisphere so it was very cold and windy. The temperature was in the 40s with strong winds and lower wind chill temperatures. We used our large Park Hyatt umbrella as a windbreak.

OCEAN ROAD TO ADELAIDE

After a couple more glitches we finally picked up our Toyota Camry rental car at the airport. The next cab driver was worse than the one we had yesterday. This man was mad that the cab ride was too short, especially from this glitzy hotel. We were told to take a cab and back charge Goway to the Hertz office in town. He grumbled the whole way until I told him he should get a different job. He refused to help us with our luggage. We walked away without closing his trunk. He slammed the trunk and cursed us. Interestingly, the Aussies never tip, which we found strange but something we could get used to. Melbourne is the capital of the state of Victoria, we were heading to Adelaide, the capital of the state of South Australia. The distance was 480 miles and we had three days to explore the country.

The Ocean Road was winding and narrow so the driving was slow. We could not reach the town I planned on so we stopped at a tourist information office. They called ahead and made a reservation for us at the Arabella Country House, a B and B east of Princetown. When we drove up at dusk Arabella looked like and ordinary ranch style motel but we were pleasantly surprised with the exterior. Half of the home on this immense farm was the owners' residence and the other half had four guest bedrooms with a large great room for guests to lounge in front of a fireplace, visit read, play games and have their breakfast. The owners, Lyn and Neil Boxshall were friendly and attentive. Hurricane Francis was bearing down on our son's home in Okeechobee, FL so Neil kept us alerted via the Internet as to the storm's progress. He was once a dairy farmer, got tired of the daily chore of milking cows and turned to beef cattle.

PORT CAMPBELL NATIONAL PARK

We came to the most dazzling section of the drive. The road snakes along the cliff tops for incredible breath taking views. We stopped several times walking boardwalks along the coastline to see how the

Southern Ocean has gnawed the limestone cliffs for ages, creating a badland-by-the-sea. There are columns of resilient rock formations named the Twelve Apostles, standing tall amidst the crashing surf and more dramatic formations at Bay of Martyrs and Bay of Islands. It is a photographer's wonderland.

Our goal for this fourth night was the Arrondoovong Homestead B&B, which I had picked from a Fodor's guide. The guide said it is a 500 acre grazing property, an 1850s bluestone homestead with 2500 sheep. I had called ahead asking for dinner as well but the owners Jeanie and Bill Sharp had made other plans for the evening so we were left on our own. We drove north for 20 minutes to Hamilton for a nice meal at the Strand Inn. We also found a liquor store in Hamilton that sold Yellow Tail wine. The wine is hard to find in Australia—it is all shipped to the United States.

We took Lyn and Neill's suggestion and were heading for Ann's Place in Robe, southeast of Adelaide. Ann's Place is shorefront property where we could watch the rough seas of the Southern Ocean. Ann's was immaculate with comfortable guest room with TV, a spacious bath with spa tub, a large guest living/dining room. We crashed for a nap. Then, while I wandered off to a Laundromat near the B&B, Jay chatted with a surgeon and his wife from Adelaide. We went to dinner with them at a pub nearby. I tried kangaroo steak for the first time. Jay stuck to beef. No adventure in that man.

ADELAIDE

We asked Ann to serve us breakfast at 7:30 so we had time to find the airport and turn our car in before noon. Adelaide is known as the Festival City, renowned for its celebrations of the arts and bountiful harvest from the vines, land and sea. 90% of resident live in the fertile south around Adelaide. Locals worry more about bushfires than taxes or crime. This state produces most of the nation's wine. The city trees are filled with parrots fleeing the state's scorching northern desert. We were here in the early spring and still found many parrots squawking in the trees. We stayed at the Radisson Playford Hotel in town. Our room was nice but couldn't hold a candle to the Park Hyatt in Melbourne. The Rundle Mall is carless and reminded us of the squares in Europe.

BAROSSA VALLEY

We were picked up at 9:00 a.m. by Adelaide Sightseeing for an all day tour to Barossa Valley, the largest wine-producing region in Australia. The drive to Barossa, northeast of town was scenic, meandering along the Torrens Gorge. The tour took us to three premium cellar doors where many wines were tasted but we found none we like as much as Yellow Tail. We saw 400 year old vines that were still producing. Lunch was at the Jacobs Creek Visitor Centre in the heart of the valley. Back to the Radisson at 5:30 p.m. then walked a block to a popular café where the waitress was kind enough to warn us that we could easily share a dinner.

KANGAROO ISLAND

A private limo service picked us up at 8:15 A.M. for our early flight on Emu Airways to Kangaroo Island where we were to tour the island then overnight at the Kangaroo Island Lodge. We had the Radisson store our luggage, we took only overnight bags. We also learned that the large hotels have laundries in their basement where you can do your own laundry. We didn't need to bring so many clothes. The Kangaroo Island tour was in a minivan with just a few tourists. We saw rugged, unspoiled terrains, but the weather was too windy and cold for our thinned out blood. Wildlife is the island's greatest attraction. The most interesting sights are on the south coast exposed to Antarctic winds. The cold wind penetrated our wind breakers and sweatshirts. The fur seals and sea lions were fascinating. A baby sea lion wanted to play with the visitors at Seal Bay. He had no fear of humans. The Lodge was disappointing, however. We learned that we did not have to stay overnight. The island is only ten miles offshore. We could have taken a plane or even the bus back to Adelaide. We flew back to Adelaide the next mid-morning. Checked into the Radisson again and received our second set of free drinks. This is all right.

COOBER PEDY

Had Sunday at leisure and repacked for our Sunday side trip, 527 miles northwest to Coober Pedy, in the Outback, known for its opal riches. The Radisson kept our luggage once more for the three days we would be in Coober Pedy. This trip promised to be one of the highlights of our vacation. Opals are the reason for Coober Pedy's existence, the site of the world's richest opal field. Summer temperatures can reach 118 degrees but in the dugouts the temperatures remains a constant 72 to 75 degrees. 70% of the 3500 residents live in dugouts. Our original reservations said we would be noodling during our city tour. Noodling or fossicking (rummaging) through the piles of rock to find your own souvenirs of opals. The practice was stopped when a journalist backed into an open mine and broke her leg. The pits are straight down, about six feet in diameter enough to get a miner down and his haul up by a crane device on the back of a pickup truck.

The interesting thing is you can join the Coober Pedy Golf Club for just $25 and have reciprocity at St. Andrews in Scotland. Of course, here in the desert you would have oiled greens and drag a board to even out your puts.

We elected to stay in an underground room at the Desert Cave Hotel. The restaurant, bar and shops were underground, also churches, even houses. We bought some unset opals home for Diane and me to be brought home, duty free, and set by a master jeweler in the Tampa mall. The shop was Umoona Opal Museum and Mine.

We walked in town and found the grocery/department store when we arrived and, thankfully, bought fly nets, worn over sunhats. We were in the Outback surrounded by cattle stations with thousands of cows and gazillions of flies.

The next day we were scheduled to take an all-day Mail Run to deliver packages, mail and even tires to various cattle stations. Mail is only delivered on Mondays and Thursdays. The van was an air-conditioned Hummer type vehicle equipped to handle two dozen passengers and packages on the roof. The Outback is dry, hot, and dusty. Even the horses wear face masks to keep the flies from drinking the water from their eyes. We were so glad we bought the fly nets. The trip was arduous but we would not have missed it. We traveled 385 miles on packed red dirt roads, through the dingo-fence, longer than the Great Wall of China, runs 3,200 miles to 5,800 miles, depending on which boast you believe. It effectively sections off the southeastern third of the country to protect grazing sheep. The land is so barren that square miles are needed to feed the cattle.

When we arrived at the Peake Station, an outstation of Anna Creek, the largest cattle station in the world, consisting of six million acres, 100 square miles, the size of Belgium, the wranglers, including Aborigines, were practicing for a branding contest.

In the distance we saw a herd of wild camels. The mailman said there are an estimated half million wild camels in the Outback, left over from the days of the Afghan cameleers. Now they are shipping the camels back to the Middle East because Australia's camels are so pure bred. We approached Coober Pedy in the cool desert evening under a canopy of thousands of brilliant stars. We were exhausted but much more informed about life in the Australian Outback.

THE GHAN

The legendary train was named after the hardy Afghans and the camel which provided the only means of transport into "The Red Centre" in the early days. We chose the Gold Kangaroo service, including sleeping compartment and meals.

We dined with an Australian couple, enjoying their stories and recommendations. The champagne welcome party was too late for us so we retired to our too-small sleeping cubicle. The clackity-clack of the train wheels did not help our sleep. We soon realized we are not train travelers, unless we could have an entire private car.

ALICE SPRINGS

We arrived at noon and were met by private car to transfer us to the Alice Springs Resort, a lovely hotel with large guest rooms. Alice Springs is surrounded by the Mac Donnell Ranges. The Springs, is an oasis in this vast land, with a population of 27,000 in the middle of the desert. It was a short walk to town where we experienced another unusual Aussie event. Once a year, on the third Saturday in September the Henley-On-Todd Regatta is held. The highlight of the all-day event is a race of boaters, dressed in bottomless watercraft scampering across a dry riverbed. In the past 42 years the Regatta had to be cancelled twice because there was water in the Todd River. What a hilarious sight, watching seemingly sane people race in bottomless craft, even bath tubs, through the deep course sand of the Todd River. The multi-event program attracts many local and international participants from the audience. They were paddling canoes with sand shovels. Signs on the trees warn of "No Nudity On The Beach, Riptides and Man-Eating Sharks", but lifeguards are present in case of trouble. The show culminates in a battle of three large ships, a Viking, a Pirate and a Navy ship, including cannons, water guns, and choking black smoke. Watching this event under shady gum trees, cold beer in hand and friendly Australians is a memory not soon forgotten.

AYERS ROCK—ULURU

Since this was only a three day trip to Ayers Rock and Kings Canyon, the hotel kept our luggage for us in Alice Springs. We were picked up at 6:30 a.m. taking only overnight bags, by Australian Pacific Tours, traveling southwest through the MacDonnell Ranges. It was a pleasant stop at Fullerton's Camel Farm where for just $5 I had a short ride on a camel. The ride was smoother than I expected. My camel, Mona, didn't even spit at me when I gave her a hug and a kiss to thank her. We lunched here with me trying camel burger, Jay stuck to his hamburger. No adventure in him.

We had time for a quick lunch before a 2:30 p.m. tour of Kata Tjuta (the Olgas), 36 rocky domes dominating the western skyline of the park, containing numerous hidden gorges and chasms. We walked into majestic Olga Gorge, the deepest valley between the rocks; saw our first caves with Aboriginal paintings dating back thousands of years. I had the opportunity to taste a bush flower, looking much like the bottle brush flower we know in Florida. The flower is used as a sweet treat for the Aborigine children. It tasted like brown sugar syrup.

At last we were seeing one of the wonders of the world, Ayers Rock, Uluru in the Aborigine language. It is one of the world's largest monoliths; an immense magnetic mound located on a major planetary point much like the Great Pyramid in Egypt. The Rock rises 1056 feet above the desert floor and extends over 3.5 miles beneath the surface. The girth is over fifteen miles. Uluru is sacred ground to the Aborigines and large signs ask the visitor not to climb the Rock but the request is ignored, dozens of people climb it. Only in recent years were the sacred sites and parks returned to native tribe's ownership. At sunset we were bused to an area where dozens of other tour buses and tour companies sponsored a wine and hors d'oevres party for their groups. There were at least 200 to 300 tourists enjoying this spectacular sight and the party. We had breakfast in our room for the meals at the Sails Restaurant at Uluru are very expensive.

At the Sails Resort, we did not know how to turn off the air conditioner. Jay was so cold that he couldn't join me for the 4:30 a.m. tour to Uluru to see the colors in the morning. We had to check out immediately to head for Kings Canyon. It was a long ride to Kings Canyon Resort, the only place to stay within the park, four miles from the actual canyon, especially with just an overnight bag for luggage. The walk in Kings Canyon was too difficult for Jay to maneuver with his limited vision. We should not have come on this side trip. We at last relaxed with a warm soapy soak in the large hot tub with a picture window and a view of the barren hillside behind the cottage.

DARWIN

We had an early morning pickup to take us back to Alice Springs Resort, where we were flying out to Darwin, in the Northern Territory. The Top Enders are isolated from the rest of Australia by thousands of miles of desert and lonely scrub land. The lush tropical city of Darwin, the gateway to the region where people from fifty different national and cultural backgrounds live in what they regard as the real Australia. Darwin is very close to Asia and during our visit there was a terrorist attack on the Australian Embassy in Indonesia. Security at the airport was stricter than any we had seen in the States. The year in the tropical north is divided into two seasons, Wet and Dry. We were in the Dry time (May to November) so we enjoyed idyllic tropical days with cool evenings. Private car transported us to the Novotel Atrium Hotel on the waterfront looking out at the Timor Sea, east of the Indian Ocean.

We walked the town streets and found a grocery store, Woolworth's, where we could replenish our wine and breakfast supplies. In the evening we walked the streets again and saw a multitude of bats at sunset and heard hundreds of parrots in the trees squawking at us incessantly. Had breakfast in the room, packed an overnight bag while leaving our luggage with the hotel again. We were picked up at 6:30 a.m. by Australian Pacific Tours for a Kakadu Art Sites and Wildlife tour with an overnight at the Gagudju Crocodile Hotel in the park. We traveled across the Marrakai Plains and into Kakadu National Park. We visited the Warradjan Aboriginal Cultural Center to learn the historical significance the park hold for its traditional owners. We joined a guided boat cruise on the Yellow Water billabong, Kakadu's most famous wetland area. It was the end of the wet season so the wildlife was not as profuse as normal. There were, however, saltwater crocodiles, birdlife, water buffalos, wild horses, water lilies and various unusual plant life. Out light skinned Aborigine guide was half Aborigine, half Swedish. She had never seen her father, was raised by her mother and loved her work, the park and her mixed heritage. After a picnic lunch we traveled to Nourangie Rock to view the ancient galleries of artwork. The red-ocher stick figures date back 2,000 years and the x-ray paintings date back about 9,000 years. These paintings in cave shelters record the evolution of the land and people of this region over the last 40,000 years.

We dined at the Gagudju Hotel, a Holiday Inn, with Jay sharing a dinner of ostrich steaks with a delicious sauce. At last he tried something new. We then had another boat ride on the East Alligator River with two Aborigine guides and a stop ashore for a demonstration of bush life tools, crafts and medicine. There really are no alligators here but the river was misnamed by pioneers that mistook the crocodiles for alligators. This trip was much more interesting than the one on the Yellow River billabong but again we were here at the wrong time of the year to see a lot of wildlife. It was a long bus ride back to Darwin and the Novotel Atrium Hotel. Along the highway the driver stopped so we could examine and photograph huge termite mounds that were twice as tall as a man. At sunset we were treated to wine and snacks by the tour company at the Bowali Visitor Centre to take photos of the setting sun over the western Outback desert.

CAIRNS

We had to be ready at 4:50 a.m. for our 5:50 a.m. flight from Darwin to Cairns, Queensland. There was no other option for the flight. We arrived at the Sebel Reef House room in Palm Cove, north of Cairns at 10:00 a.m. The hotel provided limo service from the airport. We were so glad we opted for Palm Cove rather than Cairns, a large city. The beachside hotel reminded us of the island of St. Thomas. There was a perfect climate, like in St. Thomas with tropical flowers lining the streets, there were brick walkways, guest laundry, private balconies, frig, coffee maker, his and her bathrooms, beautiful decorations, very spacious rooms and a great restaurant. It was only a short walk to cafes, casino, wine store, bus service, sandy beach. We ate dinner at a street café, then relaxed with a glass of wine on our balcony enjoying the ocean breezes.

The next morning we were picked up by the bus service for the Quicksilver catamarans that takes tourists out to the Great Barrier Reef from Port Douglas. The Great Barrier Reef is Queensland's indigo answer to the Red Centre. Known as Australia's "Blue Outback" the reef isn't a single entity but instead a maze of 3,000 individual reefs and 900 islands, most of which are populated exclusively by seabirds and turtles. It stretches from Brisbane to Papua New Guinea, over 1,000 miles. It is the largest living feature on earth and the only one visible from space. Despite the high speed of the catamarans it was a 90 minute ride out to the Reef. I was disappointed with the Reef in comparison to the colors and life of the Reef in comparison with the Caribbean reefs. Jay was disappointed in the semi-sub also. I did see giant clams and blue coral that are not in the Caribbean but no sea fans. The two-foot rock bass were so tame that you could pet them. It was an exciting and exhausting day.

The next day we were picked up at 8:00 a.m. and transferred to the Sky rail Rainforest Cableway car for our journey to Kuranda, a village in the rainforest. We toyed with canceling this day trip but it became one of the highlights of our Australian trip. After a delicious barbeque lunch we visited the Koala and Wildlife Park with an informative guide. We had a chance to pet a kangaroo. After the park we were put on army duck amphibian boats and taken on a most interesting trip through the rainforest and into the waterways. Following the duck boats we sat on stone seats in an open amphitheater and watched Aborigine Dancers perform dances accompanied by haunting didgeridoos and stick instruments. After the show we were taken to fields where we could practice spear or boomerang throwing and didgeridoo playing. It was a day full of fun and new sights.

SYDNEY

Sebel Reef limo transported us to the airport in Cairns for our final flight in Australia to Sydney. A private car took us to the Sydney Harbor Marriot Hotel, a large city hotel, but well-located, just a half block from the Circular Quay. Found the Goway office to thank them for a wonderful trip, had a leisurely lunch in the Sydney Tower Restaurant, the city's tallest building. Seeing the city from 1,000 feet was almost as good as flying over it.

The weather was deteriorating but we had our last planned trip of this marvelous vacation. We were collected at 7:00 a.m. for an all day trip to the Blue Mountains National Park, one of the most spectacular wilderness areas in Australia. These 3500 foot mountains were once the bed of an ancient sea. The blue color is from the evaporation of oils of the eucalyptus forest. After lunch he took us to Euroka Clearing, deep within the National Park, to view kangaroos in their natural environment. We saw joeys peeking at us from their mother's cozy pouch, but were happy to board the River Cat for the ferry trip down the river into Sydney Harbour.

SYDNEY TO MELBOURNE

Our Hertz car was delivered to the hotel; there was no drop off charges to leave the car in Melbourne. We had five days to explore the coast of New South Wales and Victoria. There were 550 miles to drive through narrow, winding roads back to Melbourne. We often dined at Wineries, stayed at B & B s, the temperature was dropping. I got sick from exhaustion and driving. The best part of our trip back on Qantas in first class was that they gave us pajamas to change into and rest. We could take them home as well. I made a final mistake on this long journey in that I did not make a reservation in LOS Angeles to overnight before heading across the country for home. It was truly an interesting adventure, one we are happy we took. We can't imagine not experiencing the Outback when traveling to Australia. We salute the people of the Outback. They are as hardy as their surroundings, often eccentric, colorful characters. Remote, isolated, communities attract loners, adventurers, fortune seekers, and people simply on the run. In this unyielding country you must be tough to survive.

$\mathcal{C}$HAPTER 42

50TH WEDDING ANNIVERSARY

Our daughter planned the most wonderful 50th wedding anniversary party for us. We had a welcome party on Friday at the hotel where most people were staying which including refreshments and drinks. Following was an appointment at the beauty parlor across the street from the hotel for the women to get their hair done. After that we were picked up by limousine from our house and transported to the Eaglebrooke Country Club where the guests had their own entrance. There was a sit-down dinner for a couple of hundred people, an open bar, and a combo/singer for dancing. I read a long speech on where everyone came from and how we had met over the years. We had relatives, friends, nannies, previous workers, even the Sand Dollar buyers, plus a Secret Service agent we met in 1994.

On Sunday we provided a catered brunch at our house for all the guests; we wanted to show off the beautiful house we had built for us plus entertain everyone once more. I remember Diane telling us a long time ago that the best gift we could give our children is that we are still together, as most of our friends still are.

REPOSITIONING CRUISE ON HAL VEENDAM

I first saw the ad in Travltips magazine for a repositioning cruise of Holland America's Veendam ship ending up in Tampa, only 35 miles from home. The Veendam would be transiting the Panama Canal and traveling 1000 miles up the Amazon to Manaus before docking in Tampa for the season. We had always wanted to take both of these trips and what better way to celebrate being together so long. Because Jay, to pass the time, can't read books with his limited vision I made arrangements with our Public Library to take along several audio books that he could listen to on our newly purchased CD player. We booked through Travltips, who scheduled two cocktail parties for the 39 travelers. This was the first trip up the Amazon for the captain of the ship also. It was our third cruise so we tried to act as nonchalant as the other extensive travelers.

Because of the length of the cruise and the destination we splurged and booked a verandah room that had a chaise lounge, a chair and table on the porch. We figured we earned it over the many years; we were in the process of now spending the children's inheritance, as parents are expected to do. Because of the length of the cruise and destination we splurged and booked a verandah room. On the porch we had a chaise lounge a table and chairs. In the cabin we had hanging lockers, two night stands, with two drawers in each, nine drawers in a vanity, a minibar, a jet tub, king bed and two foot locker drawers under the bed plus space for our suitcases. The frig came in handy for we were allowed to bring soft drinks, wine and champagne aboard from port visits but not hard liquor. Vodka was easily smuggled aboard in ever present water bottles.

Service on the HAL ships was impeccable. Fresh fruit was always available in our stateroom; a laundry facility was accessible to guests, plenty of activities were provided, hand sanitizers were everywhere, and we were expected to use them. With a guest capacity of 1266 and a crew staff of 560, the mandatory use of hand sanitizers was crucial. Dress code was casual, but no jeans were allowed in the dining room.

Two Captain's formal dinners were planned where men had to wear a jacket and tie. Our dinner guests sharing our table were the same throughout the cruise; unfortunately, we would have liked to have various dinner guests to meet more people. One couple at our dinner table was on their 42nd cruise. After the turndown service many clever animal shapes were left in our room. They were cleverly made from fresh towels.

SEATTLE

Our first port of call was Seattle, the largest city in Washington State and the Pacific Northwest. Disembarking always involved carrying our photo ID which was scanned every time we left or arrived on the ship to keep track of passengers.

We chose to walk to Pike's Place Market, a distance of five miles round trip. The Market was as we remembered it, laden with colorful flowers, luscious fruits, vegetables, unusual mushrooms and overflowing with seafood of every imaginable variety. The salmon fishmongers threw large fish from one employee to another putting on quite a performance.

AT SEA

It was a day to get back into our regular morning gym routine. We only had to climb from the 9th to the 11th deck to reach the gym, equipped with every machine imaginable. After a gaming lesson at the casino I joined the kitchen tour and cooking demonstration. The weekly consumption of tons of food is mind boggling. I took part in every activity provided, not wanting to miss a thing.

The Captain's formal reception was scheduled for this evening. I wore my red long 50th anniversary dress and received rave reviews. The crew liked the color; several ladies said I got an "A" and one couple along our way stopped us. The man said "I just have to tell you that you look like a million bucks". What a nice complement.

LOS ANGELES

Early arrival at 7:00 a.m., departing at 3:00 p.m. We learned of a free trolley to downtown Long Beach where we bought a case of coke for Jay, root beer for me and six beers. The store cashier said we could take our buggy to the trolley five blocks away and they would retrieve the carts for us. What a pleasant surprise. No problem bringing the drinks aboard with one fellow even carrying a bottle of Scotch. We brought Vodka from home as the prices on the ship are extremely high.

AT SEA

I went to 8:00 a.m. mass in the movie theater room the first Sunday we were on the ship. HAL always carries a priest onboard on longer than ten day cruises. On this ship there was a minister and even a rabbi, especially if Jewish holidays occur during the cruise. All three were on this ship plus a doctor and nurses in the infirmary. The Captain announced that we have travelled 2600 nautical miles from Vancouver.

The second Captain's formal dinner was held this evening. In the reception line we thanked the Captain for getting us safely past Hurricane Otis, which became a category 3 storm. The ship was rolling all night. The winds and seas were high with another Hurricane, Stan, brewing in the Pacific. A third hurricane was heading for the States. He also said we might miss Acapulco because of the storms. It was a disappointment, but, as in flying "if the pilot doesn't want to go, neither do you". The night could be rough, he advised. I started taking Dramamine; Jay never did have a problem with motion sickness.

We had several days at sea but we never were bored. Jay listened to his audio books and I participated in many activities including a "Survivor" type show and a performance for the audience put on by the guests, including the priest, minister, and rabbi.

The afternoon guest lecturer was Richard Holt, an expert on the Panama Canal. His grandfather was one of the original engineers that built the Canal; his father was a pilot on the Canal, as well. Holt's lecture was most informative, we were eager to see this engineering marvel.

The next morning we heard an interesting lecture on the construction of the "Big Ditch" presented by a third generation Panamanian. She related the history of Panama.

Instead of the midnight buffet to display the artistic talents of the chefs a Sunday afternoon was taken for this picturesque buffet. The food was exceptional; you hated to bite into the various animals and forms.

ACAPULCO, MEXICO

Storm had abated enough that we were able to visit Acapulco after all. There was only one tour we had booked, the famous cliff divers. The Captain said we would be at the dock by 11:00 a.m. Unfortunately he also had to announce that the side thrusters were not working and we would try to kedge ourselves into the dock but the winches were not strong enough for the bow, spring and aft lines. We at last were at the dock but late so the morning and afternoon cliff divers tours were combined and we got to see these insane men dive from the cliffs after saying a prayer at the small grotto built at the diving site.

We were disappointed in Acapulco in general. There was no pride to clean, fix or paint the buildings. We did see an Applebee's, a Walmart Super Store, and a bingo/gaming parlor on the way to the divers. Of course, if we had come on our honeymoon, as originally planned it would have been much different—before it was "discovered" by tourists.

SANTA CRUZ, HUATULCO, MEXICO

This small village in the rugged southern Mexican state of Oaxaca (wah-HAH-kah) is within 150 miles of Mexico City, but is a world away from the metropolis. Huatulco lacks industry and affluence but has a large indigenous population. We arrived on an overcast day so it took only an hour to see the village, the open air church, and find a store that sold pure vanilla to take home. Saw a tourist with a cast on her leg. This was no place to find your way home from a small village like this.

PUERTO CALDERA, COSTA RICA

We had booked the "Skywalk in the Rainforest". It was not what we expected. We had a 45 minute bus ride to the mountain top and walked downhill for 1.5 miles. We crossed three suspension bridges, watched crocodiles sunning themselves on a sand bank in the river on the way to the mountaintop, saw a couple of toucans in the distant trees, heard two Macaws flying high, red mushrooms on the walk, and many parades of leaf cutter ants carrying loads far exceeding their own weights. This was the only wildlife we saw on the entire trip. It was not the lush rainforest we had envisioned.

We were advised to get up early the next to enjoy the Costa Rican coast, the Golfo Dulce, but after the Skywalk we were not impressed with Costa Rica. The show this evening was a Jamaican comedienne Mathilda as the dummy, and Dennis Murray as the ventriloquist. They were so funny that we bought their DVD.

We had seen three different couples leaving the ship with casts and broken legs that had to make their way home from these small Mexican villages. We were so happy that no sad incident happened to us.

PANAMA CANAL

The Panama Canal is an incredible engineering feat, opened in 1915 and still operating well after the Panamanians took over on December 31, 1999. The Panama is a lock type canal that is approximately 48 miles long and unites the Pacific and Atlantic Oceans, saving ships thousands of miles. Since its opening, about 874,000 ships have transited the waterway. The Canal's three sets of locks, each of which has two lanes, serves as a water lifts which elevate ships 85 feet above sea level to Gatun Lake. Here they cross the Continental Divide, to then be lowered back to seal level on the opposite side of the isthmus. What is amazing is that 58 million gallons of water is used for each lockage and it is ultimately flushed to the sea. There is so much rainfall in this area that Gatun Lake and damming of the Chagres River supply all the water for the locks.

Though vessels use their own propulsion for the greater part of the transit, they are assisted when passing through the locks by electric locomotives which use cables to align and tow the ships. Depending on its size, a vessel can require the assistance of four to eight locomotives. Tug boats may also be required in the chamber with the vessel. The Veendam with a beam of 101 ft. just fit in the 106 ft. wide chambers.

ORANJESTAD, ARUBA

The days at sea were numerous and filled with activities. Our next stop was Oranjestad, Aruba. We found a market where we bought four bottles of wine, vermouth and two liters of vodka, all well priced. We had no trouble bringing all aboard but we did learn that vodka bubbles when shaken so Jay lost his water bottle but the guards let this little old lady through with no trouble.

ST. GEORGE'S, GRENADA

Our table group agreed to meet ashore and have an island tour for a fraction of the cost booked through the Veendam. The quality of the Amazon River is so full of silt that the ship will not be able to make fresh water and the laundry rooms will be closed.

After our island tour of 3.5 hours we welcomed the air conditioned ship, then rushed to the laundry to do our last one before we reach the Amazon. The next day King Neptune presented a proper ceremony for the "pollywogs" that had never crossed the equator before by ship.

King Neptune had to come a day early so the navigation pool could be refilled before we reach the River.

AMAZON RIVER

The Amazon is a gigantic system of rivers and forests covering almost half of Brazil and extending into neighboring countries. The volume at the river mouth is 46,000 gallons per second, 6000% of the output of the Nile. The Amazon varies in width from one to thirty five miles but the mouth of this great river is more than 250 miles wide and actually relatively shallow. With the river six feet below normal our Captain was concerned that we would be digging our own trench. We did see many riverboats, the main transportation mode for this area, high and dry along the shoreline. Our destination city of Manaus is 1000 miles upstream and can be reached only by boat or plane. Manaus is the furthest point for ocean going vessels.

It was amazing to see the brown Amazon rushing past the leisurely Rio Negro (Black river), acidic from the vegetation, and having no mosquitoes. The two rivers have densities so different that they do not mix for several miles. This "Meeting of the Waters" occurs about 8 miles from Manaus.

BOCA DE VALERIA

This half day visit was a truly Amazonian experience. Boca is a typical primitive Amazon village with around 75 residents. Many of the local homes are stilted for the rainy season. The natives were friendly and invited tourists into their homes. We took pictures with the chief, saw the schoolhouse, chapel, bought hand-made crafts, and saw the muddy swimming hole with children drinking the silty water. At the bar we could even buy an ice cold beer for $1. This was a phrase that all these primitive people knew how to say in English: ONE DOLLAH. ONLY ONE DOLLAH.

It was off this village that we saw the pink dolphins, known in Brazil as "botos". Of all the dolphins they are known to be the most intelligent, with a brain capacity 40% larger than that of humans.

SANTOREM

Santorem is nearly impossible to reach overland. In the 1920s Henry Ford established the Ford Industrial Co. of Brazil near Santorem to raise rubber trees for tires. We had booked the Walk in the Tapajos Forest, which was a big mistake. The trip is not for seniors. we told the shore excursion official our opinion of the tour. We did learn that the Brazil nut trees do not bear fruit until they are 100 years old, are 100 feet high, and that we could not bring a bagful home. They must be roasted immediately, after they are harvested from the ground.

MANAUS

Manaus was once the fifth wealthiest city in the world in the 19th century. Furniture was shipped from Europe, all made by hand. The residents were so rich from the rubber trees that they sent their laundry to England. Entire buildings were bought in Europe, dismantled, shipped up the river and reassembled on site. The Amazonas Opera House had rubber in the pavement so the noise of the carriages would not disturb the audience. The parquet floors were fitted without the use of nails or glue. The wealthy rubber barons lit their cigars with $100 bills yet the natives were extremely poor. This city of two million people, without sewage treatment, dumps all their waste into the river. There is so much squalor; the sidewalks are paved with small 3'x3' booths of vender selling everything from tools to underwear, pirated CDs and DVDs. The government doesn't provide jobs so the vendors are allowed to hawk with no license but the must pay a fee, read insurance, to the "big boss", probably the major, $3 real per day. During our first trip to the Municipal Market we managed to get some interesting pictures of native life, enjoyed some cold cervesas, bought some $6 real vodka, poured it into our water bottles so we could smuggle it aboard the Veendam. We hunted for shelled Brazil nuts we could take home but learned that they must be roasted before eating or they taste bitter if not consumed within two days of picking. The raw Brazil nuts taste more like coconut than roasted nuts.

PARINTINS

There were seven beautiful young local girls scantily dressed with feathers, g-strings, and coconut bras passing out free cold bottles of water. We opted for the tricycle trip, which are jury-rigged, tricycles, man-powered, with a makeshift awning and decked out in palm fronds for these special visitors. We saw no cars, only motor bikes, motor cycles and the common Moto Taxi. As in Manaus, raw sewage ran down the gutters into the Amazon River. Parintins was our last stop in the Amazon. The Boi-Bumba Festival, held in June rivals Rio's Carnaval. Everyone is a member of the red or blue teams and houses, phone booths, taxis; even Coca Cola bottles are either red or blue. It is the only time Coke is bottled in blue bottles.

We are headed to Barbados on our way home to Tampa. It was nice to see clear green water again after the brown, silty Amazon. We were advised that Hurricane Wilma is at Cancun, heading for Florida tomorrow. The captain advised us that we would not be going to Half Moon Cay in the Bahamas because of the Hurricane we would instead go to St. Kitts.

The HAL chefs put on the Grand Buffet at noon today, usually the midnight buffet, but this made more sense for elderly, tired travelers. The buffet was a showpiece of many beautiful displays.

Before we retired the captain announced that there had been a diving accident in St. Kitts, we would be stopping in St. Thomas around 1:00 a.m. to offload the diver so he could use the hyperbaric chamber for decompression. We knew St. Thomas had a chamber for Jay was the first one to use the compartment when he got the bends while diving. We decided to stay up and see St. Thomas as an approach from the sea which we hadn't seen in many years. We were surprised at how lit up the island is now.

The good part of this cruise is that it dropped us off in Tampa, 35 miles from home. The Customs and Immigrations lines moved quickly and we found Diane waiting for us at the curb. She said that all the passengers looked very much alike, all seniors and white haired.

The Captains log said we had traveled 11254 nautical miles. We experienced a vacation in two areas that we had dreamed about for many years: the engineering marvel of a Panama Canal transit and the Amazon River. This cruise filled our memory book with many happy adventures, but it did not get even a dime from us at the casino.

CHAPTER 43

We got our newsletter out late in 2007 because our daughter gave us for our December birthdays, a sky dive. And we did it!

You don't get many pilots jumping out of a perfectly good airplane, like us. But for the first few times you jump you are attached to an instructor and when he goes, you go. We left the plane at over 12,000 feet; free fell for about 6,000 feet and then when the chute opened it was so quiet and peaceful. My instructor always jumped barefoot and I wondered about his landing on the gravel patch but he did it without losing too much of his feet. I found it very noisy at first for you leave the plane at 150 miles per hour or so. My birthday is on the 17th so I went first and Jay then had to go on the 29th, or risk being called a sissy by his two children. His son and my brother were to try it later in January but they were saved by bad weather. We jumped in Lakeland, where they have never had an accident. Jay would like to try it again but I don't have that on my bucket list. Been there, done that.

Other than losing our sanity in December of 2006 we have been in great health. Jay continues to curse his failing eyesight, especially with my requiring a magnifier more often.

We bought our manufactured double wide home in November of 2006 but did not want to leave our home in Deerfield at Christmastime. I could drive the 20 miles from our home built for us in south Lakeland and put away the items like dishes, linens, clothes, etc. Cypress Lakes had the lifestyle we thought we had in our home but in 3.5 years of living there not one person invited us in for a cup of coffee or a glass of wine. This was after I invited the whole street to our first Christmas Open House. At Cypress Lakes we can do as much as we want or as little. There is a full time social director, many dances, plays, a library, restaurant, two pools, a gym, shuffleboard and tennis courts, cards every day, all on the Cypress Lakes property, where Jay can drive the golf cart, if necessary.

Our trip in 2006, August 9 to 23, was a land/sea tour to our last frontier, Alaska, with Holland America Lines. We so enjoyed the Veendam on our long cruise in 2005 that we wanted to book with them again. We had eleven days on land and four days from Skagway on an HAL ship back to Vancouver where we were to fly home to Lakeland. Our Pinochle group booked a cruise to Alaska a few years ago but we were more interested in seeing the land. What surprised us is that Alaska is twice the size of Texas.

ALYESKA PRINCE HOTEL & THE KENAI PENINSULA

Alyeska is the native name for Alaska. We found Alaska to be more beautiful and rugged area than we imagined with an abundance of wildlife, mountains, vastness, and more flowers than I could ever believe loved this cold weather. Of course, the Alaskans saw this as balmy, summer weather. The Alyeska Prince Hotel, a ski resort, had a superb restaurant on the mountain top. We slept on a thick featherbed and covered with a heavier one and it was August. We had a two hour ride to reach Seward where we boarded the Glacier Explorer for the Kenai Fjords. We saw puffins, fur seals, otters floating on their backs asleep in the icy waters, many seabirds and a pod of ten or twelve Orca (killer) whales that cavorted, slapped their tails but also sang to us. The crew advised us that this was most unusual to have them sing. It was a special welcome to this last wilderness of the United States.

ANCHORAGE

A three hour bus ride took us back to Anchorage where we stayed at the Hilton and, unfortunately, never saw the moose that had the run of the yards o0r the streets. In the morning we were transferred to the McKinley Explorer train, with reserved seating for our eight hour trip to Denali Park. HAL owns the rail cars with the largest viewing windows. We sat in the upper level and dined below. The trip was interesting, picturesque, the crew friendly and entertaining.

DENALI PARK

We had two nights at the McKinley Chalets in Denali. The Chalet had three rooms, a bedroom, kitchen area and a sitting area but we were up at dawn to see the wildlife and had little time to enjoy the Chalet or visit the stores, on site or across the street. We were taken on a bus trip into the interior of the park, where private cars cannot travel to see the caribou, grizzly bears, moose, and Dall sheep (white dots high on the mountain top where no predators can reach them).

We took a tour that visited the Husky Homestead kennels of the Iditarod Champion, Jeff King. We learned about the racing, the gear and got to snuggle Husky puppies. The Alaskan Huskies are not the large, blue eyed Siberian dogs you see in the movies. They are small but are born to run and pull. When the sleds are hooked up they get so excited and all bark, "Take me. Take me." We ended our stay in Denali with a dinner show, Cabin Night Fever. It was a rowdy show, lots of fun, with salmon and ribs served family style, along with all the accompanying dishes. The waiters were also the performers. To call a waiter to your table you twirled your napkin over your head.

FAIRBANKS

We reboarded the McKinley train headed for Fairbanks. After a city tour we traveled south along the Richardson Highway passing

North Pole, AK to Rika's Roadhouse, an important stop for miners in the early 20th century. Rika's has a fur shop that rivals anything in New York City. Then we went on to Gold Dredge #8, owned by HAL. It seems this cruise ship line; Holland America is heavily invested in Alaska. It owns trains, hotels, dredges, saloons, boats, all the money-making opportunities. The size of this river walking dredge was mind-boggling. From the immense piles of dredged material we were given a "poke" (that is, a small canvas bag containing a pan for hunting gold nuggets.) Our two pans amounted to $15 worth of nuggets and it cost me $16 for a locket to hold the nuggets. A true American enterprise. At the dredge we were served a delicious miners stew in cast iron pots along with hot biscuits, all served family style, on picnic benches.

TOK

Our next stop late in the evening was Tok, Alaska, a small historic crossroads on the Alaskan and Glenn Highways. It reminded us of the Australian outback. There were only a few stores, not many houses, and a fascinating gift store with displays by an expert taxidermist. The unusual name, Tok, in one version is derived from the Athabascan word for "peaceful crossing". Another version is from the English words for "Tokyo camp", and yet another account is from the canine mascot of one of the Engineer units that built the highways.

CHICKEN, ALASKA

The next morning we turned off the Alaskan Highway to travel down the Taylor Highway to Chicken, AK., the most entertaining stop on the entire trip. Chicken is a living gold mining history. Susan Wren. (Owner of the Chicken Creek Saloon and the rest of downtown Chicken) purchased the property fifteen years ago. It was originally a hotel. There is a café, emporium, saloon. even a Chicken Poop(the outhouse). Population is about 100 in summer and 60 in winter. Legend has it that miners working the creeks 100 years ago hunted ptarmigan as a food source but since they could not spell the work they christened their new home Chicken after the bird they though most resembled the ptarmigan. We reluctantly left Chicken, Alaska after our group supported Susan's Emporium, buying most of their souvenirs at her store.

EAGLE, AK

Eagle is another isolated settlement where the winter mail comes in by ski plane. Population is 120 with 19 students in the four classroom school. (Only two are used presently)> There are no restaurants in Eagle so HAL provided box lunches for us. Children leave their shoes outdoors and keep another pair indoors. The citizens of Eagle used the Wickersham courthouse to hold a mock trial for our group followed by the citizens putting on a bazaar of their handicrafts across from the courthouse. I volunteered for jury duty and, of course, the culprit was guilty. We would have enjoyed looking at the crafts of these people if the weather cooperated. It was cold and blustery. It was much too cold for our Florida blood.

YUKON QUEEN TO DAWSON CITY

We boarded the Yukon Queen for our 102 mile trip down the Yukon River. A welcome hot meal was served on the Yukon Queen. Dawson City was most interesting with dirt roads and elevated wooden sidewalks. If you don't like your neighbor you just move somewhere else, usually in the wintertime when the land or the river is frozen. Dawson City was the original capital of the Yukon Territory. Three men discovered a fist-size gold nugget on a tributary known at Rabbit Creek, later renamed Bonanza Creek. This started the Klondike Gold Rush then work came to Dawson of the discovery of gold in Nome, so Dawson by the end of summer lost more than 8000 people.

We chose the City Walking Tour for the morning. Some of the building had scantily clad statues of girls in the upstairs windows beckoning the men for some pleasure. Our guide for the tour, "Gabriella", was dressed in turn-of-the-century costume. She led us to the closed but preserved buildings that were the bank, the mortuary and the SS. Keno steamship. There were over 250 steamships that plied the Alaskan waters in the 1890s, ninety or so on the Yukon. We met various "ghosts" along the way. The first ghost was in the bank covered up in a dogsled display. He startled everyone when he unexpectedly jumped up and said he was looking for his wife, Rose, both deceased for 100 years now. We found Rose at the Keno after a visit to the mortuary where we heard more tall tales of the olden days. Rose mistook Jay for her lost husband and he played along. This tour also included a bus ride to the Bonanza Creek but w had no luck finding any gold.

With the city tour we received two tickets for the museum or the Canadian Parks. We visited the museum then walked to the Jack London cabin originally located in an isolated rural area but later brought to the city as a tourist attraction. He had a very rugged home, just an elevated wooden platform bed with an animal skin on it, one chair, and a stone campfire for cooking and heating. Outside there was an elevated cache cabin for food supplies. We then walked to the fancier Robert Service cabin for a reading of his famous poetry by the same "ghost" that was in the bank sled. He was a fantastic reader and a lover of Service's poetry. The Service cabin included a real bed, dresser, living room furniture, a dining table, even windows.

On the evening of our second night in Dawson we walked to "Diamond Tooth Gertie's" casino for a rollicking can-can show. After the show we walked a couple more blocks to the Downtown Hotel's Sourdough Saloon, home of the Sour Toe Cocktail. If daring, you buy a Yukon Jack shot at the bar (orange flavored liqueur), then in a dark corner booth a toe is put in the glass. For a certificate you must down the shot and have your lips touch the toe. It looked gross but surely the toe, looking real, must be fake. We were housed in the bright colored Jack London building in Dawson and were thankful for the heavy drapes and featherbeds to sleep on and under in August, 2006.

We had another 8:00 a.m. departure for Whitehorse, now the capital of the Yukon. We travelled down the Overland Trail; a winter road that connects Dawson with Whitehorse. For the first time Dawson was not cut off from the rest of the world for almost eight months of the year when the Yukon River froze over.

It was a long eight hour drive with a lunch stop at Minto Resorts, a rustic place owned by HAL. A hot buffet lunch was provided by the cruise lines since there are no restaurants or settlements for miles. We pulled into Westmark Whitehorse in the evening. This city has a population of 23,000 and is the home of the main campus of Yukon College. Jay and I walked to a tent market a few blocks away that was held only on Thursdays. We shared an elk burger and in the cold wind we quickly perused the crafts at the other tents then made a dash for the hotel. The hotel creaked all night as if there were footsteps in a room above us but we were on the top floor.

The next morning we had a city tour of Whitehorse but more interesting was a trip to "Uncommon Journeys", commonly known as "Club Med" for sled dogs. At this musher's we could pet the working dogs and the puppies. Their sled dogs have been sent all over the world to well-heeled clients who have been with the Taylors on guided tours. Rod and Martha Taylor said they sleep with the newborn pups so they become acclimated to human company thus becoming ver sociable dogs. One dog is scheduled to travel to Palm Beach, Florida where the new owner is building a refrigerated lap pool for the dog to exercise in comfort.

We were returned to the Westmark for a buffet lunch before boarding the bus for the 2.5 hour trip to Carcross, Yukon Territory to meet the historic narrow-gauge White Pass and Yukon Route Railroad for our journey to Skagway where we would board the HAL ship, Volendam, for a four day cruise back to Vancouver. There were many photo stops along the way with the most interesting was the smallest dessert in the world, only 660 acres.

The ride down the White Pass & Yukon Trail was jerky and cold. One hundred thousand men and women headed north from Skagway but only 30 to 40,000 actually reached the gold fields of the Klondike. Because all prospectors were required to bring a year's supply of food with them up the White Pass, which climbs from sea level to 3,000 feet at the summit. The WP and YR, the rail built by gold, is an engineering marvel that was literally carved from sheet granite cliffs. Building the 110 miles of track was a challenge in every way. Some work took place in winter with heavy snow and temperatures as low as 60 below. The parlor cars were heated by small pot-bellied stoves.

SKAGWAY

The most interesting part of Skagway to us was not the shops but the waterways with pink and king salmon struggling upstream to reach their birthplaces for breeding. The current was very strong, sometimes with rapids to climb, but the fish were determined. It was only a two block walk to the Westmark Inn, Skagway; in fact the town can be walked in less than an hour. The population is only 850 year-round residents. One two-story shop had a façade of 8,800 sticks of driftwood.

Before casting off at 8:00 p.m. we chose another visit to a Musher's Camp with a ride by Sled Dogs. A six-passenger wheeled cart is hooked up to a sixteen dog team and these amazing animals pulled us uphill through the woods. Again we had a chance to pet puppies and learn from a different trainer.

GLACIER BAY

We picked up the Glacier Bay Park Rangers at 6:00 a.m. and they disembarked at 4:00 p.m. We heard but never got a photo of a glacier calving. Entering the Bay, you cruise along shorelines that were completely covered by ice just 200 years ago.

KETCHIKAN, AK

There was just a day to explore this city of 8,000 residents Ketchikan is known as "Alaska's First City" because it is the first town travelers reach when ferrying north. The town is named after the Creek. It is in this Creek where many salmon end their long journey to breed and die in these shallow quite waters.

The town also has the world's largest collection of standing totem poles and has the heaviest rainfall in North America, measuring its rain in feet, not inches. But we were all eager to see Creek St. Historic District. Formerly known, as "The Line", Alaska's most notorious red light district from 1902-1954. This zigzagging boardwalk above the Creek supported at 30 "sporting houses" of ill repute in its heyday. At Dolly's the flashy madam at the door wanted $5 just to tour the sporting house. Jay figured he had his own Dolly and sporting house at home-he didn't need to pay $5 just to tour this lady's house of ill repute.

We opted for the horse and buggy ride through town then walked to the salmon hatchery where fry are raised in spawning tanks and released back into various streams for replenishment. The hatchery is also a nursing home for injured birds. They had two eagles recuperating in sick bay. Surprisingly, the eagle has a wing span of eight feet. They are truly majestic-looking creatures. It's no wonder they were picked to represent the USA.

VANCOUVER, B.C.

We and were transferred to the airport for an uneventful flight back home after a most interesting and adventurous vacation in frontier Alaska. We were enthralled with the land portion of this holiday and welcomed the restful cruise back to Vancouver. Our major interest was in experiencing the vastness, wild life, and ruggedness of what was once called "Seward's Folly" but is truly a national treasure.

CHAPTER 44

HONOLULU, HI

The next year the Ledger called in January 2007 and said if we changed our yearly payment to monthly we could take advantage of a trip to Hawai'i for only $2886 for two persons. We couldn't pass up this opportunity to see the islands in our last state of the Union. Like Alaska we always wanted to see this State.

Because we would be arriving in Hawai'i at night we reserved a room before and after the cruise at Celebrity Resorts W., an easy walk to downtown and to restaurants. We would be travelling from Tampa to Dallas, Los Angeles and then on to Honolulu, HI. It was a ten day cruise on the Pride of Aloha, which must have been a foreign registry ship for we had to call in a foreign port per Federal Regulations.

HILO, HAWAI'I

The big island is the gateway to the Volcanic National Park that presents a spectacular ongoing drama of earth-in-the-making. It is here that the gradually shifting archipelago is directly linked to the Pacific Plate's source of molten lava. Volcanoes are prodigious land builders. Kilauea and Mauna Loa, two of the world's most active volcanoes, are still adding land to the island of Hawai'i. Mauna Loa is the most massive mountain on Earth. It rises 56,000 feet more than 27,000 feet higher than Mount Everest, much of it underwater. Pele, the fire goddess is the sacred living deity of Hawai'i's volcanoes.

As superb voyagers, Polynesians from the Marquesas Islands migrated to Hawai'i more than 1600 years ago. They sailed across 2,400 miles of open seas in double-hulled canoes. They brought along items essential to their survival, pigs, dogs, chickens, poi, sweet potato, coconut, banana, and sugar cane. The Hawaiian Archipelago once celebrated as islands of evolution are now islands of extinction. The arrival of people changed forever the conditions that fostered the original diversity of life. Forest disappeared as people cleared the land to plant crops and establish communities. Settlers introduced numerous alien plants and animals.

FANNING ISLAND OR TABUAERAN ATOLL

At only 900 miles distant from the Hawaiian Islands Tabuaeran Atoll is the closest foreign post south of the Hawaiian. Fanning Island is an atoll ringed with palm trees. The atoll is administered as part of the Republic of Kiribati in the Marquesas. Because we were spending the day at Fanning the ship had a barbeque for us ashore. The atoll has a population of 2,500, principally Gilbertese settlers brought from Kiribati by the Fanning Island Plantations to work in the copra (the meat of the coconut) industry. Most houses on this atoll are made of material obtained from the coconut and pandanus trees. Later in the day, we chose to stand in line to get our passports stamped by Fanning Island Immigration. We had visited on 10/25/2007.

To increase the opportunities of the islanders the government has placed greater emphasis on education. Primary education is free and compulsory for the first six years. Higher education is expanding. Students may study in other countries of their choosing, usually in Fiji.

MAUI PLANTATION AND IAO VALLEY

We visited two of Maui's most beautiful and popular attractions. Our excursion began with a guided drive to Iao Valley State Park. One of the highlights of the park is the Iao Needle, a 2,250 foot cinder cone pinnacle that dominates the surrounding lush terrain. We enjoyed a walk in the park, viewed an utmost impressive valley and then visited the unsurpassed sight of the Maui Tropical Plantation. We saw bananas, mangoes, papayas, coffee and macadamia nut trees. We bought souvenirs in the Gift Shoppe of mixtures of macadamia nuts for the family and us and had them shipped home. We were then treated to a coconut husking demonstration.

LUAU KALAMAKU ON THE ISLAND OF KAUAU'I

The luau on the island of Hauau'i was a theatrical luau, where the actors portrayed the story of the Polynesian migration to Hawai'i. The show culminated with a fantastic fire dream featuring fire poi balls and a traditional fire knife dance. In a climactic ending, Pele, the fire goddess, her sister, and prince of Kauau'i pay homage to Kauau'i mythology. There were also many hula dancers, of course. It seems whenever a Hawaiian puts on a grass skirt she can't keep her hips still.

Our menu included salmon, pork, mahi mahi fish, purple and gold sweet potatoes, macaroni salad, fresh fruit, poi, jasmine rice with star anise; dessert was, of course, pineapple upside down cake, rice pudding and chiffon cheese cake. We didn't try the poi because we heard it was too bland although the Hawaiians love it.

HONOLULU, HI

We had dinner at a beachside restaurant, and then strolled the streets of Honolulu. This being Halloween, most residents were in costume, either going to parties or just showing off their outfits. We returned to our reserved room for a good night's sleep before heading home. We were reluctant to leave this tropical paradise for it reminded us of St. Thomas with its balmy weather and tropical breezes.

At the age of 80 Jay had an emergency appendectomy this year, at the end of March. There is concern because he is on Coumadin for his atrial fibrillation. They wanted to thicken his blood before the surgery.

Diane and her husband Hamed took a trip to Egypt where Diane finally met Hamed's family. They left in August and we took care of Barney while they were away.

CHAPTER 45

In 2008 we agreed to join Bill & Sandy Mason (my Red Hat Queen) on a week's cruise to the Western Caribbean. We wanted to go on the cruise because of the chance to try the zip line rides in the tree canopies on both Belize and Roatan, Honduras. If we can skydive we certainly can zip line.

Our next door neighbor, Bob Sutton, drove the four of us to the Port of Tampa, and will pick us up when we return in a week. We left the dock in Tampa on May 18th. After a day at sea to get acquainted with the ship we arrived at Grand Cayman. I thought about swimming with the sting rays again but passed on this excursion because we had been there a few years ago with Bob and Fiona Smith and it was much more fun with people joining me in the water. We were anchored out quite far as the approach to the island is very shallow.

About three weeks before our departure date an article in the local paper stated that a woman's harness broke and she fell to her death in Honduras. The cruise line cancelled that trip and refunded our money. Later we learned that the woman was far too heavy (225 pounds is the upper limit) and although she signed a waiver, the operators should not have taken her. Thus the Legend cancelled that trip to protect themselves. We learned that the trip is still available in Honduras but on the docks, not through the cruise line. The Honduras trip would have been much easier for you are bussed to the site, plus you have 13 rides in the canopy rather than the five we had in Belize. It was an extremely long and difficult trek up the mountain to the tree line and especially tough for Jay. The path we climbed was rocky and steep plus he was carrying the backpack with water and heavy camera.

GRAND CAYMAN, CAYMAN ISLANDS

After a day at sea to find our way around the ship, our first stop was at Grand Cayman. I thought about swimming at Sting Ray City again but we had been there a few years ago with Bob and Fiona Smith. It is much more fun when others are in the water with you. So we passed on this event because Jay can't swim due to the trauma his eyes have endured over the years. Bill Mason was usually off golfing and Sandy was no company for us swimmers like Bob and Fiona Smith were in the past. We walked around the shopping area after being tendered to shore. We were anchored out quite far as the approach is very shallow. Jay had forgotten his knit shirts in his packing so we searched for long-sleeve light-weight knit shirts for our land tours, to no avail. We did see large iguanas caged in the shopping malls and noisy cockatiels to attract the tourists. The drinks ashore seemed quite expensive so we returned to the ship early to enjoy our martinis in our room or on our balcony.

COZUMEL, MEXICO

Prior to our tour we inspected the elaborate shopping mall Cozumel provides the cruise passengers. There were outdoor escalators to the second floor filled with fancy jewelry shops, bars, restaurants, and kiosks selling trinkets.

This day, Wednesday, 5/21/08, was to be an exciting one for I was to swim with the dolphins, get a kiss from one and a ride plus a handshake. Jay came along for an extra charge of $25 for all spectators. He sat on the shaded balcony and tried to take pictures and movies although he could barely see my group across the pool but perhaps it was the cervesas that blurred his vision this time.

Each participating guest had to wear a life jacket. Mine was much too large so I was fighting it throughout the event to keep it from decapitating me. A smaller, tighter one would have worked much better even if I couldn't breathe.

We were bussed to the Dolphinaris not too far from the ship docks. We were in the water about an hour and split into several groups of about 10 persons. (It was a popular tour). We swam out and on cue a large dolphin appeared to give us a kiss on the cheek then turned to present his two belly fins for a handshake. We then scattered in the water so the mammals could swim between us. We were instructed to pet them but not on the face.

The dolphin swims under your extended arms, turns on his back so you can grab hold of his two belly fins for a fast ride across the pool. The largest male in the aquarium tried several times to approach me but we didn't connect. It must have been my deodorant. A juvenile was then sent out to give me my ride. Mine was just too short a ride, but I thanked my new friend and he smiled and swam away to join the other dolphins. For the memory book I had to buy the expensive, $70 DVD, for this exceptional experience.

BELIZE, BRITISH HONDURAS

On Thursday, 5/22/08, we were in Belize where we were to ride the zip line in the tree canopy. We were both scheduled for this exciting adventure. What we didn't know was that we had to walk uphill for about 500 feet over a ricky and dangerous jungle path into the rainforest. Fortunate for us it hadn't rained in some time. It was an arduous trek and had we known we would have opted for the Honduras trip on the docks where you are bussed to the mountain top. Jay carried the heavy backpack the entire way without an offer to help from the crewmen following the two slowest and oldest guests. The entire group of younger people cheered us when we reached the top where we could sit, drink some water, and learn about the mechanics of the ride, before proceeding to the area where we would be harnessed up for our jaunt in the trees. After we were outfitted in the complicated harness we climbed another 20 feet to the first platform. One by one we had our chance to fly through the canopy and marvel at the incredible feat of clearing the jungle and the construction of this zip line so high above the ground.

There was a crewman to send us off of every platform and one to receive us at the next platform. Good thing for the third ride had us heading for a cliff wall at high speed. We would have made a smear on the cliff if the big fellow hadn't knocked the wind out of us and stopped us before we splattered the wall. There was another ride or two then an interesting rappel down about forty feet to a lower platform. Nothing to worry about for the man on the lower platform totally controlled your descent. The last ride was a long one back to the caves where we were outfitted and another short rappel (old hat by this time) back to the ground. We were honored as Jay and I at 76 and 81 years of age were the oldest people this outfit had ever had on their zip lines and we did it without incidence. You are never too old to try something new.

ROATAN ISLAND, HONDURAS

At Roatan Island, Honduras on Friday, 5/23/08, we joined Bill and Sandy Mason for a tour of Roatan. Sandy did not spend much time in the casino on this cruise. She said the machines were not paying. Bill golfed a couple of days. One day he flew to an island that had only the golf course on it. Golf carts were waiting at the airport instead of taxis. The Roatan tour was interesting with a display of Garifundas. The men were dressed as women and masted to represent the times when the men were hiding from the British soldiers or be slain. They were probably all descendants of slaves. The tour included a short boat ride to see some shipwrecks and a stop at a roadside stant to taste local jellies and jams. Later we were happy to return to the air-conditioned ship for dinner and the show.

Because of our stop in Roatan I learned on my return home that I cannot give blood platelets for a full year as Roatan is malaria infested—even if I never left the ship the mosquito can find you on the ship. Had I known I could have taken anti-malaria shots prior to the cruise? Next time I will consult with Bloodnet.

Another day at sea with a final dance show after dinner. The dancers were to be applauded for performing on a rolling and pitching stage. Then back in port on Sunday 5/25/08, for our transport home by our accommodating neighbor, Bob Sutton. We thanked Bob with a bottle of Crown Royal and a coconut rum cake for his wife. All in all it was a good cruise with new experiences and memories to be added to our travel scrapbook.

Jim had to give up his paintball operation in Okeechobee for it was just too isolated a location. There were no motels or restaurants near his home for people to get a snack. All food items had to be provided by him. He and Pamela poured their hearts and souls into this business and we are sorry that they had to give it up. He rented out his property and home in Okeechobee. The tenant is taking very good care of his possessions. They needed a home for their horses, and his twenty acres provides this for them. Pamela is living with her parents in South Carolina, Jim is living with us temporarily. Both of these young people want to live in a log cabin in Tennessee eventually.

In our working days we could keep a job as long as we wished. Not these days, with the job market so dismal. It is so sad for these youngsters.

$\mathcal{C}$HAPTER 46

Jim and Pamela marry in 2009 at Hollis Gardens on 8/8/09. They had rented a tent and had their catered reception at home. In the fall of the same year we made a trip north for Jimmy's graduation from high school. We enjoyed meeting his girlfriend's family with whom he is staying. We also met a few of his friends and saw Sally and her boyfriend along with his Grandma Hartley. We spent some time looking at houses with Jim and Pamela and bought him a four bedroom home that he is now renting.

VENICE, ITALY

Our long awaited trip to the Greek Islands began with a flight to Venice, Italy which we had visited in 1984 with International Weekends. So much had changed since that time. In 1984 there were more pigeons than tourists, this time it was reversed. We opted for the bus service to the ship provided by the Holland America Cruise. We had enjoyed the trip through the Panama Canal and up the Amazon River so much that it would be Holland America ships whenever we could manage it. Their ships are usually smaller, than the new behemoths so the lines are not as long for food service. We were scheduled for the Nieuw Amsterdam, which had 2,000 tourists and 900 crewmen. This was twice the size of the passenger list when we went through the Panama. The overnight trip was arduous but we survived. We had a four hour layover in Gatwick which was much tougher. We did not arrive in Venice until 4:00 p.m. by the time the HAL bus arrived at the ship we could only eat and collapse in bed.

My planning of the trip included a visit with our friends in Solothurn via Eurail Pass and then travel by Eurail again to Paris, spend a few days with Cathy Mackenzie, the agent on the Vice-President's detail when the Gores arrived at Sand Dollar. Prior to the trip we bought expensive gondola serenade trips in Venice for our first shore excursion but we missed it because I had forgotten to set my watch to Venice time. They left without us. My fault, so no refund.

SPLIT, CROATIA

We chose no shore excursions on this, our first cruise stop for we could walk to the Diocletian Palace built by the Roman Emperor for his retirement in 305 AD. After Diocletian the Romans abandoned the site, so the Palace stood empty for several centuries. It once housed about 9000 people. The Palace has been declared a UNESCO World Heritage Monument because of its degree of preservation. We only explored the Palace basement on the ground floor with its many stalls selling various crafts and Croatian souvenirs. The Palace basement had thick walls of about two feet and barreled ceilings.

PIRAEUS, (ATHENS), GREECE

We would be leaving Athens at 4:00 p.m. so we chose a shore excursion of only four hours titled Athens and the Acropolis. We saw a little of Athens on the bus ride to The Acropolis, known also as the Citadel of Athens. We learned that acropolis means a hilltop and there are many acropolises in Greece but on the one in Athens is the best known in the world and thus called The Acropolis, without qualification.

We trudged up the steep hill along with hundreds of other tourists, absorbing the beauty and magnificence of The Acropolis. We carefully wound our way up the 'ess' shaped walkways to the building known as the Propylaea, or gateway building. The Propylaea was begun in the year BC 437, with the architect finishing the construction in five years, an incredible feat considering that the many Doric pillars are six feet in diameter and twenty nine feet in height. There was no heavy equipment in those days. One stoa or public walkway was broad enough to allow the horses, wagons, and golden chariots to enter. We puffed our way to the top of the hill which was about 500 feet above sea level. This was a lot of climbing for the elderly.

The Acropolis has had a long and checkered history having been destroyed or pilfered by Persians, Turks, Byzantine Emperors, invading barbarians, Franks, and Ottomans in their heydays. Even Lord Elgin, a British nobleman and diplomat, famous for removing many marble statues from The Acropolis to a museum in London. Throughout its history the Parthenon had been converted to a Christian Church with all its accompanying changed, then a mosque, including a minaret, but it really is a temple to the Virgin Athena, Goddess of Wisdom and the patron Goddess of Athens.

The building once housed a colossal statue of Athena, forty feet high sculpted by the renowned ancient Greek architect, Phidias, who also supervised the construction of the Parthenon. The Parthenon is considered the most perfect and magnificent ruin in the world. The structure, completed about BC 438 replaces an older temple to Athena. The roof tiles were of white marble necessitating the numerous pillars that were over six feet in diameter at the base.

The Greek Ministry of Culture was carrying on a program of reconstruction to assure the stability of the ruins so the Parthenon was closed to the public during our visit. The Parthenon was built on the ruins and foundations of a more ancient temple, which dates back to the middle Stone Age. Lord Elgin was supposed to take artists to Athens to sketch and make molds of the bas relief statues of the Parthenon. Instead he became known as the perpetrator of the largest heist in history. After residing in a London museum for two centuries the Elgin Marbles might be on their way home to the new Acropolis museum in Athens.

As we climbed the hill to get a closer look at the Parthenon we passed the Erechtheum we could see the southern portico, or porch, facing us known as the Porch of the Caryatids. Instead of columns there were six draped female figures engineered so their necks, the slenderest portion of the statues could support the massive roof of the porch, while remaining graceful and feminine. The Erechthum is the most sacred and mythical of all the temples in Athens. It was the most ancient sanctuary on the Acropolis, really not called a temple but a house, built by Erechteus, who was buried within its walls. The view of Athens from this hilltop was breathtaking. We can only imagine the city during its Golden Age.

ISTANBUL

The Dardanelles is a narrow strait in northwestern Turkey connecting the Aegean Sea with the Sea of Marmara. The water flows in both directions in this strait, from the Sea of Marmara via surface current and from the Aegean via an undercurrent. Like the Bosphorus, closer to Istanbul, it separates Europe (the Gallipoli peninsula) from the mainland of Asia. The University of Leeds recently revealed that there is, in fact, an underwater river that flows through the Mediterranean and under the Bosphorus (caused by the difference of density of the two seas) that would be the sixth largest river on earth if it were on land.

We picked two shore excursions in Istanbul; the first was The City Walls and the Spice Bazaar. The City Walls were not much to see but the Spice Bazaar was all we imagined. Our guide, a paunchy local Muslim, who spoke good English, loved his work and Istanbul. He said he would never leave this great city. He led us to his favorite kiosk in the Bazaar, where we could sample anything we considered buying. The Spice Bazaar is the oldest bazaar in the city, known for its exotic spices and second in size only to the Grand Bazaar, both very large covered shopping complexes.

Istanbul is a megacity that is overwhelming with its people and its merchandise. It is an inspiring city full of Mosques, Muslims, history and character. The history dates back to the 7th millennium BC or maybe older. Istanbul historically was known as Byzantium and later Constantinople. It has served as the capital of the Roman Empire in the fourth century, the Eastern Roman (Byzantine) Empire until the 13th century, and the Ottoman Empire, until the Republic of Turkey was proclaimed independent in 1923.

The next day we chose the Best of Istanbul shore excursion. The 2010 census puts the population at over 13 million people, second only to Moscow. When Constantine I defeated Licinius in 324 AD he effectively became the Emperor of the entire Roman Empire. He immediately laid out plans to convert Byzantium to a city of Christianity and Greek culture. Numerous churches were built across the city. The establishment of Constantinople was one of his noted accomplishments. He converted all residents to Christianity. Constantine built the Hagia Sophia that remained the largest cathedral for over one thousand years. The St. Sofia cathedral later became a mosque, today it is a museum. We were taken to the Hagia Sophia, which was within walking distance of the Blue Mosque. The Sophia was a vast empty space today that must have been awesome in its prime.

The Blue Mosque was much too crowded for us but we dutifully waited in line, doffed our shoes, put on their slippers, and proceeded with the multitudes into the sacred mosque. Those dressed not to the liking of the attendants at the entrance were given shawls to cover their bodies. We were warned on the ship to dress appropriately for the Turkish people but there are always some in a crowd this large that will do their own thing, no matter how many warnings are given.

Although the Blue Mosque's interior is covered with over 20,000 handmade blue tiles we found the crowds so oppressive that we had to exit quickly to get some fresh air. This mosque, also known as the

Sultan Ahmed Mosque, while still being used as a mosque, has become a popular tourist attraction in this largest city of Turkey. It was built during the reign of Sultan Ahmed who was criticized because it has six minarets, the same number as the holiest mosque in Mecca. The Sultan solved this problem by commissioning his architect to build a seventh minaret in Mecca.

TOPKAPI PALACE

The immense Topkapi Palace was our next stop where we were to have lunch (thankfully—and sit). The Topkapi was built by Sultan Mehmed II, conqueror of Byzantine Constantinople. The structures were renovated in 1459, and consist of hundreds of rooms and chambers. The treasury once resided at Topkapi. The Palace once held as many as 4000 residents. It was the official and primary residence of the Ottoman Sultans for 400 years. It sits on the acropolis of Saraglio Point, a promontory overlooking the Golden Horn, (a Bosphorus inlet) and the Sea of Marmara with the Bosphorus in plain sight from many points of the palace.

While we did not see the famous Basilica Cistern that holds 20,000,000 gallons of water we were familiar with cisterns since they are required by law in the Caribbean islands. The Basilica Cistern is the largest of several hundred ancient cisterns that lie beneath the city of Istanbul. The Basilica Cistern was built in the 6th century during the reign of the Byzantine Emperor Justinian I. The walls of the cistern are 13 feet thick; the water has traveled down several Roman Aquaducts, also built by Justinian. During the 1985 restoration 50,000 tons of mud was removed from the cistern and a platform was built to replace the boats that were used to tour the cistern.

CARPET MERCHANT

We were taken to a carpet merchant's establishment, served warm Apple Tea and watched a young girl display carpet weaving techniques while several assistants spread various Turkish rugs on the floor enticing us to buy and ship a rug home. We were just too tired to really enjoy the offerings of the Grand Bazaar but I did succumb to street hawkers that insisted I buy a silk rug for only $30.00 US. This treasure sits at the front entrance of my humble manufactured home.

MYKONIS, GREECE

Wisely, we didn't plan a shore excursion for Mykonos. Istanbul had worn us out so we walked the waterfront of Mykonos, searched for wine to take aboard the ship. Then sat and enjoyed a bottle of beer at a beachside café as we watched life go by on this island full of brilliant white-washed homes. It was a restful day ashore after the clamor of Istanbul. We lunched at a delightful outdoor café covered in vines of bright pink bougainvillea, and kidded with the staff.

EPHESUS, (KUSADASI), TURKEY

This ancient city of Ephesus was already inhabited during the Neolithic Age (around 6,000 BC). The city was one of the Greek cities in the Ionian League. Then later in the Roman period it was the second largest city in the Roman Empire. Only Rome was larger. Ephesus had a population of 250,000 during the 1st century BC, which made it the second largest city in the world. The city was famed for its Temple of Artemis(Temple of Diana) and considered one of the Seven Wonders of the Ancient World.

The tour I chose for Ephesus was Ancient Ephesus and the Virgin Mary's House. It was another all day tour. We started with a walking tour of the ruins of Ephesus. Our excellent guide pointed out that even back in the original days the homes had sewer lines and indoor toilets. The women did not like going to the public toilets where men sat only two feet apart on marble seats discussing business, while doing their business. On chilly days they would send their slaves down to warm the marble seats.

We did see the clay tiles used as sewer lines, while the drinking water must have been supplied via Aquaducts during the Roman Period. Aquaducts are associated with the Romans but they were devised much earlier in Greece, the Far East and the Indian subcontinent. Seeing the two story ruins of the Library of Celsus, built in 117 A.D., as a monument and sarcophagus to Celsus, who is buried in its entrance, was awesome. The capacity of the library was 12,000 scrolls. There were double walls to protect the scrolls from temperature and humidity. It was built in a territory that traditionally was Greek to its core. This library was an indication that Public Libraries were built throughout the Roman Empire, not just in Rome.

The walking was difficult for Jay with his poor vision and he scratched his arm on one of the rough stone walls. Because he is on Coumadin for his atrial fibrillation, he bled profusely. On the tour bus a doctor and nurse attended to his wounds and asked if he wanted to go to a hospital. I was glad he said no for I could imagine being stranded in a Turkish hospital, not knowing the language or their ancient methods of treatment. After all, we were in one of the most ancient cities in the world. We welcomed the chance to relax on the bus as we climbed Mt. Koressos to the house of the Virgin Mary.

HOUSE OF THE VIRGIN MARY

The House of the Virgin Mary is both a Christian and a Muslim shrine. Mary was taken to Ephesus by Apostle John, who built the house for her out of rectangular stones. Mary did not want to live in the city so she chose this remote spot on a mountain top to live out her remaining days. At the beginning of the 19th century a bedridden Augustinian nun in Germany awoke with the stigmata and had vision of the house near Ephesus. This led to the discovery of the domain. The small T-shaped stone building consists of a bedroom on the right and a kitchen on the left. A small stream runs under the Virgin's house and supposedly has healing powers. On the exit road from the shrine there were hundreds of pieces of paper stuck into the wire fencing, all prayer requests. The atmosphere was quiet and serene, a truly holy place.

THIRA, (SANTORINI), GREECE

Santorini, an island in the south Aegean Sea, is the site of the largest volcanic eruptions in recorded history though what remains today is a water filled caldera. Santorini and Anafi, an island to the east of this island are the only two locations in Europe to feature a hot desert climate, where the precipitation is too low to sustain any vegetation. Many plants depend on the scant moisture provided by the common early morning fog condensing on the ground as dew. The island acquires only ten inches of rain per year, has no rivers, and water is scarce.

In recent years a desalination plant has provided running but not yet potable water, to most houses. The town is perched on the crest of the caldera with high steep cliffs of almost 1,000 feet. The bus ride up the narrow, steep roads to town was a hair-raising experience. We started walking up the wide sidewalks made of field stones, there was a short two inch step that Jay did not see and he tripped and fell on the rough stones and proceeded to begin bleeding profusely again. Fortunately, a local resident took us to a drug store that was opened this day for the cruise ship in port. We were able to buy an effective spray bandage that stopped the bleeding but the trip was ruined for him. He wanted to go home and forget about the other shore excursions, other Greek Islands and the Eurail passes leading to our friend in Paris with a place for us to stay in this expensive city.

As he drowned his sorrows in Greek beer at a restaurant just below the pharmacy, I was able to climb the rest of the hill and see some of this quaint island with the stone sidewalks, whitewashed homes, and steep stairs leading to restaurants with dining areas that enjoyed spectacular views. Fortunately, we were able to get a refund on the only remaining excursion that I picked for Olympia: Ancient Olympia and Zorba.

KATAKOLON, (OLYMPIA), GREECE

Olympia is a sanctuary of ancient Greece and is known for being the site of the Olympic Games in classical times. The games dated back further than 776 BC, with the first games being held in Olympia in honor of Zeus. During the Roman Period the games were opened up to all citizens of the Roman Empire. In Modern Olympia the Olympic flame is lit by sunlight reflecting on parabolic mirrors in front of the Temple of Hera, then transported by a torch to the place where the games are held.

We chose to not take the shore excursion I had booked and instead walked around the town, enjoying a beer at a saloon near the center of Olympia.

AT SEA

We had another day of rest before disembarking in Venice. We had contacted Evert and Henrietta Bogart at their ski cabin in Tschappina, Switzerland, to learn that they wanted us to come on Wednesday, September 1st, not Tuesday, August 31st, for they would be arriving in Solothurn on Tuesday night. So I had made a reservation for Tuesday night at the Ca Loredon, a bed and breakfast in the heart of Venice, for Tuesday night. We disembarked the Nieuw Amsterdam ship and found the elevated train near the docks to the water taxi, the main mode of transportation in Venice.

When we got off the water taxi there were men waiting with strange carts that could take our luggage but yet climb the stairs over the canals that we had to cross. Thank God we hired one of these carts for we would not have found the B & B without the guide. The Ca Loredon was not the most enticing place. The narrow steep stairs were too dark for Jay to reach the upper stories where our bedroom was located. The hostess cleaned a room for us near the eating area.

Our guide was there early the next morning and helped us down the dark stairway with our luggage. He told us where to get off the water taxi to reach the Eurail station. We managed to get on the empty train heading to Solothurn. I had bought two expensive passes for three countries, France, Switzerland and Italy but we would have to forego our stay with Cathy Mackenzie in Paris and fly home from Zurich.

We walked the two blocks to Evert's doctor, who was kind enough to fit us in. Without x-rays he told us that Jay had not punctured his lung from a broken rib when he fell in Santorini.

In Solothurn we did the typical tourist activities, had a beer under the clock tower, walked the town, visited a chocolate factory, found a pharmacy for pain pills for Jay. Solothurn is representative of all Swiss villages, everyone walks. There are not many obese Swiss people.

I had spent a lot of time on Henrietta's computer and telephone making a complaint to Holland America and changing reservations to return home from Zurich instead of Paris.

We had forgotten that we had stayed in their large basement room previously, and how cold the floors were on bare feet, or the icy ring on the toilet seat and how the temperatures drop at night, despite having a cozy featherbed. We were ready for Florida temperatures again.

Before we departed Henrietta took us on a drive to an area we had not been before to a chalet on the mountaintop where couples were dancing polkas inside while on the sunny verandah we shared a cheese fondue and watched hang gliders take off from an open farmer's field after a swift running start.

In the early morning hours we sadly left Switzerland and the Bogarts. We used our Eurail passes to reach Zurich. The trip home was uneventful. We were happy to be back home where everything is familiar to Jay, and he can't trip on an unseen curb.

CHAPTER 47

2010 started out with Dolly's cataract surgery. Unfortunately, I told the doctor performing the surgery that I wanted to see the golf ball land on the green. That was a mistake because I do not see that far anymore and I must use a magnifier more often, which frightens Jay for I am his only chauffeur.

The Veteran's Hospital in Tampa has an excellent low vision clinic and I drive Jay there every few weeks to see the glaucoma specialists or the low vision experts where he is able to get his glasses, computer with printer and Zoom Text on the computer, magnifiers, and the Merlin Reader which has changed his life for he can put a newspaper under the reader and enlarge the font as much as he needs. He uses a 32 inch TV as a monitor and has a 26 inch TV as a second monitor.

We have been totally occupied with monthly visits to Lauren, Jay's sister, who has moved from her independent living unit in St. Petersburg to assisted living after she fell and broke her pelvis bone in February. She was in the full nursing section for a few weeks then moved to assisted living where we know she is given her medication by the nurses. We have also hired a caregiver (a nurse friend of Diane's) for her who is getting her involved socially, which she never did on her own. She has totally lost her memory, she is taking medication for depression, dementia and Alzheimer's disease, although she does recognize us when we visit her. It is so sad to see someone not remembering anything of the past even a few minutes ago. The only blessing in her new arrangement is that she can no longer smoke where she now resides but she thinks she gave up smoking 50 years ago.

We did travel to Phoenix in October to visit Steve & Debbie Siskowski. My brother, Lars and his wife, Karen Dykes picked us up at the airport and drove us to their new home in the high desert of Cornville. We spent a few days with them and they drove us back to Phoenix where we again spent a few days with the Siskowskis. Later the Siskowskis drove us to Tucson, or Oro Valley, for our weekly reunion with the Ethyl/Pinochle Club at the Oldenkamps. Lars and Kathy Dykes joined us for a dinner in Tucson, and stayed in a motel rather than driving home.

On the last night there Jack fell on his way to bed. He was taken to the hospital that night and required surgery the next morning. Jack's wife, Laurie, could not drive us to the airport as she usually does. Our trip home was a nightmare because of weather conditions in Dallas. I think that Cathy and Greg Heffelfinger got home to Richmond before we reached Tampa.

Laurie had moved the car and Jay was looking at the car instead of where he was walking. He had tripped over a parking curb at the desert museum in Tucson. The men at the museum were most helpful and stayed with us until the ambulance arrived. We had a long trip via ambulance to the nearest hospital. After hours in the emergency room he had nine stitches put in his brow where his glasses had cut his brow.

With Jack's falling and Jay tripping over a curb he didn't see we decided to call it quits for the yearly reunions. We are just too old for this travel business, although there are many places we would like to still visit.

CHAPTER 48

We are blessed that we have seen as much of this planet as we have, although it was not via sailboat as we had dreamed of and planned for so many years.

Places that we would still like to see is a safari in Africa, the Taj Mahal, in Agra, India, the Angkor Wat Temple in Bangkok, taste Thai cuisine in Thailand, revel at the wildlife of the Galapagos and marvel at Machu Pichu, visit Rio at Carnival, swim in the warm springs of Antarctica, visit Patagonia, Ireland, Scotland, Scandinavia, and Russia. I am afraid we have run out of time and mostly because of Jay's vision. We can't risk his falls again because he can't see where he is walking. He is most comfortable at home where he knows where everything is and can sometimes even put articles away.

We must be satisfied with the countries we have seen and written about in this dialogue.